SPLIT BRITCHES

Lesbian Practice/ Feminist Performance

EDITED BY SUE-ELLEN CASE

London and New York

First published 1996
by Routledge
11 New Fetter Lane, London EC4P 4EE

Simultaneously published in the USA and Canada
by Routledge
29 West 35th Street, New York, NY 10001

Typeset in Sabon by
Florencetype Limited, Stoodleigh, Devon

Printed and bound in Great Britain by
TJ Press (Padstow) Ltd, Padstow, Cornwall

British Library Cataloguing in Publication Data
A catalogue record for this book is available from the British Library

Library of Congress Cataloguing in Publication Data
A catalogue record for this book has been requested

ISBN 0–415–12765–3
0–415–12766–1 (pbk)

CONTENTS

PLATES

ACKNOWLEDGMENTS

Each of these plays was produced in the spirit and practice of collaboration. When preserving these experiences in the form of written texts, the attempt to list credits in a conventional way is an attempt to describe the impossible. It is the work of three women working interchangably as writers, directors and performers, with the assistance of many other creative artists: designers, choreographers, musicians, and managers and muses. The following is a list of people who were there at the beginning, showed up at crucial times, or have been here all along. These are our essential team members: Alice Forrester, Maureen Angelos, Susan Young, Joni Wong, Stormy Brandenberger, Laka Daisical, Karena Rahall, Charlie Spencer, Debra Miller, Heidi Sama Blackwell, Rose Sharp, and Stacy Makishi.

These plays are a product of time and place as well as of people. They emerge from an atmosphere of possibility that extends from the nomadic community of alternative artists touring Europe in the 1970s through chaotic boom of downtown performance and performance spaces on the lower east side of New York in the 1980s to the theory and practice of lesbian desire and queer representation in the 1990s. The following is a list of fellow travellers on this journey.

Our partners, our teachers and our inspiration: Spiderwoman Theatre, Hot Peaches, The Bloolips, and Women's Experimental Theatre. All the women of Women's One World (WOW), who have been our community, our support, and our friends, especially Pamela Camhe, Jordy Mark, Robin Epstein, Holly Hughes, Amy Meadow, Eva Weiss, Carmelita Tropicana, Lynn Hayes, Terri Dame, and many others. The venues that gave room for the performances and believed in our work, and supported and produced us at crucial times: WOW, Women's Interart, La Mama, Etc., PS 122, One Dream, Dixon Place, Franklin Furnace, The Oval House, Gay Sweatshop and the Drill Hall Art Centre in London, and Hampshire College, University of Hawaii. Those who described, argued, critiqued and documented what they saw: Alisa Solomon, Marilyn Stasio, Sue-Ellen Case, Laurie Stone, Kate Davy, Jill Dolan, Vicki Petraka, Linda Hart, Peggy

Phelan, Juli Burke, Elin Diamond, and Terri Helbing. And the larger community who made important contributions of time, money, spare rooms, free dinners, critical comment, and friendly encouragement, and who have worked to keep Split Britches visible: Joy Tomchin, Deborah Light, Christina Biaggi, Telma Abascal, Phylis Chesler, Adrienne Collins, Angela Stewart Park, Anne Engel, Mary McIntosh, Shaz Nassauer, Rebecca Trowler, Judy Rosen, Virginia Mayer, Madelaine Olnek, Karen Kvernenes, Ingrid Berkhout, Neil Kirshner, Shara Antoni, Margo Lewiton, Ronnie Geist, Ellie Covan, Meryl Vladimir, and Ellen Stewart. And to Talia Rodgers, who brought the project to Routledge and saw it through.

their new play, *Lust and Comfort*. They have led workshops and developed projects in colleges and universities in Great Britain, the United States, and Hawaii, such as *Honey, I'm Home*, the *Alcestis* project at Hampshire College and *Valley of the Doll's House* at University of Hawaii. With the Five Lesbian Brothers, they produced Ginka Steinwachs' *Monsieur, Madame* for the Goethe Institute in New York in 1991, and their first play, *Split Britches*, was produced for PBS in the summer of 1988.

Yet this is the first anthology of their plays to be published. Given their celebrated status, the rather late appearance of their work in print may seem startling. Complex historical and personal factors account for its tardy timing. This is how the book was finally produced. Weaver, Shaw and I first conceived the project as we sat together in Honolulu in 1993, when they were working on *Valley of the Doll's House*. I knew that I would be spending the next year at Swarthmore College, where they would provide me with student assistance for projects. Although Shaw and Weaver would be in London much of that time (and Deb Margolin would be expecting her second child), they agreed to put their papers in order in their apartment for students to photocopy and compile. When the first student, Terri Senft, a graduate student at NYU, arrived at the small, walk-up apartment near their performance space, known as WOW, she discovered four large, green plastic tubs under the bed. Weaver and Shaw had divided all their notebooks, script fragments, programs, budgets, press clippings, interviews, photos, and other addenda into these four tubs. Senft and I met to explore the first tub. I looked around at the tiny, old apartment where Weaver and Shaw had lived, with Shaw's daughter, for fifteen years. I admired their dedication amidst a kind of poverty of space and material goods. I wondered at the contradictions between the numerous press clippings, awards, and sold-out bookings I found collected in the tubs, the records of prodigious talent and artistic labor, and the bare minimum of material comfort I found in their fourth-floor walk-up. The door into the apartment did not seem all that secure to me. The entrance to the building was also fairly accessible to anyone who might want to enter. Moreover, the building looked as if any fire would consume it greedily in a matter of minutes. So Senft and I agreed that she would photocopy everything in the tubs – at least one copy of these historical documents would exist outside of the apartment. As Senft's time eroded, she turned the job over to Alicia Newman. The photocopying took almost two quarters. At the same time, the students were constructing an inventory of items in each tub. NYU Performance Studies offered photocopiers and the means to copy all of the videos that record the performances. The final stages of editing were assisted along by Rebecca Rugg, who researched the bibliography and generally checked all details.

Since the different versions of the scripts did not agree with one another, and were typed across random, sometimes unnumbered sheets of paper, I decided we had to begin constructing scripts both from the written records and from transcriptions of the videos. Tellory Williamson, at Swarthmore College, began this monumental task. Vicki Patraka offered her transcription of *Little Women* to aid in the process. I began to feel the tension of the moment when great performance, lively within its communication, in fact, the kind of performance that has built communities becomes printed play-script. Having witnessed how these texts devolved from various fragmentary, differing scripts – the attempts of the actors to remember how they best played the sequence, the transcription of the dialogue off videos – I realized with both pleasure and sadness how the delicate, passing show becomes transcribed into the unyielding typeface of print; how the many variations, produced by specific audiences, different occasions, actors' instincts, and ensemble creation become reduced to that final choice; how the slight gags disappear behind the page, and the sweat dries into printer's ink.

This move from performance to page is an unusual one in the late twentieth century, when playwrights and directors determine rehearsals. The 'poor-theater,' itinerant-actor nature of this work builds its stage with window shades painted as scenes, as in *Beauty and the Beast*, stored in a large suitcase for the next appearance in the park, found objects from thrift stores that determine how the scenes will play, strewn across the bedroom floor, and scripts that function like *commedia* 'sides', on which only the single actor's words are written. Split Britches reaches back through history in the tradition of what is called popular theater, but really means poor people's theater: the *commedia dell'arte* players in the town square, the German players at the market fairs, night-club acts, vaudeville shows, cabarets, all the way back to the women mimes outside the Athenian theaters. They continue the tradition of the unprinted, ever-changing, improvised, homeless, show. They exhibit the enduring wisdom of poor theater, in which you can't buy masquerade, you can't import it, like those huge elephants carrying Italian effects up to Louis XIV's spectacles; no, you have to make it yourself from nothing – from the everyday – even the discarded everyday that lingers in secondhand clothing stores. Cast-offs become costumes, found somewhere along the endless racks in the Unique Boutique on the lower end of Broadway in Manhattan, or the idea for char-acters and the contradictions of their lives is discovered in a deserted, old store window that advertises *Dress Suits to Hire*.

In the 1980s, the Reagan decade, in which being poor was 'out', and the tradition of the poor artist faded before the spectacles produced by Robert Wilson, or Peter Sellars, and regional theaters organized boards of directors, and subscription seasons, Split

Britches insisted upon its poverty as its style and its politics. Even its sometime home, the WOW café, ran anarchically and out of poverty. As Peggy Shaw once related, 'the decisions are made by whoever shows up on Tuesday night,' and the power resides in the one who 'knows where the plug is, or can find the extension cord.' Intended as such, desired as such. Not meant to romanticize poverty, but to make it, along with anarchy, accident, and collectively, count; to imagine what these conditions might produce; to contradict the politics and aesthetics of affluence.

Yet, even amidst poor theater traditions, Split Britches makes a unique contribution. *Commedia*, after all, offers the stories of fathers and sons, vaudeville capitalizes on sexist humor, and all produce endless reruns of the heterosexual imperative. Split Britches stages women's poverty, women's humor and fortitude. They celebrate lesbian desire, love, and troubled long-term relationships. They narrate the Jewish-identified woman's distance from the sexist traditions of her ethnic community. Not as realism, nor as the 'natural' condition of women and lesbians. When they put on a dress, you know it's a dress – it still hangs on its hanger around their necks, in *Beauty and the Beast*, and *Belle Reprieve*. When they stage lesbian seduction, they assume butch–femme roles, movie-star identifications, mythic beauties and beasts. When Margolin dons the *yarmulke*, it's alongside the tutu in *Beauty and the Beast*, or the revealing costume of the prostitute in *Little Women*. They have created a tradition of theater, then, and taught it in workshops, passed it along to people they apprenticed to their projects, shared in collaborations with other groups. The yawning gap of the canon awaits them as they cross the stage onto these pages, and criss-cross the critical passages of feminist and lesbian critics such as Jill Dolan, Kate Davy, Elin Diamond, Vivian Patraka, Lynda Hart, and my own, but it will be changed by them and history will be made to account for those it usually renders invisible.

WEAVING SPLIT BRITCHES

Originally, Split Britches was composed of Peggy Shaw, Lois Weaver, and Deb Margolin. Shaw and Weaver first met in Berlin in 1977 where Shaw was performing with a male drag group, Hot Peaches, and Weaver with the feminist theater group Spiderwoman. Spiderwoman's costumes had been lost in the shipping process. They heard another American troupe was playing in town, so they subsequently borrowed costumes from Hot Peaches. Weaver remarks that, for a multi-ethnic, radical feminist theater, the fancy, sequined gowns of the drag queens set their scene in a completely different style. Yet this borrowing, this cross-dressing cross-over between the homosexual subculture and radical feminist political theater would later prove to be one of the unique contributions Split Britches would make to theater history.)Meanwhile, Shaw and Weaver fell in love. Shaw left Hot Peaches and began working with Weaver in Spiderwoman's next show, *An Evening of Disgusting Songs and Pukey Images*. The tales told in various critical essays, and in interviews, present various versions of what happened next. 'Disgusting and Pukey' seemed to compose a utopic blend of differences among women: lesbian, straight, women of color, white women, old, young, women of size, thin women, etc. However, these same differences apparently caused a rift within the ensemble. Rebecca Schneider, in her article 'See the Big Show: Spiderwoman Theater Doubling Back,' quotes Gloria Miguel of Spiderwoman as saying, 'Some of the women who were lesbian wanted to make Spiderwoman an all-lesbian group . . . and – over our dead bodies.' Then she quotes Muriel Miguel as reporting that 'My feeling was that the pressure of the white women in the group got too much for me' (242). Jill Dolan, in *The Feminist Spectator as Critic*, notes that 'history has it that Shaw and Weaver left Spiderwoman because of sexuality-based conflicts' (136). It seems that ethnic and sexual differences caused Spiderwoman to split their next work into two shows. The Miguel/Mayo sisters produced *Sun, Moon, and Feather*, while Shaw, Weaver, Pam Verge, and Naja Beye began work on what would become *Split Britches*.

Now rather than imagining this split as merely within the context of these two groups, it might be more productive to see just how it acts out its historical moment. The turn of the decade into the 1980s was the time when women of color began to test feminism for the way in which it produced whiteness and middle-class values within its critical practice and its sense of activism. *This Bridge Called My Back* appeared in 1981 to herald the beginnings of such a confrontation. Likewise, some lesbians and what would become sex-radicals were challenging feminism for its moralistic stand against pornography and lesbian sado-masochistic practices. In 1982, the history-making Barnard conference drew the line between the lesbian s/m community and the feminist anti-porn adherents. Thus, the sense that feminism might provide an all-encompassing critique gave way to explorations by new, more narrowly focused activist groups and critical writings. Spiderwoman's split reflects this change. As Spiderwoman, the focus tightened onto Native American experiences and issues, with only a very minor interest in staging the lesbian. Weaver and Shaw, on their way to creating Split Britches, moved into an all-white, but increasingly lesbian-focused theater practice. By 1985, when Split Britches and Spiderwoman restaged 'An Evening of Disgusting Songs and Pukey Images,' each of these so-called 'differences' had become exact enough in its own articulation, and strong enough in its own practice to afford the staging of coalition.

Meanwhile, back in the summer of 1980, Weaver began to develop a piece based upon her family history. Along with Shaw, and other members of Spiderwoman, they constructed the characters of Weaver's two aunts and one great-aunt who had lived in the Blue Ridge Mountains of Virginia. They titled the piece *Split Britches*, based on the pants women wore in the fields, which allowed them to urinate without stopping work. In 1980, they performed the piece at the first WOW (Women's One World) Festival in New York. By 1981, after a successful run of the show, Shaw and Weaver left Spiderwoman to work on their own. They 'discovered' Deb Margolin around that time. She began working with them as a script writer, but was eventually cast in the role of the third aunt. The trio first performed the play at the Boston Women's Festival in 1981. They toured *Split Britches* through Great Britain, Germany, Italy and the Netherlands, to return for an off-Broadway run in 1983. By 1982, the trio had begun to work on their second play, beginning to sense that they had become an ensemble that would continue to work together. They took the name Split Britches as a sign of their continuing labor in the arts, permeated by the personal, private 'leaks' that would nourish their imagination and fortitude.

Together, Shaw, Weaver, and Margolin composed and performed *Split Britches* (1981), *Beauty and the Beast* (1982), *Upwardly Mobile Home* (1984), *Little Women* (1988), and *Lesbians Who Kill* (1992). They agreed that any member of the troupe might use the name Split Britches in solo performances, or in other collaborations, but only Shaw and Weaver have done so. As Split Britches, Shaw and Weaver collaborated with Isabel Miller in adapting her novel *Patience and Sarah* to the stage, with Holly Hughes in the creation of *Dress Suits to Hire* (1987), with the troupe Bloolips in *Belle Reprieve* (1991), and with James Neale-Kennerley in *Lust and Comfort* (1995). As a duo, Weaver and Shaw performed *Anniversary Waltz* (1989) on their tenth anniversary and Shaw retained the name Split Britches for her solo piece, *You're Just Like My Father*, in 1994. This volume brings together representative texts from both the work of the trio known as Split Britches along with certain of the plays developed in collaboration.

Beyond their work as Split Britches, these three performers have also moved out to carve their own place in the broader field of performance. Deb Margolin has garnered much critical attention for her one-woman shows, such as *Gestation* (1991), *Of Mice, Bugs, and Women* (1994), and *Carthieves! Joyrides!* (1995). Lois Weaver and Peggy Shaw made their film debut in Sheila McLaughlin's *She Must Be Seeing Things*. Weaver now serves as the co-Artistic Director of the London-based theater, Gay Sweatshop, a nationally funded gay and lesbian touring company in the UK. With the company she has created new shows, such as a project around the construction of beauty called *In Your Face*, founded Queerschool, a performance training program for lesbians and gays, and launched a monthly experimental performance series called One Night Stands. Shaw is touring her solo piece *You're Just Like My Father* in Great Britain and the United States. She is also performing the role of Billy Tipton, a passing woman, in *Slow Dance* at the American Place Theater.

WOW

Split Britches has been associated with the WOW Café since their inception. They have been nourished by WOW and nourished it with their labor, creativity, and performance skills. WOW began as a wish Weaver and Shaw formed for a festival of women's theater projects while they were touring with Spiderwoman in 1979. They invited companies they met on the road to come to the festival, even though it only existed in their imagination. Back in New York, they formed the group Allied Farces in the summer of 1980, along with Pamela Camhe and Jordy Mark, in order to organize benefits, costume parties, and other assorted events to raise money for this festival. The festival, called Women's One World, took place in October, 1980 in the Allcraft Center at St. Mark's Place. Weaver, Shaw, Verge and Beye performed *Split Britches* as their contribution. After the festival, the Allcraft management invited the organization to stay on and to continue producing performances. They began calling themselves the WOW staff and bringing in acts. In 1981 they began plans for a second festival. On a budget of $2–3,000 they produced eleven days of performances with groups from all over the world. Split Britches offered its second and final version of *Split Britches* with Shaw, Weaver, and Margolin.

The two festivals produced the sense that there was a wealth of women's performances and an audience for them, which encouraged the group to open the WOW Café in March, 1982. Located at 330 East 11th Street, the performance space was owned and operated collectively, throwing rent parties near the end of the month to continue its lease, and opening its doors to all women performers – with no audition requirement. Lois Weaver described it as 'community built around a theater.' At WOW, Weaver first invented the persona of Tammy Whynot, as an emcee for the cabaret evenings. Later, Tammy would evolve into a full character to grace *Upwardly Mobile Home*. Likewise, the persona of Carmelita Tropicana, the Latina lesbian comic formed through disparate functions in the café. Holly Hughes first performed there, writing comic fragments that would later cohere into performance scripts. Sarah Schulman staged her early plays. Split Britches were housed there as regulars, premiering *Upwardly Mobile Home* on its small stage. Eventually, WOW became one of the best-known spaces for women's performances in New York. It was one of the only spaces for openly lesbian material.

Weaver and Shaw provided a daily presence at WOW. Their personae and butch-femme role playing helped to form the atmosphere and the style of the space. Weaver taught classes in acting and directing, disseminating a new tradition of performance. Influenced by Brecht's *Saint Joan of the Stockyards*, they created *St. Joan of Avenue C*, with Weaver directing, Shaw designing, Margolin writing, and Alisa Solomon serving as dramaturg. This early experiment brought together their characteristic blend of concerns: the materialist politics of real estate and food distribution, alongside issues of gender. In 1985, as the rent went up, they moved downtown to East 4th Street, across from La Mama. The new WOW is a fourth-floor walk-up that seats around fifty spectators. Something like 'blacks' (stage curtains) indicate a stage space. Even that convention is contested by Shaw: 'I'd like to take down the curtains and let the real estate show through.' The names Lois Weaver, Peggy Shaw, and Split Britches continued to be regarded as almost synonymous with WOW. Soon, the evenings were overbooked by new groups and enthusiastic audiences. The Five Lesbian Brothers began performing there. The *Village Voice* reviewed the shows.

In the past few years, as Weaver and Shaw began to spend more time on the road, their presence at WOW diminished. As Shaw recalls, there was one show that marked the end of their consistent time in the space. In 1989, Shaw and Weaver made a video with Bloolips, Spiderwoman, and Hot Peaches entitled *Odyssey*. The quest was for Shaw, who got lost somewhere 'uptown' after receiving an award (the Obie). Yet Split Britches stays on, if only sporadically. Margolin is presently directing a new piece in the space, and Weaver and Shaw still participate in the annual retreats on July 4th weekend, during which the WOW season is planned. They make a wish list, which Shaw insists always comes true.

THE CREATIVE PROCESS

How does Split Britches work on its texts and performances? Lois Weaver supplied notes on the process, which I will try to reproduce, in a slightly more finished form in this section.

They might begin with a structure of polarity, such as butch-femme, or, in *Beauty and the Beast* the idea of 'Glitter and Guts.' They might explore an obsession, such as Weaver's with Tennessee Williams, Margolin's with Wuornos, or Shaw's longtime desire to play Stanley in *Streetcar Named Desire*. They have also begun with a frustration, such as trying to afford to live in New York in the mid-1980s with Reagan's re-election, with the fact that 'all our lesbian friends were getting jobs and houses in the Hamptons, while we couldn't afford the rent.' These frustrations led to *Upwardly Mobile Home*. They have responded to unsolicited suggestions for a piece, such as 'you should do *Little Women*.' One source was a newspaper clipping on the case of Aileen Wournos, a serial killer, for *Lesbians Who Kill*.

Once settled upon a starting place, they begin to make lists. For example, a list of 'what we have always wanted to do on stage.' This resulted in bits like strip, sing in harmony, kiss, serious comedy, romantic comedy, which they strung together to produce the format of *Little Women*. Along with show business desires, they make a list of social issues occupying their attention at the time, such as the anti-pornography/censorship debate, gentrification, violence, identity, intimacy. They also list stories they'd like to tell, such as: Shaw's 'fat lady' and Margolin's 'I am feminine,' in *Upwardly Mobile Home*; Weaver's 'the cow is sick' in *Split Britches*; Shaw's butch nightmare in *Belle Reprieve*; the Katharine Hepburn/James Dean coming-out story and the song Margolin and her sister sang together as children, in *Beauty and the Beast*. They collect the cultural icons they want to subvert: 'I want to be in America' in Yiddish, in *Upwardly Mobile Home*; lip-synching 'It's Impossible' as Perry Como, in *Beauty and the Beast*; Ed McMahon as the 'belly laugh' in *Lesbians Who Kill*.

Characters are also based on a bipolar split. They choose characters who consist both of someone they love, or want to be, and someone whose behavior or politics they also detest. For example, Margolin embodies the orthodox Jewish man who thanks God every morning that he is not a woman. Weaver plays the Salvation Army woman, who works with the poor, but condemns lesbians (*Beauty and the Beast*). Weaver:

> We create characters we both love and hate – satire, but not from a hateful place. Take the Salvation Army Lady. I have a lot of love in me for those Salvation Army ladies. I grew up with Baptist preachers' wives. They were the first women I was in love with. At the same time, they would be the first women to hate me and who I am now. But still, it's like loving a part of yourself and your past.

Within the shell of that contradiction, they add sub-characters that further enliven their own ambivalences, such as the rabbi in toe shoes, or the Salvation Army woman as Beauty to the lesbian Beast. Then they adorn these character complexes with identification fantasies they have with famous performers: Marilyn Monroe, Tammy Wynette, Marlon Brando, or Sid Caesar and Imogene Coca. Yet, in spite of this proliferation of contradictory personae, they continue, within the characterilogical axis, to play themselves. As Shaw said, 'I always play myself.' Their dialogue speaks their own personal experiences, opinions, and actual interactions onstage. The actors are never 'lost' in a character, but act a character within the narrative, until that narrative shifts, or is broken up by a song, or by an identification with some popular culture star. Sometimes, as in *Beauty and the Beast*, a visible layering of characters, through costumes, registers the accretion: Margolin wears the toe shoes, the rabbi's shall, a dress around her neck on the hanger, etc. The name of the troupe, Split Britches, resonates through their conflicting, heterogeneous nodes of character.

With characters and major conflicts in mind, they then begin collecting things from thriftshops, gifts, and generally 'found objects': a 78 rpm recording of the 1930 performance of *Shanghai Gesture* in *Upwardly Mobile Home*, recordings of Mae West and Gypsy Rose Lee, and cloud diagrams for *Little Women*. These props, costumes, and inspirational items lead to bits and episodes within the performance. The performance, then, is more a response than an intention. Characters develop in the interstices among collective improvisation, personal memory, political agenda, and material conditions.

At the same time, they begin working up musical pieces with Laka Daisical, or movement with Stormy Brandenberger. Together, they improvise comedy bits and schtick. Then it's a matter of collecting all of these elements together to mix, match, cut, and paste them into a preliminary outline. They identify episodes that need to be fleshed out. Weaver functions as the director, dramaturg, and editor, leading the discussions. Margolin functions as scene writer, sitting at the typewriter, catching phrases, ideas, and images which she fashions into dialogue and monologues. Shaw writes monologues, songs, and attends to the visuals of sets and props. At this point, they bring in other artists to help execute their ideas: set design and costumer, Susan Young; paintings, Nancy Bardowil and Matthew Owen; lighting, Joni Wong.

They begin rehearsals. Weaver directs, but they all continue to write and revise. Margolin writes the transitions between the developed points. As Weaver describes it: 'We then drag this material to its knees and do public performances – this is where WOW has played an essential role.' They continue to revise from the performances – sometimes up to a year and a half. This is particularly true for the earlier scripts, such as *Split Britches*, *Beauty and the Beast*, *Upwardly Mobile Home*, and *Little Women*. In the later scripts, *Lesbians Who Kill*, *Belle Reprieve*, and *Lust and Comfort*, the different parts of the process overlapped. The performances were considered complete after two to three months of work. In this later period, other kinds of support also hastened the process. Writers such as Margolin and Holly Hughes played a larger role, writing the scripts independently. Theaters such as La Mama and Gay Sweatshop offered space and technical equipment. Collaborators also played a more formal role, such as James Neale-Kennerley, the director and co-author of *Lust and Comfort*, and the collaboration with Bloolips.

I think the plays also evidence the thrift and economizing that poor people and women have learned to practice. The residue of the novel, *Little Women*, and the research into Louisa May Alcott's biography still reside in the text. There is no wasting of the precious matter of women's work and its results. Their sewing continues to hold in the thrift store clothes. The domestic sphere is inscribed in thrifty uses of basic household items, such as painted sets on window shades. *Split Britches* does not presume technical support. For years, they turned on the light that catches them, or turned to change costumes from their own upstage trunk. They assume responsibility for their own housework. At WOW, and in certain of the texts, Lois Weaver plays the gracious host, inviting the audience in to the space: getting them settled, solving any little problems that might occur in the house. Their endless and thrifty labor produces this specifically female and lesbian 'body' of dramatic literature.

THE LESBIAN CRITICAL RECEPTION

Interestingly, many US academic feminist critics have received the work at WOW and of Split Britches primarily as lesbian performance. In fact, writings on Shaw and Weaver's performance strategies, within the context of WOW, as well as part of Split Britches, have composed the dialogue around issues such as how 'lesbian' is visible in performance, how a lesbian address is constituted, the unique nature of a lesbian audience reception, the relation of lesbian performance to community or subculture, the dynamics of lesbian desire within the system of representation, the function of butch-femme role playing, and the lesbian uses of camp. If performances other than lesbian ones composed any significant part of WOW's format, they have played a lesser role in its critical history. In her early article, 'The Dynamics of Desire,' Jill Dolan first notes that 'most' of the spectators are lesbians' (1988, 69), but then continues to write that 'Lesbian desire is always assumed in WOW Café performances' (70). Alisa Solomon, in her initial piece on WOW, asserts that 'Feminism and lesbianism appear in the show, not as issues, but as givens' (1985, 100). Kate Davy contends that 'WOW productions represent lesbian sexualities on the stage and presume lesbians as the audience.' Davy even broadens the focus out beyond the theater: 'The world as constituted by lesbians and inhabited by lesbians is the premise from which most WOW productions proceed, a premise whose consequences radically shift the nature of the performance address' (1992, 231). Side-stepping, for a moment, the question 'what is a lesbian?' we can, however, determine what performance practices these critics associated with lesbian.

For Alisa Solomon, in 1985, the emphases fell on the collective nature of both the artistic work and the economic base of WOW. At that time, individualistic, capitalist practices were allied with patriarchal ones within the feminist critique. Since WOW was, 'essentially,' a separatist space, it aimed to create a space for practicing alternatives to that dominant order. As a separatist space, notes Solomon, WOW also provided safety and support for women who were trying to develop their talents and skills within a violent and restrictive patriarchal tradition. Permission to perform was linked to the 'safety' of an all-woman space, and the equalizing (sharing) of power through collective development. Solomon identifies what were considered to be the signature practices of lesbian feminism in the late 1970s and early 1980s, collectivity and separatism, as the practices of WOW. In my own article, 'From Split Subject to Split Britches' (1989), though making passing mention of butch-femme role playing, the function it serves is to mark a community on the streets, outside the theater, that moves inside and plays, semiotically, to the spectators. My critical investment, in that article, is in constituting a 'collective subject' that transverses social and aesthetic frames:

> Who is the subject of this drama? She is the site where all of these personae collect. Yet the actor is also her character on the street.... The rapid succession of characters alienates the audience from any empathetic relationship to a single character.... Setting this dynamic within the lesbian context of social and sexual relationships, particularly the butch–femme parody of gender roles, the subjects of Split Britches do more than split .... the collective subject of Split Britches.... accumulate(s) vortices of representation and reception of gender throughout several historical periods while retaining a contemporary setting in social class and ethnic identity.
>
> (142–144)

Combining a materialistic feminism, like Solomon's with strategies of representation, I situated lesbian, as a social practice, alongside the workings of class and ethnicity within the subject position. In this analysis, an alternative performance practice would house all of these disruptive forces, collectively, in one heterogeneous subject. Both Solomon and I are still presuming, hoping, to extend a single feminist critique across differences.

In 1986, Kate Davy began her work on how lesbian performance constructs the spectator, specifically referencing WOW performances. Davy seeks to fashion a lesbian address in performance that effectively excises both the 'male subject' and 'sexual difference.' She configures separatist practices as strategies within the system of representation. However, she cleverly complicates that separatist address with WOW stagings of 'butch–femme iconography:'

side-stepping sexual difference by replacing it with sexual simi-
larity, while at the same time retaining gender, or the residue of
sexual difference that people 'wear' in stance, gesture, movement,
mannerisms, voice and dress.

(48)

Here, separatism is aligned with butch–femme role playing. The
masquerade of gender, butch–femme role playing, within a separatism based on gender (women-only), both contradicts and corrects,
as Davy interestingly develops, the latent essentialism that separatism
might empower. Davy's deployment of butch–femme practices as a
correction of essentialist assumptions, written in the mid-1980s,
reflects the historical move toward a lesbian critical and social practice that would abandon, and later, even attack the tenets of early
lesbian feminism.

Jill Dolan, in 1987, continues to develop a focus on butch–femme
role playing at WOW. She perceives it as providing a kind of utopian
disruption of the gender-regime: 'In the lesbian performance context, playing with fantasies of sexual and gender roles offers the
potential for changing gender-coded structures of power' (1988, 68).
Dolan follows in the separatist sense of creating a (utopic) alternative to the patriarchal order. However, unlike early emphases on
collectivity, she aligns, as Davy had done, 'lesbian' primarily with
gender, or more specifically, against gender, through butch–femme
role playing. (While lesbian theory is beginning to distinguish itself
from feminism, it also remains allied with it in retaining gender as
the primary category of oppression and disruption.) This fidelity is
even more evident in Dolan's larger argument within which her
discussion of Weaver and Shaw's butch–femme role playing is
housed. She raises the problem of pornography, the representation
of sexual or seductive acts within the feminist debate, and solves it
with an emphasis on same-sex, or gender, reception theory.

My own argument in 'Towards a Butch–Femme Aesthetic,' appearing in 1987, uses the performance of Split Britches to mobilize
an attack on the homophobia embedded in feminist critical strategies.
Still prior to the actual development of a sex-radical position within
lesbian theory, this article nevertheless seeks to explore the performance of seduction rather than gender play. Shaw and Weaver were
kissing on stage (and off), flirting with each other and the audience,
and sexualizing their dramatic encounters. Lesbian, then, appears
in the play of seduction, as artifice, through butch–femme role
playing. In this argument, butch–femme is more about desire than
gender. While the article critiques the latent heterosexism in feminism, it does so from within feminist discourse. (The move away from
gender towards the representation of lesbian sex, however, reflects
the historical moment of the late 1980s, when the sex-radical

position would finally exit the feminist discourse, to move into a new theoretical and activist alliance with gay men. Yet the article still locates the power of disruption as agency in the subject position – once collective, and here divided into two reciprocal roles.

With the 1990s came the debates over identity politics, the evacuation, by poststructuralists such as Judith Butler, of agency and the subject position, and the complex, psychoanalytic studies that would make the subject into a scenario rather than a character. Lesbian studies have been securely launched and are entering a period of self-criticism. Teresa de Lauretis, in her path-breaking article, 'Sexual Indifference and Lesbian Representation,' arrives at Weaver's performance strategies, as femme, in the film *She Must Be Seeing Things*, and at WOW. What de Lauretis shares with the above commentators, is a concern with lesbian visibility through butch–femme role playing and how it works within the system of representation. For de Lauretis, passing, an issue that would occupy much writing in the 1990s, in critiques both of 'race' and sexual orientation, troubles the butch–femme role playing. While the butch is historically visible, de Lauretis illustrates, how can the femme be seen? This conundrum is tied to de Lauretis's other point, which she aims at Davy and Dolan, that 'lesbian' cannot 'be,' as in an audience of lesbians, but is produced within a scenario of desire. Lesbian is an effect within a triangulated gaze, set before visible heterosexual practices. De Lauretis produced a psychoanalytic mapping of desire. 'Seeing' the lesbian is now understood through the lenses of The Gaze. Invisibility becomes as important an effect, in this analysis, as visibility. If Weaver, as femme, disappears within a heterosexist ('hommosexual', as de Lauretis puts it) economy of the visible – looks like a straight woman – then seeing her must imply the desire to do so, and, with that, the dynamic of internal, even unconscious factors.

In 'Identity and Seduction: Lesbians in the Mainstream' (1993), Lynda Hart reviews the debate occasioned by WOW and the butch–femme role playing Weaver and Shaw perform. *Anniversary Waltz*, Shaw and Weaver's retrospective on their performance and relationship, offers Hart a perfect vehicle for her critical review. Following Butler, Hart would exit the politics of identity and visibility. She seeks to correct the 'problem' of identity with the process of identification. After describing how Weaver and Shaw play Hepburn and Tracy to one another in their seduction scene from *Beauty and the Beast*, Hart writes: 'Rather than showing their lesbian "identities," they demonstrate the construction of their desires through the history of identifications. Identity itself thus loses its meaning as a fixed construct, and sexuality is performed as a historical process that is both social and psychic' (130). Hart then moves even further into a Lacanian model to find 'lesbian' in Shaw and Weaver's performance to enter the realm of the visible through 'hallucination.' The conditions of spectatorship overcome a consideration of performing, within such Lacanian critiques.

At this point, it might seem we have moved quite a distance from the actual performances of Split Britches. If we consider, however, the numerous treatments afforded Shakespeare, or even a contemporary playwright such as Pinter, or Beckett, we can perceive how (the critical reception of unique and influential performance, while returning to simple description, also writes that performance into the philosophy and history of its times.) These articles are a testament to the strength of image and action Split Britches provides to feminists and lesbians. Some readers who are familiar with these articles may have felt a kind of mounting tension in the dialogue as authors refer back to one another and disagree openly with their assertions. Others, familiar with the early practices of feminism and materialism, may feel enriched and excited by a dialogue which unfolds through contradiction and self-criticism. While, as one of the players, I do not want to disguise my role in the process, neither do I want to use this opportunity to 'get the last word.' Any summary or conclusion here would be pretentious. Yet I want to attempt to describe what I believe is happening in the present moment.

As lesbian 'identity' is troubled by an insistence on more complex and fluid processes of visibility and the initial stage of lesbian theory retreats behind (some of) us, the limits, the boundaries of what constitutes lesbian become more intriguing. As neither WOW, nor Split Britches can be 'simply' lesbian any longer, the complicating presence of Deb Margolin, the heterosexual who has worked in this context, comes to the fore. The presence of Margolin in the troupe is reminiscent of that early alliance in feminism among lesbians, straight women, women of color. It harkens back to the 1970s Spiderwoman model. Margolin's continuing work with Split Britches is inspiring in the way that it keeps that tradition alive. Playing alongside a butch–femme couple, who draw multitudes of lesbian grassroots community people to their performances, Margolin continues to make the point that her aesthetic labor is gynocentric in dedication and her world is not restricted by the heterosexist imperative. Yet, following the above critiques, Margolin's role also raises these questions: How is this lesbian theater, with Margolin performing and writing in it? How is it not?

'Queerer Than Thou: Being and Deb Margolin,' by Lynda Hart and Peggy Phelan employs the example of Margolin to dismantle critical attempts to secure lesbian as an identity. They raise the sore scepter of exclusivity, 'queer border patrols,' as they put it, to unsettle the earlier analyses cited above. Yet circulating their co-authorial desire through Margolin produces a coy production of lesbian identity through denying it. Keeping to my earlier promise,

to side-step the debates around identity and observe what performance practices are aligned with 'lesbian,' I will sketch out, in the
following discussions of the actual plays, shifting appearances of
lesbian, when Margolin is on or off stage, and in the texts she did
and did not write. I will argue that, while Margolin never plays the
heterosexual woman in the classic sense of the word, i.e. never with
a man, a certain effect is produced by her presence in the scene.
Shaw and Weaver play lesbian differently when Margolin is present
on stage than when she is not. They also write the lesbian scenes
differently than Margolin.

For, as many have argued both theoretically and historically
before, lesbian social lives have been ghettoized, producing different
styles of social 'intercourse,' in the ghetto and out. Certainly, as
conditions improve, assimilation greatly diminishes the effects of
ghettoization. Nevertheless, the current attacks by fundamentalist
Christian organizations, neo-nazis, and the new right continue to
threaten and harass lesbians, creating paranoia (or justified fear),
closeted behavior, and feelings of violence. The later plays of Split
Britches, *Lesbians Who Kill* and *Lust and Comfort*, effectively stage
these dark times and their pernicious effects. Consider, however, that
Margolin wrote parts of *Lesbians Who Kill*. As a Jewish-identified
woman, in these times of renewed anti-Semitism and anti-affirma-
tive action decisions, she also feels and understands the effects of
the backlash. Also, her commitment to imagining the lesbian position remains clear. So how does she write lesbian seduction? The
individual plays compose a complex picture, but one style does
emerge that I will discuss briefly here.

Margolin's passages of associational wordplay that bear the
burden of seductive language in *Lesbians Who Kill* are lyrical and
exciting. They morph a kind of wild proximity, indicative of seduction. The prime example of this style may be found in the play on
the word 'sloe' (see page 194 in this volume). The contributions
Shaw and Weaver made to the script signify differently. Let me
caution the reader here that the point of this comparison is not that
one style is lesbian and the other is not but, as before, to see with
what differing performance and textual practices 'lesbian' is aligned.
For example, Shaw and Weaver created the lip-synching sections.
Now, lip-synching has long been a practice of the gay subculture –
particularly drag queen shows. One of the most new drag acts of
this sort is by a performer called Lypsinka. Weaver and Shaw have
adapted that practice to lesbian theater. Kate Davy, in her article,
'Fe/male Impersonation: The Discourse of Camp' makes an intricate
and revealing comparison between certain gay male theatrical practices and those of Weaver and Shaw. But, for the purposes of this
investigation, it suffices to perceive lip-synching as bearing the mark
of the subculture. Weaver and Shaw are acting in the tradition of

bar shows, etc. For butch–femme role playing, a practice adapted from drag queens wittily inverts the direction of gender masquerade within the tradition, and complicates its signifying practices.

Likewise, *Lust and Comfort*, developed in the context of Gay Sweatshop, resonates with styles and concerns of the current 'queer' community. Beginning the narrative, or more precisely, one of the narratives, with the transgendered, or transsexual person, reveals an investment in the current discussions within the community about the new contribution that critique makes to 'queer'. The play, then, starts off with one foot deep into the community's 'real' estate. Likewise, following scenarios around who will 'top' whom reflect sex-radical sex play. These and other markers flag community issues and practices as diverse and ephemeral as the community has become.

In other words, Margolin's passages offer seductive wordplay, whereas Shaw and Weaver offer inventive recyclings of subcultural, gay and lesbian performance practice. To test out some of the stylistic differences, compare Shaw's speech on butch in *Belle Reprieve* to Weaver's monologue on femme that works through the myth of Cassandra. Margolin scripted that passage. Then look at Weaver's re-de-construction of femme in *Lust and Comfort*. All of this debate, hopefully, leads back to the plays and performances themselves. I have cited articles above that would, if read in full, lead to different approaches to these performances that might enliven various readings of them.

SPLIT BRITCHES

This play marks the initial collaboration of the trio and is the project from which they took their name. The material originated in Weaver's family history. Referring to the tradition of women's performance art, Weaver as 'Cora as Narrator' informs us that

> a lot of artists were drawing from autobiographical material. They were going back to their roots. So I decided to go back to my roots. I went back to the Blue Ridge Mountains of Virginia where I was born. And through a series of oral history projects, you know, tape recordings, photographs, and so on. . . .

she begins the story of her family generations. Vivian Patraka, in her insightful and meticulous introduction to the first publication of the script in *Women & Performance*, notes that this beginning of the idea of a 'continuing performance group took shape – a group I see as departing from both the universalizing rituals of cultural feminism and the documentary realism of representative women's experience, which so often was the core of earlier feminist collective performance' (1989, 59). So, while this project may have found inspiration in the women's performance tradition at the time, it strays from realism and ironizes the standard elements of the documentary. The slide show, which typically documents such projects is turned into *tableaux vivants*, with actors moving from pose to pose, as the black slice of the projector segments the live space. Later, as in the placement of slides 21–22, the convention returns to interrupt the narrative flow of the performance. The intervention of *tableaux* jolts the observer back from narrative and empathetic response to see the memorial, historical function of this piece, as well as to create, in the Brechtian sense, a critical attitude about just why and how these women were forced into poverty.

Poverty plays a significant role in the depiction of these lives, but not as oppression heroically overcome, or sadly endured. Instead, their poverty is the motor of necessary labor and thus strong women. It is a force for decision-making, such as eating biscuits without jam to provide for the future, and to save wood, no matter how aesthetically carved, for the fire. While this is rural poverty, Split Britches will continue, in its future plays, to incorporate urban poverty as a similar productive force. As we watch Della make biscuits and see the perfect dough emerge during the performance, we can see how gender produces a different perspective on domestic need. Think, for example, of Sam Shephard's *Curse of the Starving Class*, in which the son returns repeatedly to a refrigerator, where he finds nothing prepared for him to eat. To cook for oneself is a given in *Split Britches*. Later, in *Upwardly Mobile Home*, coffee is brewed onstage. They spread peanut butter on crackers. Prepared coffee, at Burger King, is Tammy's fantasy of a morning luxury.

Rural life is represented by the sound of bugs, the stories spun in the realm of flies – their sound, their swatting. The play resonates with the sonoral landscape of the country. In this script, musical numbers include songs of the country, from the hymns of the calling of the chickens, to singing the sound of the cow. The dialogue includes storying through animals, such as the story of the turkey opening out into a full dimension – dreaming through them as they live with them and listen to them. The human imagination is intertwined with those animals. This ecology is not one of humans isolated among humans that will set the later, more urban-based plays, but humans among other species.

Cora (Weaver) plays the simple or slow people who live among poor white trash. There is no thought to separate them out from the group. Those of us from white trash backgrounds are familiar with this 'slow' character. Cora evidences their wisdom and quality of life, even their seductive ways, as Della is drawn to dance with Cora and kiss her. Yet Cora's unadorned will threatens to flash out beyond control – the same laws of reason or sociality can't be counted upon in her case. And time is all present time for Cora –

grandma is still upstairs, dead on the bed, in the present moment.

Emma (Margolin) is the philosopher. Sounds, events, interactions lead her off into meditations on life and death. The sound of flies inspires ruminations on death, aging, and dreaming. She can think herself into high gears of association and disassociation, crescendoing up from a blind turkey to 'two hundred girls swattin' the bugs. Feel my muscle. I built this wall myself. Take a trip to California. Walk on your fingers.' Each character is isolated in her own memories and dreams and interconnected, sporadically with the others, in sharing fantasies or discussing housework.

There is a darkness in the piece, in spite of the flights of fancy and the humor. The style of Split Britches plays on the razor edge between the horror and oppression assigned to women by the dominant society and the creative liberation their imagination and labor provide them with for survival. *Split Britches* concludes on the lesbian fire burning inside of Della (Shaw). The fire so hot that it 'can make ashes out of me if I ain't careful.' Kept in the closet of her pocket: 'lookin' up at me just as cute and sweet as a pretty girl . . . but then it starts to hurt. So you got to beat it. You got to put it out.' Earlier, Della's strip, down through the protective layers of the clothes to her underwear and her whiskey liberates her to sing Besse Jackson's 'Bull Dyke Women.' But the words are actually 'B.D. women' – a secret language for the initiates. Her flirtation with Cora, their dance together that Cora can't admit, stops with Cora's indirect condemnation: 'the preacher's comin.' This first play stages the power of the closet, the fragile moments even closeted people may find to express their desire, their truncation, and finally, the agony of the secret and the pent-up need.

In 1981, with little historical precedent, then, Weaver and Shaw set out to create lesbian on their stage. In her article on the play, Patraka quotes from an unpublished interview Rhonda Blair conducted with Weaver and Shaw. Shaw begins:

> 'It's very new, being a lesbian. The word and the people being out in the world is very new. . . . So we're trying to find out what a lesbian is. Or what I am. We're trying to find out without all these other constructions or rules. . . .' Weaver continues, 'When we worked on *Split Britches*, we wanted to create characters that people would identify with and like, and then realize . . . "Oh, my God, I like a lesbian."'

> (1989, 60)

Two different processes are at work here: first, to represent lesbian and second, to represent her to 'others'. Della's role acts lesbian out, while Cora's and Emma's roles reveal how those 'others' find themselves in relation to lesbians and live among them. For Cora, there is the latent attraction, managed through indirect discourse and moral regulation. Emma is not involved, in that sense. Margolin has invented a character who witnesses, accepts, allows the private space, finds the parameters of playing with, but also serves as monitor – the border of lesbian – where it stops.

BEAUTY AND THE BEAST

Beauty is an ongoing theme in the work of Split Britches. Woman as object of the gaze is traced from this play, through Tammy Whynot in *Upwardly Mobile Home*, the issue of pornography that runs through *Little Women*, Blanche and Stella in *Belle Reprieve*, and Weaver's show around the politics of beauty, *In Your Face*. Although Margolin's character of Khurve plays out the issue in *Little Women*, it is generally Weaver's roles, the femme roles, that situate the issue. In this play, beauty is situated within ethnic and religious debates, social issues of the time, gender issues, and lesbian desire.

The play heralds the beginning of the long rule of Republican politics, informed by the conservative Christian agenda, that would dominate the US scene up through the present. The Salvation Army officer serves as the guide. At once the Pat Nixon-type hostess and the revivalist tent show salvationist, Beauty calls for the audience to sacrifice something – to repent. She summons the memory of repentances by Johnny Cash, Patti Smith, Bob Dylan – 'celebrities for God' she calls them. The relationship between political and entertainment success through the embrace of Christianity is emphasized throughout the play. That same rhetoric is also undone as empty spectacle. Even the gunshot wound to Reagan, his donning the mantle of martyrdom, so familiar in Christian narratives, is parodied. As the Beast dies, she gets up to warn 'Don't fall for it! Reagan tried it.'

In this political atmosphere, Margolin's Jewish character is set against the tide of assimilation. She flips into the Jewish stand-up comedian who tells anti-Reagan jokes. Wearing the *talis*, and sporting *payes*, she parodies the style of joke-telling that male comedians used in their shows in the Catskills. She tells the audience she always wanted to be the famous theologian Martin Buber. In this play, she represents the masculine, from ethnic 'other' to the Father – the authority figure in the fairy tale. Shaw plays an old lady with purse and floral dress, who is also the Beast of butch desire. The contradictions of roles wind complexly through the religious and ethnic images national politics deploy to secure their programs of self-interest for the affluent. Each character, operating on three levels at once, demonstrates how sexism/racism/homophobia work together to produce what seem varied differences, but actually create an over-arching program of oppression. At the same time, each character evidences humor and understanding, though cloaked in assimilated prejudices. If they openly sport the dark versions of social behavior that dominant society has inculcated in them, the brainwashing also leads them into wild, insane riffs, in which alternate thoughts may surface. Like the closet in *Split Britches*, conspiracy fantasies lurk in the closeted leftist critique that hides beneath their education, such as: 'Nixon kidnapped Patti Hearst.'

Bad jokes and painful puns dominate the vaudeville sections of the play, as they intersect with the flowery, awkward simulation of fairy-tale language. This play stages the interaction between 'high' and 'low' language. As the audience wonders how the actors dare tell such bad jokes, or play such bald humor, they also begin to ask how such flowery verse dares to make things so obscure and indirect. In this way, the play challenges actors to perform one of the most sophisticated and difficult types of stage business: the 'throw away.' How do you 'throw away' all signs of 'professional' acting and writing and make the point that this is the intent? I have noticed, in watching this play before audiences less accustomed to the theater that the laughter, which is one of recognition, occurs far less than in an audience of aficionados. The sophistication of Split Britches resides in just this skill of deconstructing dominant forms through popular ones, rather than through the avant-garde tradition.

Once again, the full-out lesbian scene, the coming out/seduction played through identifications with Katharine Hepburn and Spencer Tracy, emerges near the conclusion of the play. During this scene, Margolin is offstage. The difference between this scene and Della's in *Split Britches* is that two lesbians come out *to each other*. Della is isolated in the first play, as are most lesbian characters in mainstream plays. The traditional coming out scene is played by the isolated lesbian to members of heterosexual society – often the parents, who represent its values. This coming out is blessed with a kiss, rather than a condemnation. At the end of the scene, when Margolin returns, the plot turns to other issues. As lesbian is run through identification, it is enclosed by national agendas.

The play ends as performance, retreating into itself, and insulting the audience. Hilarity is the weapon against the forces of darkness, which were consolidating their power at the beginning of the 1980s. They are represented, even named, yet the play is not pervaded by the kind of darkness that shadows *Split Britches*. It is as if its own self-knowledge, that is, its un-closeted condition, brings it to the radical edge of aggressive humor. If the women in *Split Britches* lived before the feminist and lesbian critique could offer an explanation and liberation from the restrictive mind games dominant society would inculcate in their socialization, *Beauty and the Beast* mobilizes characters, narratives, songs, and seduction through those critiques. As *Split Britches* is confined in the house, traveling inward through stories and monologues to the women's repressed desires,

Beauty and the Beast turns out on the audience and at the dominant culture. The lesbian closet of *Split Britches* becomes coming out stories in *Beauty and the Beast*: coming out against the national agenda of homophobia, racism, and class privilege.

UPWARDLY MOBILE HOME

The idea for the setting of this piece came from a Fall 1983 article in *Rolling Stone* about a marathon camp-out in Allentown, Pennsylvania. The person who could remain up on a billboard for the longest amount of time would win a mobile home. The contest became a fiasco because everyone was so desperate to win that no one would give up. People remained up on the billboard for over a year. The company that organized the contest refused any responsibility for the people's welfare, so townspeople brought them food and emptied their buckets of feces.

Split Britches wrote this dedication on one of their programs:

> This show is dedicated to survivors of all depressions; people living under bridges; in boxcars and doorways; to the homeless; to the people who can no longer afford to use pay phones; to everyone who finds it easier to make money waiting tables than to apply for a grant; to the cracked building on East 3rd Street; to all the ways that art grows out through the cracks of poverty and need.

In this play, the so-called affluent 1980s is portrayed as the time of an economic depression. This period marked the beginning of rapidly rising numbers of homeless people in the US as well as a time of the intense gentrification of Manhattan. Housing for the poor became co-ops for the rich. As the gentrification spread farther and farther through the once-poor sections of Manhattan, the resultant homeless people were forced out to the perimeters of the island. The characters in this play are camping out under the Brooklyn Bridge – about as far as you can go. Their rootless, socially invisible ways, however, also offer them protection. As Mom says: 'We're safe here, no one can see us, we're invisible.'

The characters are performers, rehearsing and playing on the street. They reveal the class privilege of reality that assigns the poor to invisibility and fantasy. In Levine's reading of ads for co-ops, she also reveals how class privilege can fulfill a fantasy – buy a lifestyle. They, as artists then, are both impoverished as invisible in that regime, but therefore safe from its violence. Alternatively, art can also play a role that is complicit with class privilege. The character of the Mother (Shaw) suggests the time of the other depression, the 1930s, as she plays a *grande dame* of the theater rehearsing a popular hit from the time, *The Shanghai Gesture*. As such, she sets up the contradiction between success in art and the staging of the lavish productions that flourish at the time that many fall through the bottom of the social net. After all, Florence Reed had made her career in the leading role, playing over 1280 performances during the depression. Yet *Shanghai Gesture* also portrays the oppression of women and one woman's financial triumph over it, but it does so within a basically, as the characters describe it, 'racist, sexist play.' As always in the work of Split Britches, the situation rides the rails of contradiction.

This group of characters are performers, who continue to work together, identify as a 'family,' 'even though they come from extremely different backgrounds.' At this point in their development, Split Britches as a troupe is beginning self-consciously to stage its own cohesion. Interestingly, in this 'family' Weaver and Margolin retain their cultural roots: Weaver as the southern Tammy Whynot and Margolin as the Jewish Levine. They play on the stereotypes of their class and ethnic backgrounds, while also exhibiting the brilliant coping strategies unique to each. They all sing 'I Want to Be in America' from *West Side Story* in Yiddish, parodying the utopic casting of the immigrant dream. Tammy displays the specifically white-trash anxiety around poverty: 'It's like we're living on the wrong side of the tracks. . . . I get so depressed when there's no toilet paper.' Margolin's Levine is doing business, with the frenetic pace of the entrepreneur, who would get a fast start on upward mobility. Weaver's Tammy is played as a sexy, blonde bombshell – she will make it up the ladder of success in her role of woman-as-object. Elin Diamond, in 'Mimesis, Mimicry, and the 'True-Real'' cites Weaver's performance as an example of the 'political potential of mimesis–mimicry.'

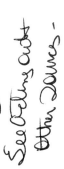

> Through subtle exaggeration, Weaver defuses the obvious fetishization inherent in that role. . . . Weaver foregrounds Tammy's exploitation 'without' (as Irigaray puts it) allowing herself to be simply reduced to it.
>
> (373)

So Tammy is both the country–western star, and the deconstruction of such a persona. She is the performer who exploits and is exploited by her persona.

Shaw is called 'Mom.' This title seems to reflect her position of authority in the group. It also relates openly to the fact that she is one in 'real' life for, since the title is only metaphorical within the play, the bit on the 'lesbian mother's legs' only makes sense within the broader context. Hardly a butch role, and only tangentially a lesbian one, within the play, the mother becomes more enigmatic than Tammy and Levine. What is her background? We have only the *chinoiserie* she wears in *The Shanghai Gesture*. She is 'unmarked' in one sense. While she exhibits all the *grande dame* haughtiness of her role in the play, she is the character who turns the materialist critique directly onto the audience:

> You have paid to see me. You will not get your money back. Your money does not pay me for my work. . . . Do you get paid what you're worth for what you do? Am I worth five dollars (*or the price of a theater ticket*). . . . I am a mother, a good mother, are you willing to pay to see a good lesbian mother? . . . Do you want to see my legs? I don't know if you have enough money to pay to see a good lesbian mother's legs.

Lesbian mother comes in here for the first time, attached to her role as performer. How much is she worth as a freak like, as she puts it, the fat woman in the circus? Is lesbian what you pay to see? Does lesbian function to titillate the audience who may look, desir- ingly, at her legs? (As in *Split Britches*, Shaw is assigned the lesbian role – there is some isolation in it as an identity, even though Weaver plays scenes with her that are seductive.) Does this practice suggest the history of butch–femme role playing, in which the butch demonstrates lesbian through her visibility and the femme accompanies her? Is Weaver slowly beginning to figure out how to play femme explicitly as lesbian? Whatever the answers, this play continues to shape those roles within a primary dedication to a gender and an economic critique. /

LITTLE WOMEN

The play was developed through workshop performances at WOW in 1988, to open at the Interartheater in New York in 1989.

PROGRAM NOTES

Lois Weaver:

> When we gathered to work on our fourth piece we asked each other what we had been thinking about. . . . Censorship in the Feminist community around the issue of pornography was the question for which we didn't have an answer. . . . But we decided to take it on and chose to put this debate against the backdrop of the moralistic tale of *Little Women*. It all seemed so simple for Jo and Meg and Amy and Beth. As we began our work, our focus shifted from the book to the author herself. . . . She became the sole supporter of her family. She was an abolitionist and a feminist (suffragist). . . . She also wrote lurid and violent tales of adventure under the pseudonym of A.M. Bernard, and sold them to periodicals. . . . Louisa May Alcott was literally a two-handed writer. . . . She hated writing 'moral pap for the young' and at

the same time was not entirely comfortable in the lurid style of thrillers. She wrote for money. . . . Louisa May became the symbol for our question about censorship.

Deb Margolin:

> Although Ms Alcott's work had seemed stilted and incomplete to me as a child, I drew strength in my efforts to draw a portrait of the strumpet from seeing that Alcott's mannered style had not been a matter of choice, but instead had arisen from the same inner segmentation that made that portrayal of an overtly sexual character so difficult for me personally.

Vivian Patraka, in *The Kenyon Review*, has reproduced the text of one version of this script along with copious descriptions of the performance itself. For those interested in reconstructing the performance itself, this work is invaluable. Along with the script, Patraka also published an excellent critical study of the play, 'Split Britches in Little Women The Tragedy: Staging Censorship, Nostalgia, and Desire,' where she argues that, although the play is specifically about censorship, written in a time of the censorship of the NEA and other funding agencies, it more broadly addresses 'cultural consensus' (7). Patraka is referring to the general consensus sought by censorship, but I would suggest that the specific feminist construction of consensus might also be addressed here.

The rift within feminist circles around the anti-pornography debates was/is deep and painful. When, as mentioned earlier, the Barnard Conference (1982) broke up in a confrontation between s/m lesbians who were pro-sex, erotics, even pornography and the feminists who were anti-porn, the debate was on. Interestingly, Split Britches includes both these factions: the pro-sex lesbian one and the feminist one that is anti-woman-as-object, etc. Later in the 1980s, Catherine MacKinnon and Andrea Dworkin drafted legislation that would remove pornography, including any material deemed exploitive of women's bodies, from the realm of public consumption. They toured the US to build support for what they hoped would be city ordinances. They also attempted to solicit signatures on petitions from individual feminists – people were almost required to take some stand in this debate. The Feminist Anti-Censorship Task Force (FACT) was formed to combat their legal strategy. They worked along with the ACLU. The National Women's Studies Association conference in 1985 was divided by debates from the two sides. Feminist presses were pressured to write statements of ethical responsibility. Naiad, the lesbian press, was attacked for its marketing of lesbian images. The debate continues through the present. In 1994 the lesbian collective Kiss and Tell published *Her Tongue on My Theory*, a book of explicit lesbian sexual images, along with a narrative about their interaction with feminist anti-porn forces, censorship in Canada, and sexual scenarios. They collect the debate around such issues alongside explicit photos to lobby for the publication of sex-radical materials from within the feminist community. In other words, the debate around these issues has lasted over a decade and is still not resolved. Split Britches performs their version of *Little Women* as an intervention into this discord.

Patraka continues to note that this 'cultural division' in the play, demonstrated by the representation of Alcott's two hands – 'the right for the children's novels and the left (with a pseudonym) for the thrillers she published,' also concerns a division of performance styles. On the one hand, so to speak, is burlesque, a 'disreputable counterpart to the more family oriented vaudeville.' Patraka develops the way that the production does not critique the sexism in the burlesque tradition, but 'reclaims the form, and with it, the desire to see bodies, from the realm of the unacceptable' (8). Patraka sets up vaudeville as the 'other' to burlesque, but I think here it is more the history of imagining the Victorian, or the girlish – the pleasure, the fantasy of prudent, modest *Little Women* that provides the cultural imaginary.

The set of *Little Women*, as in many of Split Britches productions, makes a unique and discursive contribution to the meaning of the piece. Patraka writes, 'Like many postmodern works, then, *LWTT* presents its motifs and suggestions more in spatial than temporal terms' (9). The bifurcation, the traditional Split in Split Britches, is here imaged as Heaven and Hell. In the tradition of the Morality Plays, Heaven and Hell are the other limits of the stage, situating all action specifically on the spectrum between. Split Britches locates the debate on pornography and illicit sexuality within these parameters, which historically defined it. Added to this effect are cut-out clouds. They took the concept of the clouds from Nicola Sabbattini's 1638 *Manual for Constructing Theatrical Scenes and Machines*. Sabbatini's designs for how paradise would be constructed are printed on the clouds. The designs make Heaven visible, as pornography makes sex visible. In a sense, the play explores the price and construction of visibility. The performance then explores the debate over pornography with its theatrical history as its set. History, then, is the ground upon which the debate takes place – particularly the history of the stage, of representation – since pornography represents sexual acts. On this ground, Shaw gestures the position of the fire-and-brimstone preacher who, in the heated act of moral condemnation, represents an aggressive sexual posture. Margolin acts the 'strumpet', on the other end of the spectrum, but one with more actual 'morality' than the preacher. Weaver's Louisa, the two-handed representer, plays in between. Thus, as the stage unfurls the banners of Heaven and Hell, surveying the ground of the moral and immoral, the characters collapse the distinctions within the contradictions of their characters.

If sexuality and its representation are the focus of the play, how does lesbian sexuality fit into this picture? Patraka, in a footnote, explains that the name Khurve is Yiddish for strumpet or whore. It is applied to Margolin, the Jewish member of the playing team. Patraka then discusses how 'the heterosexual as strumpet or whore' in this production, fits 'under the rubric of lesbian theater.' Referring first to Joan Nestle's description of the historical alliance between prostitutes and whores in the 1950s and early 1960s and then to Lynda Hart's essay on Karen Finlay, in which she theorizes the 'connection between the figure of the sexually explicit performer and the lesbian performer. . . . to the censorious mind,' Patraka concludes: '*LWTT* gestures to both the complex interrelationships theorized by Hart and the history marked by Nestle. . . .' (footnote 3, p. 13) Thus, from within a debate on morality and censorship, lesbian lines up with all deleted sexual practices. In this way, a coalition may be formed between straight feminists and lesbians – particularly within the political support of sex workers.

BELLE REPRIEVE

Belle Reprieve is a queer deconstruction of Tennessee Williams' *A Streetcar Named Desire*. The title is a pun on Belle Reve, the plantation where Blanche and Stella were raised, in *Streetcar*. The production was developed in London in the fall of 1990 at the Drill Hall and at La Mama in winter 1991. It toured both Great Britain and the US *Belle Reprieve* marks a turning point in the work of Weaver and Shaw. Lesbian, nested within feminist concerns in the earlier plays, making only sporadic appearances and sometimes playing as an adjunct to other representations, begins to play a leading role. The next three projects, *Belle Reprieve*, *Lesbians Who Kill*, and *Lust and Comfort* will be primarily lesbian plays, in that they will focus on lesbian, or 'queer', issues, and play within those subcultural signs. Consequently, the feminist context, which governed the critique of the earlier plays, now relocates, as lesbian becomes 'upwardly mobile.'

This play also foregrounds film as a cultural source – another turn in the work of the company. *Belle Reprieve* is based on the film iconography of *Streetcar*, more than the script. It is as much about the cultural icons established by Marlon Brando and Vivien Leigh as it is about the actual characters. Visual images from the film haunt the stage design and the construction of scenes. The earlier plays took more inspiration from written texts, such as the fairytale of *Beauty and the Beast*, or the novel of *Little Women*. The plays following *Belle Reprieve* turn more to film. *Lesbians Who Kill* plays through film noir images of women with guns and *Lust and Comfort* is based primarily on the three films listed at the top of the script, designing scenes taken directly from *The Servant* and *The Bitter Tears of Petra von Kant*.

Another first for the company is collaborating with men. For Shaw, the work with Bloolips presents an interesting return in her career. Bette Bourne, founder of Bloolips, and Shaw worked together in Hot Peaches before Shaw met Weaver, or began to perform within a feminist context. For Weaver, it would be the first time to work with men since the formation of Spiderwoman. Likewise, Bloolips had not worked with women. Bette Bourne has appeared in various Bloolips shows, including *Gland Motel* and the Obie-winning *Lust in Space*. Outside of Bloolips, he enjoyed critical acclaim for his lead role in Neil Bartlett's *Sarassine*. Precious Pearl is a long-time member of the troupe, working as set designer as well as actor. Each duo is also a couple, who have lived together for roughly the same amount of time and each duo also has a long history of gender masquerade.

The interaction of gender masquerade with members of the 'real' gender whom they impersonate brought a fertile field of exploration for all four of the actors. At one point in the notebooks, they refer to the project as 'four actors escaping from a script – a heterosexual script.' Bette Bourne is not a drag queen, but a 'radical sissy.' His female roles do not try to emulate women, in the sense of trying to 'pass,' with wigs and falsies; rather, Bourne resituates the feminine as an affect within a gay male sensibility. Precious Pearl, as Mitch, relates to that feminine displacement, both in his own 'sissiness' and his flirtation with Blanche/Bourne. They play these displacements to Weaver's full-out femme performance and Shaw's complex of Stanley, which includes both butch and 'man.' As a result, the masculine/feminine divide doubles in its complexity. After all, Shaw's Stanley plays masculine aggression to Bourne's Blanche, while Weaver's Stella seeks sisterhood with her. Through it all, Pearl's Mitch moves like the floating signifier of attentive masculinity.

Shaw notes that the rape scene was the first enigma to confront her. How would she rape Bourne's Blanche? In what way? How would their sexuality be constructed? Weaver sums it up: 'the men went for romantic friendship, which is supposed to be lesbian, while Peg and I took on the physical/carnal kind of sex usually attributed to gay male sex.' The violence in *Streetcar* posed difficulties for the troupe. Stanley is a batterer and rapist. The cast stressed this attribute as specifically macho het–male, in its stereotypical representation.

Improvising on these themes, a process familiar to Split Britches was more threatening to Bloolips. Precious Pearl, in an interview in the January 9, 1991 issue of *What's On* put it this way:

> Bette and I tend to work in quite a narrative way. . . . Allowing yourself room to search around with free association feels quite

dangerous, it starts to throw up some horrific and frightening images. In the past we've tended to centre around comic effects, but Lois and Peggy like to walk the line between horror and poignancy and tragedy and humour.

(37)

The episode of Bette's outbreak from the scene, begging to do a 'real' play in a 'nice frock' ironically leads directly to the rape. Playing a woman can have frightening consequences. So can realism.

Weaver and Shaw found that working with gay men allowed them to become more 'queer' in their performance. In this play, Shaw/ Stanley delivers a powerful monologue on being butch in the streets, in the sheets, and on the stage. The tender coming-out stories in *Beauty and the Beast*, the flashes of flirtation in *Split Britches* and *Upwardly Mobile Home* seem timid and exploratory compared to this full-out passionate affair between Stanley and Stella. Sex is the subject of the play. Stanley emerges from the audience, standing out in the dark of the house to call out Blanche's sex appeal, rouse her to rough foreplay, work into the famous shot of him on 'his' knees before her, face buried in her groin, to carry her offstage and into the bed. Butch–femme play here is not about kissing, but about having sex.

LESBIANS WHO KILL

The original idea for this script came from Margolin, who had been avidly following the Aileen Wuornos case. The idea of lesbian serial killers promised to raise many significant issues, so Margolin suggested to Weaver and Shaw that she would write it, if they would perform it. Margolin saw it as the lesbian serial killer's version of *The Brothers Karamazov*. After hearing the idea from Margolin, Weaver and Shaw describe a series of events that led them to resolve it would be their next piece. They set the discovery within an interview between the two characters in the piece: 'May Interviews June', *Movement Research* Fall 1991 4–5:

JUNE: It popped out of my mouth at the end of a very long day. We were on tour with Bloolips in *Belle Reprieve*. After surviving the usual daily harrassments, like groups of men on the street corner who need to comment on your hair and body parts, or overhearing a police officer referring to some unidentified woman as 'that cunt,' we arrived at the theater to find a difficult review of our work in the daily paper. It was not difficult because it was bad . . . in a sense those are easy . . . it was difficult because it was written from an openly misogynist point of view. The men in the group were characterized as 'hilarious and poignant' and 'anarchically farcical,' while the women were criticised as 'self-indulgent and monotonous' and 'less imaginatively and more didactically political.' It was a divisive review, and unconsciously we let it top our delicate balance of male–female politics in the group. We began to look at each other and wonder if we believed what the reviewer had said and did the men agree, and had we come as far as we thought we had in our own struggle against sexism? All these issues were too big to talk about on the eve of the last performance of a thirteen-week run and seven-month process. So after the performance, the women in the company decided to go out for a beer to commiserate the state of our sex in our society. We found ourselves in a bar that provided large-screen video entertainment for the customers, featuring women being beaten, shot and tortured. We promptly left the bar only to find that all our cars had been towed, not by the police, but by a local towing scam. When we protested that a $200 towing charge was too much for parking five minutes in a shopping center parking lot, we were reprimanded for not behaving in a 'lady-like manner.' It was at this moment that I announced to every man within ear-shot that the title of our next piece was going to be *Lesbians Who Kill*.

Gender anger, which had taken a back seat to 'queer' solidarity in *Belle Reprieve*, now takes the front seat, in the car in which *Lesbians Who Kill* takes place. In spite of the fine work of the collaborative process by both groups, the reception back into mainstream presses and audiences, and even lesbian and gay audiences, re-enacted how sexism can proceed, even within 'queer' circles. Thus, from *Belle Reprieve*, Split Britches moves into the expression of direct anger and violent impulses against such sexism.

The case of Wuornos offered the perfect metaphor for the situation. The following offers some selections from the newspaper clippings the group used for their beginning improvisations:

The Times, April 1, 1992 p. 7b: 'Wuornos said "I am no serial killer ... What I was was a prostitute." This article reports that, although Wuornos confessed that she shot and killed seven male motorists who picked her up for sex, she insisted she killed only those who had become abusive or violent.'

Sun Sentinel, December 20, 1990, reports that the police had arrested two women for the murders. The women, one blonde, one brunette, matched the composite sketches. They were found in a $25-a-night-motel in 'a rundown part of the city.'

Sun Sentinel, December 8, 1990, notes that one detective in the case 'could think only of one case involving two women serial killers: a pair of Michigan lesbians who killed "to solidify their love."'

Village Voice, April 28, 1992 p. 40, an advertisement for a line of guns 'discreetly dubbed as Feminine Protection,' 'The line includes stylish totes, evening clutches – even a garter belt holster.'

Other sources, May and June note in their interview, report that women who kill have suffered abuse. In the case of Wuornos, her father was jailed for raping a seven-year-old girl, and she was impregnated by her grandfather.

> JUNE: 'We would never be able to tell these women's stories. In our work in Split Britches we've tried not to co-opt the experience of others for political and theatrical effect. We look to where our own images and histories intersect with the issue and find our own impulses in that intersection ... our own complicity.'

So, while they might base their performance on the case of Wuornos and surrounding materials, they would never attempt to reproduce it; rather, they use it as a springboard into their own intersection and complicity with the situation.

The subject matter and the title prompt many to ask 'Do you, as lesbians, hate men?' In the interview between May/June, June answers this anxiety:

> JUNE: You mean do I hate men? 'Man-hating lesbian' is a way of dismissing our arguments against the imbalance of power in this society. Then we spend all our time disclaiming 'It's not that I hate men, it's just that I'. . . . How many women have said to me lately that they were thinking of carrying a gun. . . . it's about frustration. It's like what happens in improvisation class when you're stuck. You run out of resources and you turn to death ... I think that accounts for the mood of violence among women. We've come to the end of a long and tiring improvisation and we've run out of ideas. . . . Split Britches has always felt that our work, and a lot of other women's work, is different from traditional theater, or 'men's theater' as we call it, because we do not rely on plot or linear narrative. There is very seldom an event or climax around which a story is woven. It is primarily a theater of relationships ... so I guess the difference in this piece is that we are using a murder, but we're using it for content rather than form.

The result is a hit and run performance in a car seat.

The collaboration for this piece was unique. Margolin had the idea for two lesbians who might or might not be the killer. Shaw and Weaver invented the characters as two working-class southern women who live in a house that attracts lightning, so they sit in their car. Margolin wrote the games 'looks like is like' and 'let's kill a celebrity;' the monologues, the play on the word 'sloe,' the raspberry, the interrogation. Weaver and Shaw inserted the lip-synching sections, all the musical numbers, the use of radio announcements, the Ed McMahon belly, the 'A Man and A Woman' affair/divorce sequence, the 'slowly I turn' sexual harassment sequence, etc. The creation of the text, then, was collaborative, while Margolin did much of the actual writing. Shaw and Weaver had worked similarly with Holly Hughes on *Dress Suits to Hire*. In both cases, the issue of defining exactly who or what is the playwright is complicated by improvisation and sections invented when the actors are 'on their feet.' These conditions finally raise tensions in the group around how credits are to be given and rights assigned. Intellectual property, as it is called, is claimed by print, by writing, while the fleeting labor and inventiveness of gesture and play remain often 'lost in space.'

The play, as mentioned earlier, draws heavily from film conventions. The actors are dressed in 'clothes from a forties film' and the lights come up to reveal a set in a 'film noir style.' The ever-present gun those film noir heroines always have tucked in their purses is brandished around throughout the play. At one point, they lip-synch lines from the movie *Deception*, starring the 'bitch queen' Bette Davis. The cross between the mythos of the film noir and the case of the woman serial murderer sets the dramatic situation.

At this intersection, lesbian subcultural markings appear. Judith Mayne, in her discussion of the films of Dorothy Arzner, makes the point that lesbians have long identified with certain film stars, certain kinds of narratives, and certain filmmakers' styles. Through gossip and socializing, they have formed a kind of canon of these works. Premier among them are the film noir heroines, who seek retribution when they are 'done wrong' by men. Thus, lesbian signifies in *Lesbians Who Kill* through the practice of borrowing from this subcultural canon. Yet lesbian, in this play, is everything. It is the sex act between May and June, their intimacy, their social isolation, their mutual trust, and their paranoia. But it is also the place from which these women can turn the aggressive violence of sexism back in its own face. This impulse is so strong that it breaks through the frame of the play, as June runs out to the audience, brandishing her gun, yelling 'all you men, up against the wall!' Only theater can retain it, as well as represent it.

LUST AND COMFORT (1995)

In April, 1992, Weaver became the Joint Artistic Director of Gay Sweatshop, in London, along with James Neale-Kennerley. *Lust and Comfort* is the first collaborative project between Split Britches and Gay Sweatshop.

Lust and Comfort continues in the deployment of film images that *Belle Reprieve* and *Lesbians Who Kill* exhibited. This time, however, Hollywood films are not the fare. British and European films provide the inspiration: *The Servant* by Joseph Losey, *The Bitter Tears of Petra von Kant* by Rainer Werner Fassbinder, and *L'Amore* by Roberto Rossellini. The play even opens with the character of a screenwriter. The cultural context for allusion seems decidedly English or European. Likewise, class politics are set within the British context, with the (man)servant speaking in an English accent. These choices no doubt reflect the years Weaver has lived in London, working with the Gay Sweatshop. The association with Bloolips and their tour of Great Britain also may have brought British images and issues to the fore. In fact, the first part of the play deals explicitly with cultural crossing. The character has fled to London and is writing a screenplay about a star who was forced to emigrate in the time of 'McCarthyism and witchhunts.'

Crossing the Atlantic is also crossing gender. The sea change of cultures accompanies the sex change of genders. Butch-femme play is replaced, here, by the 'dark secret' of transsexual practice that causes the character to draw the curtains and retreat into the chambered violence of hiding. This scenario reflects the pressing issue, in the lesbian community, of Female-to-Male transsexuals (F2M). Questions raised by the issue: how is lesbian situated within transgender practices? What constitutes a sex change – merely hormone injections of testosterone, the double mastectomy, the phalloplasty? In the current urban scene, various combinations are being constructed. Thus, gender falls in with sex and sexual practice in a new configuration. Constructing the body leads the parade of gender and sexual practices. This perspective is more 'queer' or lesbian than feminist.

The language in *Lust and Comfort* is quite different from that of the other plays. The dramatic situation controls the play of words, rather than an associative sense. A simulation of the rational, dominant language that is exchanged between the upper class and its servants, and between men, takes over. In playing 'men' they play their language. In say, *Lesbians Who Kill*, the language attacks the dominant discourse from the outside – barbing and stinging and threatening. In this play, the only 'out' possible is when the actors abandon any role-playing to revert to their own names and their own relationship. Roles marked feminine, such as the strip tease, or the maid, seep in to heat up the desire between the characters. However, immediately after this seepage of desire molds a gendering, even if a simulated gendering of characters, the femme as object of the gaze makes the point of her objectification, with framed photos of her body performing 'several cheesecake poses' which conclude, literally, on a pedestal. Roles produce 'lust' but not 'comfort'. The system of representation is locked up tight by unequal power relations secured by class, gender, and seduction.

As lesbians, Lois and Peggy also play out power roles. They attempt to 'top' one another in seduction. The images are adapted from Fassbinder's *The Bitter Tears of Petra von Kant*, which portrays the power imbalances inherent in class and sexual roles in a narrative of seduction and betrayal between a powerful fashion designer and a young would-be model. In other words the servant/master role for lesbians that Fassbinder scripted play here against Losey's manservant. At first, Peggy, the designer, 'tops' Lois, but through her objecthood, Lois takes the power and 'tops' Peggy. Butch-femme, a more stable set of power dynamics, is replaced by the direct struggle for power and its reversals between women. Lesbians and women are no longer the alternative to power struggles, but embody them – even enjoy them as part of seduction. Reflecting the lesbian sex-radical practices around these issues, this play enacts the trends of the 'queer' subculture in the 1990s, just as the earlier works dramatized lesbian feminist issues of the 1980s. The debate within *Little Women* has definitely resolved itself in the direction of a lesbian-identified depiction of sexual practice. Compare this house of *Lust and Comfort* where the F2M transgendered person, sexual scenarios of servant/master, struggles to 'top' one another, and the sharing of sex-power fantasies play, to the cabin in *Split Britches*, or the mobile home to test the shrinking sense of an alternative life. Lois reveals, as part of the play, a sexual fantasy from her childhood: she bound other children in the basement, operating as their 'Madam, director, or Führer,' her father's socks stuffed down her pants to give her the biggest dick. In other words, the lesbian has taken over the phallus, reflecting all the recent works celebrating the dildo. The word 'fuck' is employed, as nowhere before, to describe lesbian sex. The man is in the woman, through transgender operations or masquerade.

Along with radical sex, however, comes the direct discussion of their own long-term relationship. Adjacent to it, are fleeting references to ageing. Lois: 'You've sucked out my fluids and dried me up like an old crone . . . sagging tits, laugh lines, crow's feet.' Peggy: 'Without that passion for you, I will get old.' Lois: 'You're not too old for me and I'm not too old for you.' They're tired – they need a break from performing – some comfort. But the phone keeps ringing. It's not Levine calling out for money, but the 1990s calling in its tough, young power plays. They can, and do, perform them. The depth, through time, of their relationship becomes visible in the playing. The stage is theirs and the stage is them. They have lived their lives and their relationship on the stage, improvising it into episodes and schtick for almost twenty years. They are the lesbian actors of their time.

SPLIT BRITCHES

A True Story

PEGGY SHAW, DEBORAH MARGOLIN, LOIS WEAVER

Conceived and directed by Lois Weaver
with additional contributions by
Naja Bey, Cathy Gollner and Pam Verge

Performed by Deborah Margolin, Peggy Shaw
and Lois Weaver
Costume design Cathy Gollner
Set design Lois Weaver

Originally produced October 1980 by
WOW Festival, New York

February 1981 by Spiderwoman Theatre Company,
with Pam Verge, Peggy Shaw
and Lois Weaver

October 1981 WOW Festival with Deborah Margolin,
Peggy Shaw and Lois Weaver

THE SETTING

The story takes place in the Blue Ridge Mountains of Virginia in the late 1930s. The set consists of a chair, a table and a bed sitting incongruously in a kitchen of an old broken-down farm. At the beginning of the play it is late afternoon, approaching dinner hour, early autumn.

CHARACTERS

(in order of their appearance on this Earth)

EMMA GAY GEARHEART – octogenarian aunt, sister of John Henry Gearheart, founder of the defunct plantation on which the three women live. Cantankerous but whimsical, possibly senile.

DELLA MAE GEARHEART – oldest daughter of John Henry and Ailey Ann Gearheart; keeps life going on the farm with feistiness, warmth and vengeance.

CORA JANE GEARHEART – youngest daughter of Ailey Ann and John Henry. She's sweet, complex and shadowy but not quite right in the head.

The stage is set and dimly lit, visible and empty of actors as the audience enters. The actor playing Cora Jane enters and walks center stage. She is dressed in many layers of old clothing, holding a hat and a pair of glasses in her hand. She addresses the audience not as Cora, but as herself, an actor, director, narrator. She offers the play to the audience:

CORA AS NARRATOR: Hello. I wanted to take this opportunity to welcome you and to tell you just a little bit about tonight's performance before we get started. First of all, *Split Britches* is a true story. It's a project I started working on about four years ago. It seemed to me at that time that a lot of artists were drawing from autobiographical material. They were going back to their roots. So I decided that I would go back to my roots. I went back to the Blue Ridge Mountains of Virginia where I was born. And through a series of oral history projects, you know, tape recordings, photographs and so on, I discovered that I in fact had a great-grand-father and a great-grandmother. My great-grandfather's name was John Henry Gearheart. My great-grandmother's name was Ailey Ann Wimmer. Well, they got married to each other . . . and they lived in a place called Copper Hill which is in Floyd County in the Blue Ridge Mountains of Virginia. And they prospered there. They had

Plate 1 *Tableau vivant* from *Split Britches*.
Standing, Peggy Shaw as Della. Seated, left to right: Lois Weaver as Cora
and Deborah Margolin as Emma
Photo: Pamela Camhe

some sons, and some cows and chickens, but then they decided to move. So they left Copper Hill, which is in Floyd County in the Blue Ridge Mountains of Virginia, and they moved to Ballyhack, which is in Franklin County in the Blue Ridge Mountains of Virginia. They brought a lot of things with them they would need. They brought their sons ... and their cows and chickens ... dried fruit and nuts ... and Emma Gay Gearheart, who was John Henry's sister, at that time ... and they settled there in Ballyhack on what was then called the old Kefauver Plantation. And they prospered there. They had some more sons. And some daughters. And one of those daughters was Blanche Teliathia Gearheart. And she got married and had some sons and daughters. And one of those sons was Russell Coy Weaver. And that was my father.

Well, I'll just tell you one more story before we get on with the performance. When John Henry and Ailey Ann and Emma Gay and all the sons and cows and chickens and so on were making that trip from Copper Hill which was in Floyd County in the Blue Ridge Mountains of Virginia to Ballyhack, which is in Franklin County in the Blue Ridge Mountains of Virginia ... along the way Ailey Ann lost her comb ... now it was a long and treacherous journey ... they were traveling by covered wagon ... and John Henry was a compassionate man and a generous man, so he stopped along the way to buy Ailey Ann a new comb. Now that comb cost him seven cents. He reached in his pocket and pulled out ten cents. He only had ten cents in his pocket at that time. He paid for the comb and put the three coins back in his pocket. And the story goes that when they harvested their crops that first fall in Ballyhack, he had the same three cents in his pocket.

Well, I've brought along a few slides of some of the Gearhearts so if the technician is ready we'll just turn out the lights and begin.

Blackout. Actors Della and Emma enter in the dark and take their places standing at the table and sitting in the chair, respectively. Cora takes her place on the bed and dons the hat and glasses she held throughout the opening speech. After actors are in position a slide projector is turned on, capturing the three actors in a still position resembling an old picture. (Note: each time a slide is called for, the three actors alter their position slightly, in semblance of a new picture being shown.)

Slide 1

Slide 2

CORA AS NARRATOR: This slide is a picture of the interior of the Gearheart homeplace. It's the kitchen, one of eight rooms in the Blue Ridge Mountain estate.

Slide 3

Seated in the lower right hand corner of this slide is Emma Gay Gearheart. Now you'll remember Emma Gay was John Henry's sister. She came to Ballyhack with the Gearhearts but spent most of her life living in other people's houses taking care of other people's children. She came back to the homeplace when she was well into her eighties.

Slide 4

Slide 5

Standing in the center of this slide is Della May Gearheart. Della Mae was the oldest daughter of John Henry and Ailey Ann and in her later years she became the caretaker of the homeplace. *mosc lode*

Slide 6

Seated on the bed in this particular photograph is Cora Jane Gearheart, the youngest daughter of John Henry and Ailey Ann. Cora Jane ... never left the farm.

Slide 7

Slide 8

Not pictured in this photograph are the eight other Gearheart children who left the farm, including Blanche Teliathia, the only other Gearheart daughter who got married, moved to town and had eleven children of her own.

Slide 9

Slide 10

You'll notice in this picture that all three women are wearing Split Britches. This was a garment worn in agricultural regions to facilitate peeing while standing.

Slide 11

Slide 12

(*From within Della Mae sings:*) With a chick-chick here and a chick-chick there. Here a chick ... (*she slides off*)

EMMA: What's for dinner, Della?

DELLA: Biscuits.

CORA: What d'ya think I ought to do with this? Sew it!

Slide 13

Slide 14

Slide 15

From the period of 1932 to 1949 Emma Gay, Della Mae and Cora Jane were the sole inhabitants of the Gearheart homeplace.

Slide off. Lights are brought up slowly from half to full, illuminating a shabby kitchen.

EMMA: What are you cookin', Della?

DELLA: Biscuits.

EMMA: I know. But what are we havin' for dinner?

DELLA: Biscuits.

EMMA: Do you think we could have some of those blackberry preserves on 'em?

DELLA: No, Emma, these are hard times.

EMMA: Della. We got one hundred jars stored up there in the spring house. Remember Cora. You picked them blackberries and she canned 'em.

DELLA: If we eat 'em now, Emma, we'll starve later.

EMMA: Just like your Mama. Always thinkin' we was gonna starve. Even when times is good.

DELLA: Hand me the rolling pin, Emma. (*She laughs*) What the hell for?

EMMA: And you're always talking for everybody. You talk for the farm, you talk for the wood, you talk for the chickens, you talk for Cora . . .

CORA: I'm hungry, Della.

DELLA: I'm cooking, Cora.

EMMA: There weren't never a time you weren't talking for every-body . . . even when they got nothin' to say.

DELLA: What j'say, Emma?

EMMA: Nothin'.

DELLA: Hand me the rollin' pin, Emma.

CORA: Don't make no difference.

EMMA: Damn bugs you got in here.

CORA: Whatcha gonna do with them bugs? Catch 'em.

EMMA: There's plenty of them for the catchin'.

DELLA: Why don't you stand up and do something for a change, Cora. Put on the plates for dinner.

CORA: I told him I wanted a hundred. And he come right around here the other afternoon and said he'd give me a hundred and twenty-five. What plates?

DELLA: The everyday plates. Since you hid away the fine china somewhere and I can't find it. I make all the decisions around here, Cora, and you're not sellin' your land. Land is money.

EMMA: Wood.

DELLA: Remember?

EMMA: Money in the bank, wood is.

CORA: Remember what?

EMMA: (*sings and is joined by Cora*) Remember the wings of Gabriel as he goes on his way to the Lord!

DELLA: Yeah, wings. They're trying to steal your land, Cora Jane, and I ain't never comin' down.

CORA: I'm going for a walk ... but that ain't really where I'm goin' ...

Slide 16

CORA AS NARRATOR: As the years passed, they developed their own way of dealing with the outside world.

EMMA AS NARRATOR: I remember when John Henry was alive, they had electric lights, telephone, and a carbide lamp out in the barn. Now John Henry's body wasn't cold half an hour before Della Mae had all these things taken out.

Slide 17

CORA AS NARRATOR: There are many stories in the Gearheart history where Della Mae would promise a family member a fine old piece of furniture ... a rocking chair, a chest of drawers ... and the very next day she would chop it up for firewood.

Slide off

DELLA: I ain't never comin' down. You should have seen 'em, Emma, you should have seen 'em. They were all down there waitin' for me, waitin' for me to sign that piece of paper, they were all down there in their city suits waitin' for me. Well when I decided to go down there I walked up them steps and into that office and I opened the door and they were all lookin' at me and at what I had on. Well I paid them no mind, I walked into that room and they all stepped back against the wall and when I got in the middle of the room I could feel the sun on my face. I would feel my scarf brush against my cheek, I could hear my leather jacket as I turned and got into that plane. And I took that plane down the runway. And took off up into the sky. And I kept on goin' higher and higher in the sky .. I left all the crowds behind me . . . the sun was getting brighter and brighter . . .

EMMA: Pass me the fly swat, Della.

DELLA: And she knew they were waitin' for her on the other side. And she took that plane up higher and higher. All she could hear was the roar of the engine and the beating of her heart. But somethin' was wrong with the engine . . . but she paid it no mind . . . she kept on goin' higher and higher . . . and she stayed up there . . .

EMMA: There don't have to be no bugs and he ain't got 'em up there . . . give you typhoid. You don't think I seen 'em? Sure I seen 'em, leapin' and creepin'. Well, it don't help much you keep that screen door open. (*To Della*) That screen door open? (*She gets no response and repeats*) That screen door open? Well don't bother! Don't bother get that screen door fixed. They come in here anyway. It's like they come a'courtin'. Only the only things they like to court is either hot from the oven, plum filthy or . . . dead. Dead as a nail. I keep my hair neat. I prefer it that way. The only reason they get in my hair so much . . . is because . . . your hair is dead! Because every time you think something . . . and then you forget it, your hair grows out a little bit. That's why old ladies have such long hair. And it's the same flies every afternoon, I recognize 'em. I wonder how they find their way. So small compared to the wood and them . . . the sky and them . . . the stars and them. Well that's durin' the day. Durin' the day. But at night is when the whinin' starts. The mosquitoes! I can feel a dream coming on. I can always feel it! And I lay down and I put out the light and the whinin' begins. And I get up and I put out the light and nothin'. So I smooth out my sheets. I'm too smart for that. And I lay down, and I put out the lights, and the whinin' begins again.

CORA: (*after much ado catching a fly*) I got it, Emma! I got it!

EMMA: There ain't no bugs in a clean house. There's peace and quiet in a clean house and don't got to be no bugs.

CORA: I got it, Emma!

EMMA: Eh. Well don't bother gettin' that screen door fixed. I'm gonna get that wood now.

CORA: I got it!

DELLA: Listen! Did you hear that, Cora?

CORA: You better leave them planes alone, Della.

EMMA: I'm not complainin', Cora.

CORA: She got to leave the planes alone.

Slide 18

CORA AS NARRATOR: The house was awful. They kept little baby chickens in there under the stove. They had calves and pigs in the pantry. And God knows what else in the kitchen.

DELLA AS NARRATOR: They all lived in one room, you know.

Slide 19

CORA AS NARRATOR: There was a family gatherin' down by the springhouse and everybody brought something to eat. Della Mae brought a great big pound cake. And I want you to know when everybody got done eatin' and it was time to have dessert, nobody would even touch that pound cake.

EMMA AS NARRATOR: Now that little Emma Gay . . . she was clean. I don't know when she washed . . . I'm sure she did . . . but I never did see her do it.

Slide off

CORA: Chick chick chick chick (*she starts dropping corn feed on the floor*) chick chick chick chick chick . . .

EMMA: (*en route from woodpile to chair*) What's for dinner, Della?

DELLA: Biscuits. I was going to surprise you, Emma, but you guessed.

EMMA: No. I didn't really guess, Della.

CORA: chick chick chick chick chick chick MOOOOOOOOOOO!

DELLA: The cow's sick.

EMMA: Don't look sick to me.

CORA: That's not the cow. (*Silence*) MOOOOOOOOOOOO!

DELLA: The cow's sick.

CORA: The cow is sick!

DELLA: Emma!

EMMA: The cow is sick.

DELLA: Somebody's got to go for help!

CORA AND DELLA: I'll go! I'LL GO!

EMMA: I'll go.

DELLA: You can't go Emma. You'll fall and break yourself.

CORA: I'll go, Della.

DELLA: You can't find your way in the daytime, how do you expect to find your way at night? I'll go, Cora you go with me, and Emma you stay here.

EMMA: You want me to stay here . . . alone?

DELLA: I'll go. Emma you go with me, and Cora you stay here.

EMMA: We keep goin' on like this, Della, we're gonna be out of it.

CORA: I know. Emma you stay here. And I'll stay with you . . . and Della . . . YOU go.

DELLA: You want me to go out there in the middle of the night with no moon over that hill all the way to Russell's house . . . and leave the two of you here by yourselves. We'll all go.

CORA: We'll all go.

EMMA: Well now I know you asked me that question. But I forgot what the answer was supposed to be.

DELLA: Emma, the cow is sick.

EMMA: The cow is sick.

DELLA: We're all goin' for help.

EMMA: We're all goin' for help.

DELLA: Get your things, Emma.

CORA: Get your things, Emma. (*She crosses over to Emma*) We're goin' over to Russell's house. We're gonna get some help for that cow, Emma.

EMMA: Russell's.

DELLA: Wait a minute. We can't leave the kitchen with the fire burning. It'll burn down the whole house.

EMMA: I got more wood over there. (*She crosses to the woodpile*)

DELLA: The cow is sick, Emma.

CORA: I'm goin' upstairs.

DELLA: Cora. The cow is sick.

CORA: There's some things I been meanin' to do upstairs.

DELLA: Cora, the cow is sick and I need your help.

CORA: I'd like to help you with that cow, Della, but . . . Grandma died. Grandma died and she's layin' upstairs on my bed. On top of all of my coupons. And I need my coupons for tomorrow because tomorrow's Thursday, and I have to go to the store. I always go to the store on Thursday. So I got to go upstairs, Della.

DELLA: (screams) I gave up everything for you! I gave up my house in town. I gave up my job in town to come back here to this farm and take care of you, and to take care of that one over there. Now I've been cooking and cleaning all day and now the cow is sick and I need your help. You better get over here and help me right now!

Cora and Della face each other humphing and stamping in a contest of wills until Della finally gives up and returns in disgust to the table where the biscuits are awaiting her attention.

CORA: I got these pieces and I'm gonna put 'em together. I got all these pieces I'm puttin' 'em together. What do you think I ought to do with this? Sew it! You think I ought to knot it or you think I ought to quilt it? Blanche thinks I ought to knot it. I got all these pieces I'm gonna put 'em together. I dyed these pieces with pokeberries. Ain't they pretty? I dyed these pieces with pokeberries. Ain't they pretty, Emma?

EMMA: That's right. You picked them blackberries, and she canned 'em.

CORA: Pokeberries, Emma.

EMMA: That's right.

CORA: Pokeberries is poison.

EMMA: That's right.

CORA: I picked the blackberries. I picked the blackberries in January.

EMMA: That's right.

CORA: No. July. I went to Blanche's house in January. That's the time I went over there and took over all of my dishes. And that's the time I was sittin' by the window that's got those little blue bottles on it. I always sit by that window. And I look out and I ask Blanche questions and she tells me. I say Blanche who's that over there and she tells me. And I say what's so-and-so doin' over there and she tells me that. But this one time . . . that time in January when I went over there and I took over all my dishes. I was lookin' out that window and there was a man lookin' in at me . . . and he was smilin' at me. He wanted to kiss me. Well I didn't want nobody to think nothin' bad about me, Emma, so I went away from that window and I didn't go back.

Plate 2   EMMA: What's for dinner, Della?   DELLA: Biscuits.
Photo: Jan Rüsz

Until the next day I went back. And he had come there in the night
to kiss me. And he wanted people to know he had come there to
kiss me because he left his footprints in the snow all the way from
the road right up to that window. He wanted to give me a bad
reputation. Well I didn't want nobody to think nothin' bad about
me, so I put on my coat and I put on Blanche's boots and I went
out there and stepped on them footprints ... all over them footprints ... a thousand footprints all over his footprints. I didn't
want nobody to know he had come there in the night to kiss me.
I didn't want nobody to think I had a bad reputation, Emma, and

I didn't want Blanche to know ... and I didn't want Della to know ... <u>nothin'</u> ...

EMMA: Where you think you're goin'?

CORA: Visitin'.

EMMA: Who you got to visit?

DELLA: You better get over here and sit down and shut up Cora because I'm cooking dinner!

EMMA: What's for dinner, Della?

DELLA: Biscuits.

EMMA: Well! Now the Devil he sure do find work for idle hands, now, don't he?

CORA: I'm visiting the Devil ... the Devil ... (*to Della's back*) the DEVIL!

Della shakes the spoon at her and Cora stamps her foot

EMMA: That child don't even know what she's saying, really.

DELLA: Like hell she don't, Emma! Like HELL she don't!

EMMA: That's ain't even funny Della!

DELLA: There she goes again, Cora.

CORA: The Devil's hungry, Della.

EMMA: Talkin' for the Devil? She must have got that from you, Della! Talkin' for the Devil.

Silence

CORA: MOOOOOOOOOOO!

DELLA: The cow's sick.

EMMA: Don't look sick to me.

CORA: That's not the cow. (*Silence*) MOOOOOOOOOOOO!

DELLA: The cow's sick.

CORA: The cow is sick!

DELLA: Emma!

EMMA: The cow is sick.

DELLA: Somebody's got to go for help!

ALL THREE: I'll go! I'll go.

CORA: I'll go, Della, I got my coat on. (*She exits*)

EMMA: I'll go. (*She starts to exit offstage through the audience*)

DELLA: Where you goin' Cora? Where you goin', Emma? Cora Cora!

Slide 20

EMMA AS NARRATOR: In her youth, Della Mae was a handsome woman, and a stylish dresser. She had a job in town, and she drove a horse and buggy to and from her house, also in town. I heard it was an unfortunate love affair that brought her back to the farm.

Slide off.

DELLA: Go on. Go ahead and leave me here by myself. Go on, Emma! Go get your wood. Don't make no difference to me if you're here or if you're not here. I'm the same woman if you're here or not here. I'm a free woman. I do everything anyway. If you were here, I'd have to pick you up and clean under you. Don't make no difference. It gets cold here in the winter. A draft comes through the kitchen and you gotta keep warm. You can't keep the fire too high or it'll burn down the whole house. I got to have my protection. I didn't always dress like this. I didn't always live like this, you know. I got to have my protection. This here (*she takes off her coat*) this is for the North Wind (*she throws it downstage*). This here (*she removes her apron, and throws it downstage*) is for the fog that comes in over the mountain. (*She starts unbuttoning her dress*) This is for all the mothers that thought I was after their little girls. (*She takes off her dress*) This is for all the little girls my Mother broke me up with because they was ... Catholic! (*She throws the dress at Emma's chair and starts removing next layer*) This is for the time in church my brother was embarrassed because he said I look like a boy. (*Finishing the removal*) And this is for the twenty-five dollars I saved up to go to the prostitute and I walked back and forth all day trying to get up the nerve. (*She throws the dress at Cora's cot and removes the last night shirt*) And this is for all the nights I cried myself to sleep (*she throws the shirt, standing in long underwear only; she goes over to her secret stash of whiskey and takes a long, luxurious slug*) And this is for Amelia. AMELIA! (*She sings several verses of a blues song from that period, 'Bull Dyke Women,' originally sung by Besse Jackson, until Emma interrupts*)

EMMA: Well now! There was an old, blind turkey! I know, because I saw him! I used to know him. And all the animals used to squabble for a place to sleep. Inside (*She pulls an old chair and drags it over to the woodpile*) But he was blind. He couldn't squabble. So he had to sleep outside and the weather was bad. First it rain. And after it rain, it shiver. And after it shiver, it got cold, huh! And when it got cold, he got mad, because ... I know why! Because the cold don't make no noise. Well. He started a singin'. Because the singin' made him less mad. <u>And the singin' attracted all the birds to him. Because.</u> <u>I know why. Because birds is attracted to singin'.</u> Even if it's comin' from an old blind-up old turkey.

Slide 21

Slide 22 (catching Emma between the woodpile and the outdoor wood, from where she will procure a huge tree trunk to drag across the stage)

Slide off.

EMMA: Well he heard it. And he thought he had made the stars squeak. How'd he know there were stars? (*She thinks*) Well. Everybody knows that. Well the birds. They started peckin' on him. And he felt it. And he thought it was time for the dancin' to begin. (*She begins a long peregrination across the stage with the tree trunk*) And it went that way. He was singin' so they were peckin' and he was dancin'. So they were peckin' and they were dancin' and he was singin' and they were dancin', so he was peckin' and they were singin' and he was dancin' and he was peckin' so they were singin' and they were dancin' ... what the hell was I talkin' about? Oh. There was an old blind turkey. I know, because I saw him. I used to know him. Well, it come to Thanksgivin' one time, and the cook come after him with a knife. And he felt it. And he thought it was time for the dancin' to start. But they killed him. And they opened him up. And when they opened him up there was ... (*she sees the bed*) a place to live in there. With a bed. With the feathers of two hundred ducks in there. (*She faces the table*) And there was a table. With bread. And wine. And fifty turkeys. And two hundred country ham. (*She sees the chair*) And there was a chair by a window. In the dust. In the light. The dust dancin' in the light. Like in church. The clean dust. Like in church. And there wasn't no bugs. And there were two hundred girls there swattin' the bugs there. Feel my muscle. I built this wall myself. Take a trip to California. Walk on your fingers.

DELLA: (*having gotten dressed again*) Emma! You seen Cora?

EMMA: Of course I seen Cora. Who do you think I see around here? I see you. And I see Cora Jane.

DELLA: Cora! Cora!

CORA: (*echoing from the audience*) Cora! Cora!

DELLA: I hear you, Cora! You better get in this house, Cora.

CORA: You better get in this house, Cora!

DELLA: You want me to get the fly swat, Cora? Cora Jane, where are you? You better get up on this porch. Show yourself!

CORA: Show yourself!

DELLA: Cora Jane, I'm going to count to three and you better be up on this porch. One.

CORA: Two!

DELLA: Two.

CORA: Two!

DELLA: Three! (*Cora enters from house left and Della grabs her by the shirt collar and holds her close.*) Where you been Cora?

CORA: I was at the store!

Slide 23

EMMA AS NARRATOR: (Cora Jane was considered mentally retarded.)

Slide 24

EMMA AS NARRATOR: She was good at needlework, and easy to handle . . .

Slide 25

EMMA AS NARRATOR: Until she got into one of her moods.

Slide off.

CORA: I was at the store!

DELLA: You're too stupid to go to the store!

CORA: I WAS AT THE STORE! It's Thursday. I always go to the store on Thursday. I go to the store on Thursday because Wednesday they deliver the kind of tobacco I always buy on Thursday! I go to the store and I buy two kinds of tobacco! I buy one for Emma and if I have enough money left over I always buy a little candy for myself. I have money to go to the store because when I collect all the eggs and I give Della twelve eggs and I keep one egg until I have my own dozen eggs. And then I go to the store. And I buy two kinds of tobacco. I buy one for Emma and I buy one for me if I have enough money left over I always buy a little candy for myself. And I buy a special kind of tobacco. The kind that's got those little red tags on it. And if I go to the store three more times and I buy two tins of tobacco I'll have enough little red tags to send away and get a cup and saucer like the one I took over to Blanche's house. And I go early to the store on Thursday because I can stop by and visit people. I visit Virginia and I visit Miss Clayter and they give me things. They give me coffee. And they give me cigarettes . . . and they give me white bread. And they save me things. They save me the coupons off the evaporated milk container. And if I go to the store two more Thursdays and they give me one coupon I'm gonna have enough coupons to send away and get a salt and pepper shaker made out of a chicken! Just like the teapot is made out of a chicken!

EMMA: That reminds me of an old blind turkey!

CORA: Chicken. Chicken.

DELLA: (*singing*) Hey diddle!

Silence

Hey diddle, the cat in the fiddle, the dish ran away with the spoon! Hey diddle, the cat in the fiddle, the cow jumped over the moon! (*She crosses to Cora's cot*) Hey diddle, the cat in the fiddle . . . (*she sits on bed with Cora*) Your coupons are dyin' upstairs! Hey diddle, the cat in the fiddle . . .

CORA: (*singing too*) I'm talkin' and nobody cares!

DELLA: Hey diddle, the cat in the fiddle . . . (*she indicates Emma*) She had such gentle hands! Hey diddle, the cat in the fiddle . . .

CORA: She could spit and chop like a man!

CORA and DELLA: Hey diddle, the cat in the fiddle . .

DELLA: The flies won't leave her alone!

CORA and DELLA: Hey diddle, diddle, the cat in the fiddle . . .

EMMA: (*rising*) I ain't never had a home of my own!

TOGETHER: Hey diddle diddle, the cat in the fiddle . . .

EMMA: Got all this land she won't sell!

TOGETHER: Hey diddle diddle, the cat in the fiddle . . .

DELLA: I'm a woman in a cold man's Hell!

TOGETHER: Hey diddle diddle, the cat in the fiddle . . .

CORA: (*crossing to table and imitating Della*) I'm tired of the back of your head!

TOGETHER: Hey diddle diddle, the cat in the fiddle . . .

DELLA: (*crossing to Emma's chair, sitting down and imitating Emma*) I didn't hear what you said.

TOGETHER: Hey diddle diddle, the cat in the fiddle . . .

EMMA: (*sitting on Cora's bed and imitating her*) Won't you come and play with me?

TOGETHER: Hey diddle diddle, the cat in the fiddle . . .

CORA: (*crossing and sitting on Della's lap in Emma's chair*) If I could have a cup of tea!

TOGETHER: Hey diddle diddle, the cat in the fiddle ...

DELLA: (*pushing Cora off her lap and quickly going to the cot where Emma is sitting; sitting down and imitating Cora*) I'm tired of you messing with my things! (*She spits into Cora's spit can and sits down on the cot*)

TOGETHER: Hey diddle diddle, the cat in the fiddle ...

EMMA: (*crossing to the table and picking up a flour-dusted spoon, waving it in the air*) I'd fly if I had wings!

CORA: Pass me the rollin' pin!

DELLA: What the hell for?

CORA and EMMA: That ain't even funny, Della!

DELLA: Hey diddle, the cat in the fiddle, the dish ran away with the spoon! (*All rise and start to dance*) Hey diddle, the cat in the fiddle, the cow ...

ALL: The cow's sick.

DELLA: Don't look sick to me.

EMMA: That's not the cow.

CORA: MOOOOOOOOOOO!

DELLA: The cow's sick.

CORA: The cow is sick!

DELLA: Emma!

EMMA: What are we gonna do, Della ... if that cow ... dies? (*She begins crossing downstage towards woodpile*)

DELLA: We'll survive.

CORA: What for?

DELLA: What do you mean, what for, Cora?

CORA: What for if the cow dies?

EMMA: And all the people I drive up and down the road. All the people I drive up and down the roads of this town ... O Day, I am a lucky woman. A real lucky woman.

DELLA: Let's go, Cora.

CORA: Wouldn't it be nice, Della, if nobody never had to go nowhere?

EMMA: (*chopping wood*) They say a prayer for me and when I go, there'll be plenty of people lined up behind my box. I can't stop to explain.

CORA: It's like dyin' if the cow dies.

DELLA: Did anyone living or dead ever need you, Cora?

EMMA: I can't stop to explain.

DELLA: Well, the cow needs me and the cow's mighty sick.

EMMA: I'm drivin' this train!

CORA: It's not the cow sick, it's you's sick, it's not the cow.

DELLA: Let's go.

EMMA: Can't stop to explain.

CORA: You're just like Mama!

EMMA: I'm drivin' this train!

CORA: Scared if it's sick. Scared if it ain't sick. If it ain't sick, you're scared it's gonna get sick. If it is sick, you're scared it's gonna die. And I don't know why you're scared it's gonna die, because everything's gonna die. And that cow is smart, too! She's just out there in the field giving milk and moanin' in the dark cause she's having a good time. MOANIN' IN THE DARK CAUSE SHE'S HAVIN' A GOOD TIME! MOANIN' . . .

Della bangs on the table with a spoon to restore order. Everyone returns to their places. The three sing a period song in the style of Stop the Trains *by the Boswell Sisters in perfect three-part harmony, at first calmly.*

Della begins looking in earnest for her rolling pin. She checks under Cora's bed, checks her table, checks the floor. She suddenly realizes what may have happened, walks behind Emma's chair and extricates the wooden rolling pin from the kindling pile Emma keeps next to her.

EMMA: What's for dinner, Della?

DELLA: Biscuits.

EMMA: Well now I don't mind biscuits, Della. But do you think we could have some of those blackberry preserves on 'em? With some ham hock. And some red-eye gravy. With some greens. And some green beans. And some bread. With some wine. And some yams. And some greens . . .

DELLA: Emma! (*She leans over and sees something in Emma's eyes*) Cora Jane! You better go upstairs and get your Aunt Emma what she wants.

EMMA: Some ham . . .

DELLA: Some ham . . .

EMMA: Some ham hock.

DELLA: Ham hock . . . go on, Cora.

EMMA: Red-eye gravy . . . greens.

DELLA: Red-eye gravy . . . go on Cora . . . I said go up and get your Aunt Emma what she wants . . . go on . . .

CORA: I'm goin' upstairs . . . I'm goin' upstairs, Emma. (*She crosses upstage, hiding in the back of the kitchen*)

Emma reaches in her pocket for her special napkin, unfolds it and tucks it into her chin in anticipation of the meal

DELLA: I bet you think she ain't never comin' down, Emma. She stayed up there. She never came down. Don't you think she's been gone a long time, Emma, I say, Emma! Don't you think Cora been gone a long time. Cora! You better get down here, Cora. I don't hear her, Emma, I don't hear anything up there. What if something happened to her? What if she fell? It would be all my fault.

Cora has sneaked up behind Della, and she and Emma exchange a glance; Emma nervously relights her pipe

DELLA: (*turning round and seeing Cora*) Cora! Why you hidin' behind me like that? Just like your Daddy.

CORA: (*putting her head in Della's chest; singing*) Tempted and tried we're oft made to wonder why it should be thus all day long. While there are others livin' around us, never molested though in the wrong. Farther along . . . (*the tempo of the hymn takes on a waltz; Della takes Cora in her arms and they begin to dance*) . . . we'll know all about it. Farther along we'll understand why! Cheer up my sister, live in the sunshine . . .

EMMA: Goin' to the dance, Della?

DELLA: I haven't been to a dance in twenty years, Emma.

CORA: . . . we'll understand it, all by and by. Farther along we'll know about it . . . farther along we'll . . . I'm dancin', Emma! I'm dancin! Farther along we'll understand why!

EMMA: I don't know how you expect to be a Christian and be thinkin' about dancin' all the time.

CORA: (*breaking out of the dance*) I think we're gonna have to stop dancin', Della. I think the preacher's comin'.

DELLA: The preacher ain't comin, Cora. I can smell a preacher comin' a mile away. Ain't no preacher gonna get past that gate, Cora.

CORA: The preacher's coming, Della.

Cora and Della sit together on the cot

DELLA: I did go to a dance twenty years ago, Cora, it was on Halloween. A masquerade ball.

CORA: A social.

EMMA: It was a social.

Everyone nods

DELLA: I got all dressed up. I wore my grandaddy's boots and I wore his pants and I slicked back my hair and I went to the dance and nobody recognized me so I danced with whoever I wanted to dance with and I smoked cigarettes and I drank whiskey ...

CORA: You better leave them planes alone, Della.

EMMA: I'm not complaining, Cora.

CORA: She got to leave the planes alone.

DELLA: Listen. Did you hear that? I got to go now, darlin'. I got to join my troops! Will you always love me? Say you'll always love me.

CORA: I'll always love ya.

DELLA: Don't ever leave me. Say you'll never leave me.

CORA: I'll never leave ya.

DELLA: I'll be back soon, darlin'. (*She salutes*)

CORA: I'll be back soon, darlin'. (*She imitates Della's salute*)

DELLA: Bye, darlin'!

CORA: Bye, darlin'! (*They kiss*)

DELLA: Bye! (*She returns to the biscuits*)

CORA: Bye! Bye! Bye, darlin'! Bye! Where do you think you're goin'? To the store! It's Thursday. I always go to the store on Thursday. Bye! Bye! Bye! You want me to stay here alone? Bye! Bye! Bye! I can't move in the dark.

EMMA: Cora Jane.

CORA: I can't move in the dark. I can't move in the dark.

EMMA: (*crossing to Cora*) Cora Jane, I think it's time we had a little foot washin' now. Come on now, get the water. Come on, now ... (*She sings*) We'll work! Till Jesus comes, we'll work till Jesus comes, we'll work till Jesus comes and we'll be gathered home!

Cora joins in and gets the water while Emma gets the foot washing basin; Cora sits in Emma's chair and Emma crouches over her

DELLA: What are you doing, Emma? Cora, don't take off your shoes. You need protection, Cora. You remember when you went to Blanche's house and she took off all your clothes and gave you a bath and you got pneumonia ...

EMMA: (*joined by Cora in song*) When the trumpet of the Lord shall sound and time shall be no more. And ... sounds eternal bright and fair! And the saved of the Earth shall gather over on the other shore ... and the role is called up yonder I'll be there.

DELLA: You think Jesus is going to call your name all day like I do? Cora! Emma! Jesus don't care about you. I'm the only one that cares about you.

Cora and Emma continue singing the hymn. In the middle of it Cora gets up and Emma sits down, and without removing her shoes, starts to pour water on her feet

Slide 26

Slide 27

CORA: (*speaking within the slide*) That's one way that Della could get Cora was through her little treasures.

EMMA: (*simultaneously*) They all used to get up there and play dolls together. Cora and Emma ... and Della too.

DELLA: (*simultaneously*) Della told me she had cash money in the bank for both their funerals ... and she did.

During these recitations Cora goes and sits on the floor at Emma's feet and Emma, seated in chair, puts her hand on Cora's shoulder. Della is standing behind the chair, stage left slightly of the other two. The next slide catches this final portrait.

Slide 28

CORA: Cora Jane Gearheart. Born in 1890, died in 1949. Emma Gay Gearheart. Born 1863, died 1952.

DELLA: Fire ain't just a thing, it's a person, I mean, it ain't a person, it's a livin' thing. Got a mind of it's own.

CORA: There was a brushfire there on the hill and they all got out there fightin' it ... I guess Cora Jane just got too excited ... she started peein' and she couldn't stop. She died the next day of kidney failure.

DELLA: I seen fires. I've felt them on my skin. I heard them cracklin' in my ear, even in the rain. Fires think. They got purposes.

EMMA: Emma Gay had a peaceful death. She died one morning in bed.

DELLA: Once I saw a whole farm burn down. And all the cows and chickens. And the fire went out and brought in other creatures from miles around ... big black birds that flew upside down next to the fire. And the fire held them there with a string tied to their wings in order to scare all the animals to death. I seen a chicken fall over and the fire went up and ate up its whole body and burped out a big white smoke! I heard dogs barkin' but there wasn't no dogs. And I got fire eatin' inside of me. I can feel it but you can't see it. And that makes me be a person with a secret. I can feel it in my eyes. I can feel it in my chest. And I can feel it in other places.

CORA: Della Mae lived for fifteen years alone on that farm, and then she finally sold it. To a stranger. And the very next Halloween that farmhouse burned down.

DELLA: I feel like that farmhouse ... and dry. And that fire can make ashes out of me if I ain't careful. Once I had fire in my pocket. I put my hand in and pulled it out real quick, and I said, why'd I do that? And I looked in my pocket, and there was the fire, lookin' up at me just cute and sweet as a pretty girl. (*She leans over Emma*) That ain't even funny, Della! But then it starts to hurt. So you got to beat it. You got to put it out, Emma. Cora!

CORA: She spent the rest of her years in a rooming house in town, and in 1974 Della Mae was buried right between Emma Gay and Cora Jane ... and to this day not a blade of grass is growin' on her grave.

DELLA: Sometimes I think the fire waits until the whole world is bored, and then it comes along to entertain 'em. But it hurts to laugh. Do you know ... by the time the men got there, there was nothin' left. It was burned right down to the ground. It's fire steals the land for real.

Slide 29

Slide out.

THE END

BEAUTY AND THE BEAST

DEB MARGOLIN, PEGGY SHAW, LOIS WEAVER

Scripted by Deb Margolin
Additional text by Peggy Shaw and Lois Weaver
Directed by Lois Weaver
Assisted by Alice Forrester and Maureen Angelos
Sets painted by Robin Epstein and Paul Shaw

Originally produced in spring 1982 at University of the Streets,
Avenue A at 7th Street, New York

Copyright: Margolin, Shaw, Weaver 1996

ORIGINAL SONGS

"Johnny Cash's Face," words and music by Deb Margolin and
Peggy Shaw
"Reagan," words by Deb Margolin and Peggy Shaw
"Alphabet Song," words by Deb Margolin

CHARACTERS

BEAUTY, played as a Salvation Army Sergeant (Lois Weaver)

BEAST, played as Gussie Umberger, an 84-year-old vaudeville hoofer (Peggy Shaw)

FATHER, played as a Jewish Rabbi in toe shoes (Deb Margolin)

In this piece characters function on several levels. There are the actors (Deb Margolin, Peggy Shaw, and Lois Weaver) who are playing the performers (Rabbi Hitchcock Rabin, Gussie Umberger, and Sgt. Joy Ratledge) who are playing the parts in the adaptation of the fairy tale (Father, Beast, and Beauty). For simplicity we have called the characters by their fairy tale names but all three of these character levels should be apparent throughout the piece.

The stage is set with three chairs, a music stand holding a placard with the title BEAUTY AND THE BEAST and cards underneath, announcing each scene, a piano and three suitcases containing props and painted window shades, which will be pulled up and attached to hooks suspended from the ceiling.

BEAUTY'S VOICE: (*calling from offstage like a town crier*) An absurd Drama of ridiculous People, Outdated Morals and Watchwords and Jokes for a Nuclear Age in a Public Bathroom just outside Baltimore, Maryland at a Refreshment Stand where Unfortunate French Fries are Sold. Starring: Gussie Umberger! James Dean! Mrs Alston! Blackie Burke! Katharine Hepburn! Natasha Macaroni! Assorted Bowery Bums for whom Things are Being Prepared! A Reknowned Shakespearean Actress, a Juggler, Mikhail Brashnikov, Perry Como, the Most Renowned Rabbi Hitchcock Rabin, Richard Nixon, Esq., the Cloth Coat of his most Humble Wife Patricia who had a Stroke a few Years Ago which was Most Inauspicious, and Many, Many Others! A Spectacular! Not to Be Missed! Come One! Come All!

ACT THE FIRST

The Father and the Beast, in the characters of Rabbi and Gussie are herded onstage by Beauty in the character of the Salvation Army Sergeant and instructed to sit in two chairs upstage, while she crosses down to speak to the audience. She has to keep an eye on them because there is the sense that they could wander off at any time.

BEAUTY: Hail and farewell as they used to say! I mean, good evening Ladies and Gentlemen, beauties and beasts! I can see you've all taken sides. The die is cast, as they used to say. A thing of beauty is a joy forever, as they used to say! (*Sergeant approaches Rabbi and Gussie, who are uncomfortably seated side by side, and goads them to join her and her accordion in singing*) BE GOOD TO YOUR ENEMIES, then the Lord above you're sure to please! How do I know? The Bible tells me so! (*Rabbi substitutes "Torah" for "Bible", which precipitates audible bickering upstage between him and Gussie over the wording. Salvation Army Sgt. stops singing, and regains control*)

BEAUTY: (*regaining control*) Well! We've got a very very exciting show here for you tonight, and I just know you're going to ignore it! . . . adore it! What a lovely *audience*! (*She repeats that twice if there are less than ten people in the audience.*) I'd like now to introduce you to tonight's internationally known group of vaudeville performing stars, just off the redeye from – I think they're from Palm Springs, Florida or something – so now lets meet them and greet them like true Christians and dedicated believers! Applaud, now! Don't forget they took the *train*!

Gussie Umberger, eighty-four years old and an inspiration to all of us! (*Beast bows*)

Natasha Macaroni, (*Father pirouettes*) Need I Say More? Such god-given grace and elegance.

Myself, Sergeant Ratledge, Sergeant Joy Ratledge! (*She waits for applause*)

And that old music hall favorite Mrs. R.J. Alston: (*Father in ventriloquist-dummy's voice*) MY ICE CREAM'S RUNNING DOWN THE STREET!

And a little later in the program we are going to be having with us Katharine Hepburn and James Dean! (*Beast bows*)

And now, Ladies and Gentlemen, we have a very special treat. We have with us a real Jewish Rib-eye. We have with us this evening, Rib-eye Hitchcock Rabin. (*Father sings a Yiddish tune*) Isn't that interesting, Ladies and Gentlemen? I find it so interesting. (*Father throws a coat at her*)

And this cloth coat! Which was worn by Patricia Nixon who I admire so much! Did you know she had a stroke two years ago April? What courage she has! And right afterward she re-did her floors! Can you imagine? She set a fine Christian example for all of us! And of course there is the Beast! (*Beast bows*)

And Beauty herself! (*Beauty bows and waits again for applause*) And I've just noticed that we have a very well known person in the audience with us this evening. Clement Cronk III, head of nuclear power in the state of Kansas, who is our honorary guest! Clement, will you please stand up and take a bow. (*She refers to someone in the audience*) Let's give him a big hand, Ladies and Gentlemen. Clement, I do so admire the great things you've been doing.

And now you can see what kind of fine people these performers are and what dedicated Christians they are. So now I want you to settle back and enjoy the show and afterwards I can't wait to talk to you about our organization! We were founded over 185 years ago, by . . .

FATHER: (*in dummy's voice*) Shut up, Mom.

BEAUTY: Right. Now let's begin.

Beauty sets a chair stage center as Beast sets the card announcing the first scene: SCENE ONE SCENE THEM ALL. Rabbi sneaks on.

FATHER: (*practially whispering*) Well maybe now I finally get a minute alone with a few intelligent men . . . you know I got to travel with these g'naven . . . these goyim . . . these madmen . . . that's all it is today is madmen . . . I'm looking for a minion . . . you know ten men . . . are there ten men? (*He begins counting in Yiddish the men in the audience. Beauty begins to clear her throat to get Father's attention*) You know, my friends, the Jew always has suffered through the ages . . . (*He sings*): L'DOR VA DOR! Hallelujah! (*He looks around, suddenly paranoid*) Is it Shabbos yet? I got to get off the train Shabbos.

Beauty clears her throat louder to get Father's attention.

FATHER: Beauty, how hard you work, and yet how sweetly you sing! Why don't you go outside and proclaim with your gentle face the conceit of Springtime, and after such a Winter the Nightlark himself will breathe your air, and the summer will come!

BEAUTY: O Father, it is always summer where you are! And work is but the soft lace in which a lady cloaks herself in usefulness. Have not all virtuous ladies done more for their paters than I?

FATHER: Nay, Beauty, nay.

BEAST: Who let the horses in here?

FATHER: I am rich, Beauty, and I only prosper that you and your sisters (*he refers to Beast*) may live like ladies, not like charwomen. Cease your toil and walk in the field with your sisters. I only wish I saw in their eyes the queenly serenity I see in yours, and heard in their voices the harps of angels as yours to an earthly heaven transports me.

BEAST: Why don't you two just *lighten up*?

BEAUTY: Yes, sweet sister, daughter of my same saintly father, you are right. How right you are! To proclaim the clear and matronly light over that which, itself being darkness, rapes in darkness and gets the day with child, a bastard baby, swaddled in the darkness that inheres in this pretentious conversation! Let us join hands and depart this house together, as it is Father's pleasure and so our own.

FATHER: Beauty! You must groom what is coarse about intelligence, that it not come forth at five o'clock like the beard of a drinking gamesman. Breed it instead to whisper from your body, out from your head like longer, softer hair; and from your bosom like two plush promises. Let it be in your step: quiet and swift with the tall green grass that grace puts under a delicate ankle as it runs. I'll live to see you married, I will.

RABBI: (*running to the audience*) YOU see what I mean . . . all this nonsense . . . I've been with them for weeks . . . HELP ME! You know, they tell me I can ride the train for less, and then I got to go Shabbos. You know I travel with these madmen, these schnorrers – Baruch Shmo! (*singing*) Yoy, yoy, yoy, yoy.

BEAUTY: (*getting his attention*) KNOCK KNOCK KNOCK. (*Pause*) KNOCK KNOCK KNOCK.

FATHER: (*coming back into the scene*) And who might that be? A suitor perhaps?

Beauty and Beast laugh

BEAST: I'll get it. (*She puts on a messenger's cap and acts the part of Messenger*)

MESSENGER: I'm sorry to have to tell you this, sir, but the market has crashed and furthermore your ships have been stolen and your fortune plundered and your American Express card cut into two pieces and returned to the company.

BEAUTY: Would you like a cup of tea?

MESSENGER: No thanks. My doctor says it makes me tense.

FATHER: (*in anguish*) When did this happen? How could this happen?

MESSENGER: About a fortnight ago, as it was reported, sir.

FATHER: How long is a fortnight?

BEAUTY: I'll look it up in the dictionary, Father.

FATHER: Nay, Beauty, it matters not. A fortnight is a fart-night so far as I care. I am ruined, and my daughters with me. Shattered is the dream. (*To Messenger*) I must thank you, sir, for the pains you took, although they are a thousandfold greater pains to me.

MESSENGER: May I use your phone? I want to call the office. (*Beast, as Messenger, turns upstage, takes off the hat, and returns as sister*)

BEAST: Well that's a fine HOWDY DO.

FATHER: Can you, most loving daughters, forgive a father who, thinking himself rich, was poor in judgement so that, lulled into complacency, let nature on his fortune take its course ... (*Father turns head from side to side to look at daughters, who turn heads in opposite direction, missing his gaze*)

BEAUTY: It is nothing, Father. We will live as we have always lived, a little poorer in fashion but much richer in fidelity to you.

BEAST: What?

FATHER: Well, we will return to till the land. As we prospered, so shall we prevent our demise. We shall return to the land like humble farmers and by my work I shall provide for you as best a poor man can.

BEAUTY: It matters nothing to me, sweet Father, for my song is every day the same and my work the work of virtue. It raineth on the rich and poor alike, as the Bible says.

BEAST: A goddamned goody-goody on the premises. We ought to sell tickets and make back the money we lost.

FATHER: Yes, my Beauty, sing for your poor father. Let me hear your song. (*They all agree to move the piano. Beast sets up next card: SHIRLEY, GOODNESS, AND MERCY. Father plays the piano and all three sing*)

ALL: Her name was Kitty
From Kansas City
And it's a pity
She wasn't pretty.
She wasn't hard to see
She weighed 543
I hope she doesn't get much fatter
But if she does it doesn't matter
Kitty, from Kansas City
Now there's a girl that I adore.

BEAUTY: She's so dumb, but you should see her dance
She thinks Rudi Valley is a street in Paris, France.

CHORUS

ALL: I love her, I love her,
It's easy to see
It's Kansas City Kitty for me.

BEAST: She's so dumb, and yet she's really queer
        She thinks Einstein is one big glass of beer.
        Oh . . .

CHORUS

ALL: I love her, I love her,
     It's easy to see
     It's Kansas City Kitty for me.

FATHER: She's asthmatic, but I never heard her wheeze
        She thinks Phillis Schlafly is an Asian lung disease.

CHORUS

ALL: I love her, I love her,
     It's easy to see
     It's Kansas City Kitty for me.

BEAUTY: She's so dense, but really she's quite sweet
        She thinks that abortion is a cold soup made from beets.

CHORUS

ALL: I love her, I love her,
     It's easy to see
     It's Kansas City Kitty for me.

ALL: They call her Kitty
     From Kansas City
     I love the girl because
     She's not the girl she was
     She can cook and she can wash.

BEAST: (spoken) And when she makes love she's the most wonderful . . .

Beauty and Father interrupt the Beast by continuing the song

ALL: Kitty, from Kansas City
     Now there's a girl that I adore.

BEAST: She's so with it, she really is quite swell
       She thinks the neutron bomb is a modern femme fatale.

(CHORUS)

RABBI: She's so gross, yet surely I've seen worse
       She thinks MX-missiles are the things you take to church.

(CHORUS)

She's so sexy, I want her on my arm
She thinks that a hicky is a person on a farm.

(*CHORUS FINALE*)

*During the final chorus, Beauty gets cardboard sheep out of the suit-
case and sets up the next scene, while Beast sets up the card: THUS
CONSCIENCE DOTH MAKE COWHERDS OF US ALL. Beauty
and Beast have cardboard sheep hanging from their necks and they
just stand there waiting for Father to begin the scene.*

FATHER: Girls, girls! How poverty has degraded you! The next thing
I know you will be snorting in the fields like animals! You work
like dogs, eat like horses, sweat like pigs ... (*She walks into the
scene and sits between them*)

BEAUTY: Yes, Father, but we sleep like logs.

FATHER: And you act like kids!

BEAUTY: And we pray like lambs!

FATHER: Sing like larks!

BEAST: (*punching Father*) Float like a butterfly, sting like a bee!

Father, after a little playful moment, sits down again, dejected.

FATHER: How could I have let this happen to me, to my beautiful
daughters? I can scarcely forgive myself. We can barely pay the mortgage on the farm.

*The following is played as melodrama, during which Father escapes
front to speak to the audience.*

BEAST: You must pay the rent, you must pay the rent, you must
pay the rent today.

BEAUTY: I can't pay the rent, I can't pay the rent, I can't pay the
rent today. (*They repeat this until they realize that Father has left
the scene*)

RABBI: (*whispering*) I ask them what it is they do and they tell me
actors! They say "I'm an actor!" Well what kind of cockapitzy! I've
been with them for weeks! Help me! I'm raising money for two new
Torahs! My shul is broke from these madmen today! They lie, they
steal! Then they tell me I'm a character! A real character! So then
I have to be an actor too! Everyone's an actor! The Jew has always
suffered for his God, Baruch Shmo! How I humiliate myself with
these madmen. One of them says he's a LesBoheme, you should
pardon the expression, it means he fools around with other men. ....
At night I cry in the middle of all this madness.

BEAUTY: (*trying to get Father's attention*) Knock knock knock

BEAST: (*getting the hat, thinking it's the cue to play the messenger again*) Most comely miss, is your father at home?

BEAUTY: (*looking at him with love in her eyes*) Yes, I'm afraid he is.

MESSENGER: I bring good news for him, news of his fortune.

BEAUTY: What news of fortune but fortune makes it news?

MESSENGER: You get all those publications in the boondocks?

BEAUTY: Rest a moment, sit you down, I'll call my father. Father, Father, F-A-T-H-E-R! (*She continues screaming 'Father' until she's worked herself into a rage*)

FATHER: Yes, my most loved Beauty, you need but call and I will come.

BEAUTY: It is the same, the messenger, who came to tell of our demise; perhaps she can re-*verse* herself and with her message pen a sweeter poem.

FATHER: (*to Messenger*) Good man, why have you come? State your business.

MESSENGER: Ahem! My business is your business, sir. Need I be bullish on a miracle? Marry, lynch me not before I tell you, sir, that your fortune's been recovered and it's said that the ship with all your merchandise, merchant's dice, if I recall it, has been found and is lodged at Port O'Storm. Geth you tither, I mean, Get you thither, and look to it.

FATHER: Do you speak true?

MESSENGER: I smoke Viceroy. (*He takes off the hat and begins to clear the stage of the chair and sheep*)

BEAUTY: O Father, great happiness, that have returned to you what (*Father interrupts, saying* 'comma') for all your work (*Father:* 'comma') was most well deserved. (*Father:* 'period.')

BEAST: I don't get my period anymore . . . it's been thirty years since my last period . . .

FATHER: (*taking Beauty's hands in his*) Now, Beauty, I will debark at sunrise to the foreign land she describes. What can I bring you?

BEAST: An older woman! Disarmament! Abortion on demand! The E.R.A. before I die!

FATHER: Yes, I will. And you, Beauty, what for you?

BEAUTY: If you have your health, Father, I have all I like.

FATHER: Nay, Beauty, there must be something . . . some small thing that will please you . . . I'll not return without a gift for you . . . tell me . . . a fur . . . perhaps a ruby, red with the blood secretly shed by all stones . . . a sapphire blue as Coltrane blew . . . what will it be . . . tell me, my dear . . .

BEAUTY: Well, there is one thing . . .

FATHER: Yes . . .

BEAUTY: O Father, a rose, and it please you, a single red rose . . .

FATHER: No more than that?

BEAUTY: In a rose I see what's in a name. A name is a name is a name, but Father, in a rose is everything. One single, beautiful red rose.

FATHER: SO BE IT! Goodbye, my darling! We will be together again soon.

Father walks to the piano and begins to play. After several false starts, Beauty sings a classic Las Vegas number in the style of "Do You Know the Way to San Jose?" After the song, Beauty crosses down to the suitcase and pulls down the window shade with a ship painted on it. Beast sets the next card: THE WATER GATE BREAK-IN. Father and Beast cross to the ship. Beast puts on the messenger's hat.

FATHER: What foreign land has fortune-hunting pulled me to? How many a man lured by fortune asks himself as he stands alone in the twilight if he's come to the right place? Nobody owns the darkness, no matter how great his fortune. I am a bit lost . . . but here's the dock. (*He sees Messenger*) What, you again?

MESSENGER: Ay, marry . . .

FATHER: Your social life is of no concern to me.

MESSENGER: Marry, sir, it seems Fate has appointed me your courier.

FATHER: Scab laborer thou art! Fate has laid off your betters.

MESSENGER: Your sex life is of no concern to me, sir.

FATHER: On with it then. Where is my ship which you as Fate's courier have promised me?

MESSENGER: I'm sorry to have to say this sir, but your fortune is lost, the market has crashed, et cetera.

FATHER: And my American Express card?

MESSENGER: TWO pieces.

FATHER: I sensed as much. Are you an actor?

MESSENGER: (*proudly, straightening up*) I'm JAMES DEAN.

FATHER: My luck! A two-bit ham and cheese!

MESSENGER: (*returning to character*) Take arms against this sea of troubles! Have you a daughter?

FATHER: Now don't start playing Hamlet on me!

MESSENGER: (*pause; then whispering a cue to Father*) Enough ... Enough.

FATHER: Enough! Enough! I must wend my sad way home, bereft not once but twice. Would I were dead! At least worms would eat.

MESSENGER: If worms ate wishes your bane would be their banquet.

FATHER: Are you starting Macbeth now?

MESSENGER: Oh, forget it! (*He exits.*)

FATHER: Off with me. If I can but pick a rose for my Beauty I can better bear the sting of these other thorns. I have no sense of humor. (*He looks around, then raises his arm*) Taxi! Taxi!

RABBI: (*to the audience*) You know, I look like a jerk but I respect myself. I respect the Rabbi, I respect the Cohen, I respect even the Ba'al Shem Tov, if you should pardon the expression. But there is one person in my opinion is closer to God than the Rabbi, than the Cohen, even than the Ba'al Shem Tov, and that's the stand-up comic. (*He assumes the stance of a stand-up comedian*)

Ladies and Gentlemen, the dollar isn't what it used to be and that's for shitsure. Used to be you could go to the movies for fifty cents. I'm finding it really difficult to support my taxi habit now ... I take taxis everywhere, and at this point I'm thinking of applying for government assistance. They have welfare, they should have taxi-fare. I'd rather take a taxi than get where I'm going. Sometimes I have every intention of taking the bus but my arm just floats heav-enward and a yellow car zooms right up to me. It's WEIRD.

Did you ever see anything that looks like this? (*He repeatedly lifts his right arm to hail a taxi and pushes it down with his left*) That's me out on the main strip trying to prevent myself from taking a taxi. I'd rather take a taxi than get where I'm going. That's a little abstract, no? I'll tell y'a a couple jokes. There was a man, he owned a small real estate firm. It was a nice firm, a Jewish firm, somewhere in Connecticut somewhere. And he had only two people workin' for him, this guy Jack and the girl Anne. But all of a sudden the bottom falls out of the market with the interest rates and the mortgages and he realizes he can't afford to let them both work for him, but he doesn't know which one to let go. Jack's a nice man, a Jewish man, he's an army buddy, been workin' for him 40 years. And Anne's a nice girk and Jewish girl, she's efficient, she's pretty, you know. So he's thinkin' about it, finally he decides whichever one of them goes to the watercooler first, he's gonna talk to. It's Sunday, he goes to bed with a heavy heart. And the next day he wakes up, his heart is smackin', but he knows what he has to do. So he goes to work, and there they are with the phones and the papers. Good morning, Jack. Good morning, Anne. He tries to pretend like nothin's wrong, you know. And epis it's one o'clock, no one's gone to the cooler. Epis it's five o'clock NO ONE'S GONE TO THE COOLER! At five past five, gets up Anne and goes to the cooler. Well now his heart is really smackin'. He's full of sadness, who knows, maybe he wished it had been the other one, who knows? But he knows what he has to do. He goes over to the cooler and there she is. And he takes her hand in his and he says, Anne, Anne, I got to tell you something Anne. I'm going to have to lay you or Jack off. So she says WELL JACK OFF, I HAVE A HEADACHE THIS AFTERNOON!! *(Beauty stands and gives him a dirty jole and he continues)* I'll tell you a joke! There was a convention of surgeons, you know, a bunch of doctors coming from all over the world, meeting somewhere like Geneva or some place like that – it don't exist, they make it up for the papers – and then after all the lectures and the papers and the drawings and the board meetings, these four doctors get together to talk. There's a man from England, the United States, France, and Italy. Gets up the guy from France and says *(in a French accent)*, "In my country, we are the only people that can take the heart from one man, transplant it into another man, and have that man out looking for work in three weeks." Stands up the guy from Italy and says *(in a fake Italian accent, adding an "a" to the end of all the words)*, "Well that's very nice, but in my country we are the only people that can take the heart and lungs from one man, transplant them into another man, and have that man out looking for work in two weeks." Then up stands the guy from England and he says in a stuffy British accent, "In my country, we are the only people who can take the heart, the liver, and the lungs out of one man, transplant them all into another man, and have that man out looking for work in one week." So finally the guy from America gets up and says, "You're all very nice doctors, Jewish doctors, but in my country, we're the only people that can take an asshole from Hollywood, transplant him to Washington, and have the entire country out looking for work in a single afternoon!"

Beauty and the Beast chastise Father for the dirty joke and force the beginning of the next scene by hanging windowshade drops they extract from the three suitcases. Two are painted as trees and the

third as a castle. *Beast sets the next card:* CAN'T SEE THE FOREST
FOR THE TREES. *Father walks among the trees singing a Yiddish
lullaby, until he comes to the castle. Two hands come from behind
the drop, grab him by the throat and pull him behind it. As this
occurs, Beast comes on, dressed in a dowdy cardigan, lip-synchs a
song in the style of Perry Como's "It's Impossible". The sound cuts
out before the song is done, but Beast continues singing. Beauty
comes out to rescue the scene and encourages Father to begin the
next scene by placing him in the chair directly in front of the castle.
Beast places the next card:* DUTY AND THE FEAST *and gets
dressed in a king's robe that one might find in a children's play.
Father is eating dinner at Beast's house.*

FATHER: What mysterious nourishment! Laid out for me as though
I were expected. Born of misfortune and suckled at a strange table!
Tis the story of every babe, and I am a child of misfortune. I know
not of its ways. (*He looks around and continues*) A sound sleep.
Never have I slept so well. My dreams were full of color; my duty
black and white: a rose for Beauty. (*He waits for the rose, then yells
again*) A ROSE FOR BEAUTY! (*Beast goes to the suitcase, gets a
fake rose and pokes her arm out from behind the castle with the
flower in her hand*) There's the perfect rose. Why strike against Fate?
I'll pick it. (*He picks the rose, and sniffs it*)

Beast appears

BEAST: Well, that really does it. You can't just go picking my roses.
You ingrate! I hire the finest cordon blah chef to serve you a decent
meal, I set up a sleeping palett for you on the marble floor there, I rise
you up early in the morning as if by magic, I put hallucinogenic drugs
in your food that enhanced your dreams and this is the thanks I get!
You must not pick my roses! My soul is in my roses. O, scar! Scar!

FATHER: No thanks, I don't smoke.

BEAST: That's *not* funny.

FATHER: Yes, it is.

BEAST: I have lived here for many years, alone and unloved. My
ugliness has kept me to myself. Many is the traveler who, lost or
broken, has found his way to my table and eaten as you have. Only
those who are heartbroken survive.

FATHER: And the others?

BEAST: I *EAT THEM!*

FATHER: Do you know this tall guy? I believe he hails from around
here . . . a messenger by trade . . . would-be actor.

Plate 3   The Beast argues with the Father
Photo: Gaye Thompson

BEAST: Hm . . . no, I don't think so.

FATHER: I can just tell he's delicious.

BEAST: I'm not really hungry. I eat out of loneliness, but I never eat the lonely.

FATHER: So one might call you a consumer of happiness.

BEAST: I reckon so.

FATHER: What wilt thou with me?

BEAST: You must stay here and live with me forever. You have stolen from me, and now I will steal from you. Your freedom is mine.

FATHER: But I have my daughters to tend to ... their love is as great as their loveliness renowned ... I cannot stay with you.

BEAST: Stay with me you must.

FATHER: All I did was pick a rose.

BEAST: All Iphigenia did was die.

FATHER: You mean it, then?

BEAST: Never words meant more.

FATHER: Grant me one thing, then: that I may return home and give my Beauty this rose for which my life will be the recompense.

BEAST: Will you return?

FATHER: I shirk my debts to no man.

BEAST: I'm not a man.

FATHER: I don't look for loopholes.

BEAST: Either you must return by sundown, or you must send someone in your stead. One of your daughters, perhaps. A curse is upon me; if you or one of yours does not return, all the wrath of a broken heart will descend upon you and your daughters; all the ugliness in my face will disfigure your spirits.

FATHER: Then I must hie me hence, these many many miles. For the last time I will kiss my children. In a way 'tis a blessing. I am a failure to them and they languish in my care.

BEAST: Yet you will be happy here. You will not languish here. I am tamed by kindness and gentle in my ways. I have suffered an awful lot. The forest breathes my breaths; the fawns and does draw close to me. The moons spins for me in a breathtaking dance; and if I wish for two things that contradict each other, leaving me to choose between one sweet thing and another, then a large green silken flower, a Vernon as it's called, springs up from the ground, and in it are the seeds of both things, and I plant them in the ground and both things grow up together from the soil, side by side, as I sleep, and when I wake I may pluck them both.

FATHER: No shit?! Then why don't you get rid of this curse and live like normal animals?

BEAST: It is the nature of the curse that I cannot wish for that. Wishing is all and I am not wishing well.

FATHER: You're no fountain of youth either.

BEAST: Time rushes. Hurry with your costly rose, and return yourself or your soul in your Daughter to me by sundown.

FATHER: As I must, so I will. The cost of rose is thorn, 'tis Beauty's knife; that Beauty's gift will cost the giver's life.

Beauty enters with an accordion and Beast with a tamborine. All three perform the next scene and song as a revival meeting.

BEAUTY: This, Ladies and Gentlemen, is the turning point, the moment of decision, the denouement. Will the father return in good faith and live out his life with one so much less fortunate than himself, or will he sacrifice his pure and lovely daughter to a life of unholy cohabitation, subjecting her to the Sodom and Gomorra of Beastiality and perhaps even homosexuality. Or, will the Beast repent of its ways and come to know that God loves even the sick and the ugly. Well, Ladies and Gentlemen, I want you to think what you might do in this situation, and we'll return to our story, but first . . . This, Ladies and Gentlemen, is *your* turning point, *your* moment of decision, *your* denouement.

There is no time like the present to repent your backsliding and come into the light of the Lord Jesus Christ your Savior. Now, you might be sitting there saying to yourself, 'Why, I have everything I need. Why should I give up my happiness, my wealth, my success, to follow in the path of righteousness?' You might be saying to yourself, 'Why tonight? Why not tomorrow? Or next week, after that trip to Las Vegas?' Well, Ladies and Gentlemen, there is no fast car or fine house that can compare to having Jesus Christ as your personal savior. There is no executive position higher than your place next to him at the throne of God. And there is no jetset vacation that can compare to that day when you'll be able to walk around your heavenly palace! And there is no time like the present! Jesus Christ can *save* you, and he can *save* you in the nick of time! Take Johnny Cash for example.

Johnny was doing fine. He had everything he wanted; he had money, he had fame, he had success. But that wasn't enough, so Johnny turned to drink and then he turned to that evil drug, heroin. His marriage was falling apart, he was losing his self-respect and then one morning after a night of debauchery, Johnny woke up and the whole right side of his face had caved in. He took one look in the mirror, Ladies and

Gentlemen, and he *knew* that something was missing from his life. At that very moment, Johnny took Jesus as his savior and Jesus saved Johnny in the nick of time.

ALL: Johnny Cash's face was original sin
It looked okay but it was all bashed in
On the right side
In the nick of time
He was saved by Jesus
Saved by Jesus in the nick of time. (*Rabbi shouts "Moses!"
in place of "Jesus."*)

The Father, the son and the holy ghost
Johnny Cash's face needs your help the most
On the right side.
In the nick of time
He was saved by Jesus,
Saved by Jesus in the nick of time (*Rabbi shouts "Moses!"
in place of "Jesus" again.*)

BEAUTY: Now you might have heard of Patti Smith. She was fast becoming a legend in her own time, a product of the 'me' generation – the limousines and the record contracts filled Patti's life but not her heart. She soon fell prey to that god of all rockstars: drugs. But Patti was a smart girl; she soon saw the light. She soon took Jesus as her savior, and Jesus saved Patti in the nick of time.

ALL: Patti Smith was livin' on the wild side
Doing CBGB's on nitrous oxide
On the right side
In the nick of time
She was saved by Jesus,
Saved by Jesus in the nick of time.

Patti Smith was livin' a heretic's life
Now she's found Jesus she's a good housewife
On the right side
She was saved by Jesus,
Saved by Jesus in the nick of time.

BEAUTY: Now you might have heard of Bob Dylan. Bob had always been considered a prophet ... not a prophet of God, but a prophet of hedonism, paganism, and yes, even communism. And it was not until Bob's name had faded from the pop charts, and he found himself alone and idle, that he saw the error of his ways. And he came to know the true prophet of God, and the rest is history. Bob made a come-back. Jesus saved Bob in the nick of time!

ALL: Dylan thought he had sub-terranean blues

Jesus got a hold of him, he's payin' his dues
On the right side
In the nick of time.
He was saved by Jesus
Saved by Jesus in the nick of time.

BEAUTY: Well, I could go on forever, Ladies and Gentlemen, listing those celebrities for God. I can even name friends like Liberace and Billie Jean King whose lives may not have taken such downward turn if they had taken Jesus as their personal savior. But I want you to look into your own hearts. I want you to make room for him, and I want you to let *him* save *you* in the nick of time.

ALL: Take Jesus as your savior and you'll go real far
'Cause everyone thinks Jesus is a Hollywood star
On the right side
In the nick of time.
You can be saved by Jesus,
Saved by Jesus in the nick of time.
You can be saved by Jesus,
Saved by Jesus in the nick of time.
You can be saved by Jesus,
Saved by Jesus in the nick of time. Amen!

BEAST: Scene . . . (*she looks around*) seven.

Beast sets the next card: THORNING BECOMES ELECTRA.
Father follows Beauty around as she puts away her accordion and
begins to set up a music stand for her dramatic reading.

FATHER: Beauty, I brought you a present. Guess what it is.

BEAUTY: A cow.

FATHER: No!

BEAUTY: A chicken!

FATHER: No!

BEAUTY: A book of verse!

FATHER: No!

BEAUTY: A babe in a basket!

FATHER: No!

BEAUTY: I cannot guess. Tell me, Father. Give me a cue. A clue.

FATHER: (*Looking at the rose*) It is something that combines the grace of all these: the spilt red blood of the cow; the stalk upon which sits the pitted brain of the chicken; the lost lands in a book of verse; the helpless babe in a basket.

BEAUTY: O Father! Didst bring me a single red rose?

FATHER: Ay, Beauty, and a thousand thorns to go with it.

BEAUTY: Father, why so sad? You're back and well, and the flower is beautiful. I missed you so much, my sweet sire! I yearned for your company! The noise of your absence frightened me. Never was *a stay louder.*

FATHER: (*taking Beauty's head in his hands, peering at her*) Do you paint your face now, my dear? I've never know you to use cosmetics.

BEAUTY: Nay, Father, 'tis worse; I paint my soul with outward show, that it not reveal fear for the heart of a Father that's broken.

FATHER: I'm not broken, I'm broke!

BEAUTY: What happened?

FATHER: After much meandering I found the dock, and cuddled herein was a boat pillaged, plundered, barely mine. That dreadful man, that beastly messenger, came to attend me . . .

BEAUTY: What did he say, Father?

FATHER: He said all the same stuff he said the first time he came: that my fortune was gone, my merchandise plundered and all that.

BEAUTY: And you believed him?

FATHER: It's funny. When mutton talks, I listen.

BEAUTY: What else happened, Father?

FATHER: I walked and I walked and with such sadness. And then I went through a forest, feeling ever so hungry and sad. I got to a castle, Beauty, a mauve and turreted castle, and when I entered, a table instantly set for me with morsels of such delicacy a king could not have turned from. I ate, and I ate. I slept and I slept. And when I awoke, a rose, like a puppet of God, popped up and I picked it.

BEAUTY: What then . . . O Father, hurry!

FATHER: A BEAST APPEARED! He was UGLY! He yelled at me for picking the rose and told me I must live with him forever! This turreted castle is to be my jail! I must return and live with him forever!

BEAUTY: You had a bad dream, Father, you are overwrought.

FATHER: NAY, 'tis all too real. I must return by sundown, or send a loved one in my stead.

BEAUTY: What mean you?

FATHER: The beast for all its beastliness seemed to sense the refinement of love: to know that if I am separated from my children, 'tis a prison to me no matter which of us the iron gaol restrains.

BEAUTY: Father, before we are parted forever, grant me one favor.

FATHER: Anything but a rose, my daughter, you before whom the rose pales in grace.

BEAUTY: Let me go in your place.

FATHER: Never!

BEAUTY: Yes!

FATHER: No!

BEAUTY: Yes!

FATHER: No!

BEAUTY: Yes!

FATHER: Well, all right.

BEAUTY: How should I get there, Father? The sun already hangs low in the pouch of the day; she will soon give birth to the dark and terrible night of our eternal loneliness.

FATHER: I'll call you a cab.

BEAUTY: No, Father, I'll take the bus.

FATHER: I don't want you taking public transportation at this hour.

BEAUTY: My spirit already transported, I care not for the stops called out to the flesh by invisible motormen.

FATHER: Then go as you will, my daughter.
The distance between two hearts for both the same;
Whichever moves, both hearts are rent in twain.

BEAUTY: I've always wanted to be Katharine Hepburn.

FATHER: I've always wanted to be Martin Buber.

BEAUTY: I've always admired a good dramatic actress.

FATHER: You know any? (*He exits.*)

Beast sets the next card and announces: A DRAMATIC READING

BEAUTY: I'll be reading tonight from Macbeth, act one, scene five. (*She corrects herself*) Act 5, Scene 1. (*As she reads the speech, she is overtaken by the angry and sexual meaning of the words*)

The raven himself is hoarse
That croaks the fatal entrance of Duncan

Under my battlements. Come you spirits.
That tend on mortal thoughts, unsex me here
  (*repeating 'unsex me here'*)
And fill me from the crown to the toe top full
Of direst cruelty! Make thick my blood;
Stop up the access and passage to remorse,
That no compunctious visitings of nature
Shake my fell purpose nor keep peace between
The effect and it! Come to my woman's breast,
And take my milk my gall you murdering ministers,
Wherever in your sightless substances
You wait on nature's mischief! Come thick night,
And pall thee in the dunnest smoke of hell,
That my keen knife see not the wound it makes
Nor heaven peep through the blanket of the dark,
To cry 'Hold, hold' (*she loses control completely*)

I won't hold. Why should I hold? I'm tired of holding. Let all the other people hold. Ooooh. This feels really good. It's good to hate. Hate is never having to say I love you. And it's fun. Just think how fun it is to say 'her, that bitch, I hate her!' And it's exhilarating. It's psychedelic. And it's enlightening. It's the perfect relationship. All those people you hate and who hate you back – it's perfect ... it's sex ... it's orgasm. Thank you.

Beast changes to new card: WHEN VAUDEVILLE MEETS THE FAIRY TALE. She gets a tutu out of the suitcase and hands it to Father.

BEAST: Get dressed, Hitchcock. This is the part of the play where you play Beauty and you meet the Beast in the forest for the first time. Could we have some music please? And some classical lighting? This is a classical piece.

Beast and Father do a ballet piece ending with Beast lifting Father. Beauty rushes out with her accordion and a chair to rescue them. They sing a Salvation Army jingle:

ALL: Salvation Army, Salvation Army
Put a nickle in the drum
save another drunken bum
Salvation Army, Salvation Army
Put a nickle in the drum
and you'll be saved.

Father is sitting on Beast's lap. They play the following scene as a ventriloquist and dummy.

BEAST: Well Mrs Alston, what a fine day we're having today.

FATHER: (*in dummy's voice*) That I know, my ice cream's running down the street.

BEAST: Why I remember when I was a young girl in weather like this, girls wore skirts down to their ankles.

FATHER: Yeah, but they started at their knees. Yuck yuck yuck!

Beauty interrupts by starting the Salvation Army jingle again.

BEAUTY: Salvation Army, Salvation Army
      Put a nickle in the drum
      save another drunken bum
      Salvation Army, Salvation Army
      Put a nickle in the drum
      and you'll be saved.

BEAST: And in fine weather like this the men are always out on the street and they say such interesting things to the women as they walk past.

FATHER: Yeah, like 'I want to suck your pussy.'

BEAST: Mrs Alston, these nice people came to the theater tonight to get away from the things they hear on the streets. They didn't come expecting to hear . . .

FATHER: Go out and get your own courage, mother fucking bitch. Suck my dick!

Beauty interrupts with another round of 'Salvation Army.'

BEAST: But think about it, Mrs Alston. Wouldn't it be wonderful if men said such nice things to women as they passed on the street. Wouldn't it be wonderful if they said things like . . .

FATHER: You want to share a chocolate soda? You want to go for a walk in the moonlight?

BEAST: What a wonderful world that would be, Mrs Alston.

FATHER: Yeah, but they'd blow it in the end, that I know. They'd blow up all the people and leave the buildings!

Beauty interrupts by playing the chords for the next song which they sing in close harmony.

ALL: Reagan, moral-shaper
      He's a slob and a woman-hater
      Reagan, baby-maker
      Just a cowboy like you.

      Bush and Reagan's faces
      Stand for bombs and for missile bases
      Blacks, queers, know your places

They could drop it on you.

If you want a politician with a John Wayne look
You can bet that he'll be there
There won't be no abortion
But the women will cook, and fuck and have kids, and
    that's fair.

Reagan, moral-shaper
Just a cowboy like you
Just a cowboy like you
Just a cowboy like you

Beast changes the card: ROME-OWED WHAT JULI-ET. Beauty sits in front of the castle with a giant knife and fork. Beast enters in the Beast robe and watches Beauty eat.

BEAST: Will you have dinner with me?

BEAUTY: As you wish, Beast, you are the master here.

BEAST: Do you find me ugly?

BEAUTY: Yes, but I think you must be very kind.

BEAST: Oh, I am kind, but I'm stupid.

BEAUTY: Oh, you're not so stupid. People who are truly stupid are too stupid to know it.

BEAUTY: Beauty you make me really happy! Marry me.

BEAUTY: (*between bites*) Unh unh.

BEAST: Why?

BEAUTY: I can't.

BEAST: Why not?

BEAUTY: No.

BEAST: I love you.

BEAUTY: What would our children be like?

BEAST: Marry me.

BEAUTY: No.

BEAST: Darling! I'll take you on a honeymoon to Olympus and feed you mint and honey with my hands.

BEAUTY: I like your fried chicken (*She smacks her lips and eats*).

BEAST: Marry me.

BEAUTY: Unh unh.

BEAST: Please.

BEAUTY: No.

BEAST: I'll be Gertrude Stein to your Alice B. Toklas. I'll be Spencer Tracy to your Katharine Hepburn. I'll be James Dean to your ... Montgomery Clift.

BEAUTY: Well, I always wanted to *be* Katharine Hepburn.

BEAST: I always wanted to *be* James Dean.

BEAUTY: I *was* Katharine Hepburn.

BEAST: I *was* James Dean.

BEAUTY: I was Katharine Hepburn and the girl who lived down the hall from me freshman year of college was (*taking on the character of Katharine Hepburn*) Spencer Tracy.

BEAST: I was James Dean (*taking on the character of James Dean*) and when I slept with a woman for the first time she threw me out of bed on the floor and told me I was sick.

BEAUTY: (*in Hepburn's voice*) Spencer used to write me poems, bring me roses in the morning, and take me for rides in her red convertible.

BEAST: I went to work the next day and passed out; I was in a coma for two weeks.

BEAUTY: One Christmas, Spencer bought me a white fur coat.

BEAST: Not only did I have spinal meningitis, but I had mononucleosis, and the doctor told me I couldn't kiss a boy for a year. (*She smiles broadly*)

BEAUTY: My mother told me that I shouldn't accept expensive gifts from girls. But I wasn't worried ... She wasn't a girl, she was Spencer Tracy.

BEAST: Then my girlfriend married a boy who thought *he* was James Dean. So I married a boy who thought he was Lauren Bacall.

BEAUTY: Then one evening, Spencer and I decided to go out to the movies together. As we were leaving the dormitory, by mistake we checked the 'dating' instead of 'non-dating' column.

BEAST: Then I fell in love with a woman at work and she fell in love with me.

BEAUTY: When we got home that evening the dorm mother was in the doorway, and she wanted to know just what had been going on.

BEAST: All my fantasies were turning into realities so I went to a

Plate 4   Beauty is called away from the Beast
Photo: Gaye Thompson

shrink and I fell in love with her too.

BEAUTY: As far as I knew, nothing had been 'going on.' But later that evening they took Spencer to the hospital in a straight jacket.

BEAST: I got all my stuff together and left Lauren Bacall. I moved in with the woman from work only to find that she thought *she* was James Dean.

BEAUTY: I found out later that she wasn't Spencer Tracy at all. I found out much later that I had been in love with her.

BEAST: Will you marry me, then, Beauty?

Beauty pauses.

BEAST: I'll be back tomorrow. (*She exits and returns immediately*) Beauty, I'm so lonely in the forest without you.

BEAUTY: Eat! It helps.

BEAST: I'll be back tomorrow. (*She exits and returns*) Marry me.

BEAUTY: I can't.

BEAST: If I can't have you no one can.

BEAUTY: You may be right but I can't consent.

BEAST: (*crying*) I'll be back tomorrow.

Beauty looks down into her plate to continue eating and is horrified . She holds the plate out to the audience. On it is written: "Your Father Is Sick, Go Home!" She faints.

Father and Beast do a short reprise of their ballet.

BEAST: (*holding Father in a dip*) So, Daddy's little girl is going home.

FATHER: I'm not your little girl. I'm not your little goil. I have a shoirt. I have a schul. I'm not a little goil. I HAVE a little goil. I'm a FATHER. (*He explodes*) I PLAY THE FATHER HERE. (*He storms off*)

BEAST: (*turning to Beauty, who has awakened from her faint*) So Daddy's little girl is going home.

BEAUTY: Thank you, Beast, for granting me leave.

BEAST: Will you miss me?

BEAUTY: In my way, I will. I'll miss your voice, your laughter, your step on my stairs. Pray for my father.

BEAST: I *eat* my prey.

BEAUTY: We're very different, Beast.

BEAST: I know, that's why I love you so.

BEAUTY: Goodbye.

BEAST: Goodbye. Don't forget! Come back in one week or I die!

Beast leaves Beauty to set the card: THE PRODIGAL DAUGHTER RETURNS. Father crosses to the piano and begins to play and sing a pop song about rejection in the style of "I Heard It Through the Grapevine." Beauty joins him reluctantly. The Beast groans from behind the castle until the groaning overwhelms the song. She enters.

BEAST: This is the part of the show where the beast dies and you're supposed to feel sorry for me. But don't fall for it! They've tried it before. They've tried it with Dracula, with King Kong. *Reagan* tried it! I bet a couple years ago you thought Reagan got shot ... he never got shot, they did it in a video workshop! I know, I was there! Moonwalkers – I bet you thought America went to the moon – they never went to the moon – those were the days of television – they did it in a television studio! Moonwalkers, all of them! Nixon kidnapped Patti Hearst. John Wayne killed Martin Luther King, I know! I was there. In every heart there's a Hollywood, where emotions are raised and stricken like sets, kisses and kindness are contracts, hopes are coming attractions. If she says she's coming back, lock the door – that way you can say she came but you didn't hear her. (*Beast dies. Beauty rushes to her. Beast sits up*) 'Nancy, I forgot to duck ... (*Beast dies again, then sits up*) I hope all you doctors are Republican.' (*Beast dies.*)

BEAUTY: Oh Beast! Oh Beast! (*She doesn't respond so she whispers*) Gussie – psst!

BEAST: Don't fall for it, Beauty! Don't fall for it, I know!

Beast talks a song in the style of Peggy Lee's "Is That All There Is?" with the following text:

BEAST: When I was young, I came home from school and my house was surrounded by fire trucks. My mother was sobbing on the front lawn because her washing machine had blown up from too much use and as I was standing there clasping onto my school books, looking at the smoke coming out of the basement I said to myself, 'Is that all there is to a fire?'

When I was ten, I found a pamphlet under my pillow. It said that soon I would start bleeding which meant I couldn't take hot baths or play baseball or go bowling and a scared as I was of that coming blood, I remember saying to myself, 'Is that all there is to being a woman?'

Then I fell in love with a beautiful girl for the first time in my life. We walked along the river, we gazed into each other's eyes for hours.

We were so in love, then one day, she left me. I thought I would die, but I didn't. And when I didn't, I said to myself, 'Is that all there is to love?'

You're probably saying, 'Why doesn't she just go straight or get a real job or do away with herself?' Well, I'm not ready for that final disappointment. And just as sure as you can't teach an old dog new tricks, I know when it comes time for me to die I'll be saying, 'Is that all there is?'

(Beauty sets the last card: THE END. Then Beast takes Beauty in her arms and kisses her. Father keeps playing as the lights black out.)

Lights up. Everyone bows, then they sing the Alphabet Song:

ALL: A you're an Afiscoten
B you're a belly-button
C you're a cantaloupe with arms

D you're a doody-head
E you're an elephant
F you're a fairy in my arms

G you're a gruesome goon
H you're a hairy hoon
I you're an icky-dicky-doo

J you're a jackass
K claustrophobia
L you're a lunatic too

M, N, maniac
O you're an octopus
P, Q, principle of queerness

R, S, T, respectably disgusting
U you pick your nose in bed
V you're a vomit-head
W, X, Y, Z

I love to go through
The alphabet with you
To show you how you sicken me

I love to go through
The alphabet with you
To show you how you sicken me

To show you how you sicken me

To show you how you sicken me!

THE END

UPWARDLY MOBILE HOME

DEB MARGOLIN, PEGGY SHAW, LOIS WEAVER

Directed by Lois Weaver
Performed by Deb Margolin, Peggy Shaw and Lois Weaver
Choreography Stormy Brandenberger
Sets by Susan Young
Lights Joni Wong
Sound design by Janee Pipik

Originally produced in spring 1984 at WOW Café,
330 E. 11th Street, New York

Copyright, Margolin, Shaw, Weaver 1996

Extracts from *The Shanghai Gesture* are reproduced
by permission of Sheldon Abend, American Play Company, Inc.

———

CHARACTERS

*A group of performers with a history of working together who func-
tion and identify as a family even though they come from extremely
varied backgrounds*

MOM (Peggy Shaw)

LEVINE (Deb Margolin)

TAMMY (Lois Weaver)

*Dawn's first light. It's dark with a slight yellow–orange glow. We
see a partially distinguishable image of a VW camper under the
Brooklyn Bridge at the base of the bridge's gray stone support structure. We hear the hum of cars and trucks crossing the bridge. A
dimly lit string of Chinese lanterns hangs outside the camper. There's
also a folding picnic table, folding lounge chair, a clothes line, a
Coleman stove and a campfire outside. Tammy, LeVine, and Mom
are asleep and hidden from view inside the camper.*

MOM: Are you still awake?

LEVINE: She's always half asleep. *dumb–blonde stereo*

TAMMY: I'm just resting my eyes.

MOM: We have one day to work on this play.

LEVINE: Don't worry, we always pull it together.

MOM: Do we have coffee for the morning?

LEVINE: Hey, listen to this! From the real estate section: (*She sits
up, her head visible through the camper window – she reads from
a newspaper*) "To the artist and investor in each of us. All around
town are investors who dream of doing something creative, and
artists who wish they knew how to turn red ink into black. To you
we dedicate Bleecker Court. Because a co-op at Bleecker Court meets
two basic human needs: creativity and financial sensibility."

MOM: LeVine, do we have coffee for the morning?

LEVINE: (*continuing to read*) "However, there is more to life here
than simply making a good investment in an exciting space."

TAMMY: Prob'ly.

LEVINE: "There's the quality of life itself. You're two blocks from
the Public Theatre, right near the Strand Bookstore and Tower
Records; up from the art galleries in Soho, down from the Bottom
Line and just east of Washington Square Park and Balducci's."

MOM: Do we have coffee for the morning?

LEVINE: At Bleecker Court, for the first time, the artist and the investor in you will finally agree on something.

MOM: LeVine!

LEVINE: Probably enough for tomorrow, Mother. *family rel* —

MOM: We have to get up early so we can rehearse before LeVine goes to work, and there's no milk.

TAMMY: (*in the van*) Hunh?

MOM: There's no milk.

TAMMY: There's no money.

LEVINE: I got some change.

TAMMY: We could change our minds.

LEVINE: The show must go on.

MOM: Who said the show must go on?

TAMMY: Oh, maybe.

MOM: Maybe what?

TAMMY: Maybe tomorrow somethin'll happen. Maybe tomorrow she'll win the contest and we can just drive away in our new mobile home.

MOM: We can leave anytime.

LEVINE: Not before coffee . . . (*She continues to read*) "Your creative needs now satisfied, you naturally move on to contemplate your financial considerations . . ."

TAMMY: Shhhh . . .

MOM: LeVine!

Sunrise. 5:30 a.m. Chinese instrumental music, slow then fast, fades up. We hear the sounds of the bridge, cars, trucks, and morning traffic which transforms slowly to instrumental music in the style of "Flight of the Bumblebee," then to a more popular song like "I'm Gonna Be a Wheel One Day." Mom gets up, gets out of the van, puts on a Chinese silk robe, lights the Coleman Stove and begins to make coffee. An alarm clock buzzes. The music stops. Inside the camper, LeVine, dressed in a black slip, jumps up and starts her stretching exercises. Mom washes some underwear in a bucket. An alarm goes off

RADIO ANNOUNCER: A sprinkle giving way to clear skies and seasonable temperatures this afternoon. Tonight it will be clear and cool, high will be around forty. Next is shadow traffic at five minutes past. We turn now to our helicopter report: Jim.

HELICOPTER PILOT: Things look okay at five minutes past the hour, Cath. Bruckner and Cross Bronx moving bumper to bumper. Choose alternate routes into Manhattan. Brooklyn Bridge one lane open – stay to your right. Two lanes closed by TV cameras covering the WUMH VW Camper Marathon on the north end of the bridge. Use the tunnel; the bridge is hardly moving. Deegan moving rather well at seven minutes past the hour. Now back to you, Cath.

LeVine continues to stretch inside the camper. Mom washes some items of clothing in the tub and hangs them on a line to dry.

RADIO ANNOUNCER: Today marks the beginning of the sixth remarkable week in the living bridge marathon. As you know five contestants began competing for a mobile home by camping out around the arches of Brooklyn Bridge six weeks ago. Under the watchful eye of millions of New York commuters, the nation's attention has focused on the two remaining contestants.

The telephone in the camper rings – LeVine answers the phone. Tammy is still in bed. Mom is sitting in her lounge chair outside.

LEVINE: Hello . . . Yes, Suzanne, this is Madeleine LeVine . . . Yes, yes, hon'. No that's not a problem . . . we can have that taken care of well before 10:30. Okay, good, good, I'm glad you called. Yes, fine, dear, fine . . . I'll see you later . . . yes. Bye.

MOM: Who was that?

LEVINE: I have to wear dirty underpants again today. My god, if I live through today it will be a miracle. Two jobs, the audition, and another fifteen questionnaires to finish, Su Yung Lee's fashion show . . .

MOM: heh-heh-heh-heh –

LEVINE: Why do you laugh?

MOM: 'Cause inside I have a joke. A very wise joke. Tonight my comic spirit runs fast along. Tonight we have a new show.

TAMMY: Shhhhh!

MOM: You have to have a sense of humor.

LEVINE: Sense of humor. What am I supposed to do now, no clean underpants for my day, fine state of affairs. People look at you and they know . . . (*the telephone rings; LeVine answers*). Hello? Yes, Jerry, good morning. I just spoke with Suzanne and she's very dissatisfied with your floor plan.

MOM: Why didn't you wash some out last night?

LEVINE: (*continuing on the phone*) I said I'd get back to her, and get to you. If we're sure the floor is laid by quarter past I can have the models in order . . . Hold on just a sec, can you? (*LeVine covers the telephone mouthpiece and looks out the window at Mom. To Mom*) I was too busy boiling water for the dishes and I didn't even eat dinner. (*On the phone*) So Jerry, cool your heels and move your ass. Okay love? I don't know . . . I'll meet you there if I can.

The front door of the camper opens. Tammy comes outside in a yellow dress and sweater with a slept-in look. Her hair is in curlers and she's carrying a cosmetic case.

MOM: (*to Tammy*) Aren't you up early today?

LeVine hangs up.

MOM: (*to LeVine*) Any luck?

TAMMY: My luck.

LEVINE: We're out of clown white. I told you that yesterday, remember?

MOM: Not even a little left?

LEVINE: I wouldn't have said there was none left if there was a little left. We've been using the little left for two weeks. And we're out of face cream.

TAMMY: My luck.

MOM: It's not luck, we've been talking about the amount of clown white for two weeks. Would you like some coffee, Tammy?

TAMMY: I had coffee already at Burger King. Jesus Christ! (*She starts to put on her make-up and comb out her hair*)

MOM: What's that?

TAMMY: I dreamt I got picked up by a woman who thinks she's Jesus Christ . . . and on her way to work yet, oooooh . . . it was a sexy dream, and I was all dressed up for work . . . with my net stockings and tweed skirt . . . she had on a skirt too. We had coffee after, she bought me coffee and wanted to know my name. I was almost gonna tell her when she started talking about how *her* camper had air conditioning and curtains, like I didn't notice. Made me nervous. I like to be able to see around me all the time, you know?

MOM: There's no milk.

TAMMY: How about some fake cream containers from Burger King?

LEVINE: Can I have some of that hot water? I'd like to wash under my pits.

MOM: Then I won't have enough for coffee, I have to have coffee, everyone else has had coffee (*meaning Tammy*).

TAMMY: It's not the caffeine that gives you cancer, it's something they spray on the beans.

MOM: You think so?

TAMMY: I liked having that dream, too bad I don't . . .

MOM: Too bad you don't dream about a script for our new show tonight.

LEVINE: We have a script, Ma . . . we have *The Shanghai Gesture*. (*She stops her calisthenics and goes for her clothes*)

MOM: It's racist and sexist.

LEVINE: Oh Mom, it's not racist and sexist, and besides, we can do something with it. It was a hit in the twenties.

MOM: The teens.

LEVINE: Revivals are really *in* right now, Mother.

TAMMY: Then it ought to be a musical. I got lots of revival songs.

LEVINE: I can't get my outfit right.

TAMMY: At least I don't hide myself in my outfit.

MOM: Your outfits couldn't hide much. Are you going out like that?

TAMMY: Mother, you always want to know everything, you talk too much in the morning.

MOM: I can handle anything, as long as it's the truth. You are what you eat.

LEVINE: I'd hate to tell you what you are. You're responsible for the way my day is going. Dirty underpants, my pits reek, and it all comes down to water. It's all water, it comes down to the fact that we have to boil water.

TAMMY: Our new mobile home will have hot running water.

MOM: I need coffee.

TAMMY: That coffee was made by fascists in Columbia.

MOM: Well it's pretty good except for that fake cream you gave me from Burger King.

TAMMY: I hope the rest of this day . . .

MOM: Tammy, I was hoping today you would sit with me, and we would think of ways to make money like the old days.

TAMMY: Mother, these aren't the old days; besides, in the old days, as you call them, we didn't ever come up with a way to make money especially doing shows on the streets. You know what I saw? The other day I saw this bum rollin' around on his back with his feet in the air tryin' to collect money for his break-dancin'. Now that's what comes of doin' shows in the streets.

LEVINE: What do you think you're livin' in now, honey? If this ain't the street, nothin' is.

TAMMY: We got the van! You gotta take a step down to arrive on the street.

LEVINE: So you're once removed from the street.

TAMMY: Yes, I *am* once removed from the street.

MOM: You'd better be careful you don't get removed from the street by the police again today.

TAMMY: It's not me they pick up, it's my stuff (*referring to her suit-case of personal items that she sells on the street*).

A red fire bucket tied to the end of a rope is lowered down into the camp site.

MOM: Would you send some coffee up to Lost Petal please?

TAMMY: I don't want to.

LEVINE: Be responsible.

MOM: Lost Petal's the one that's been sittin' up on the bridge for six weeks.

TAMMY: Well, what if there's shit in her bucket?

LEVINE: She won't shit till she has her coffee.

TAMMY: I haven't had *my* coffee.

MOM: You had your coffee at Burger King.

TAMMY: I *dreamt* I had coffee at Burger King.

LEVINE: That's the level our dreams have sunk to.

MOM: A slicing off process. A little bit cut off each day and the raw edge left to be sliced again the next day.

TAMMY: All right, all right. (*She takes coffee to the bucket and sends it back up*)

MOM: Wash your face, Tammy, you still have make-up on.

TAMMY: Mother, I just PUT my make-up on.

LEVINE: Okay troops, gather round, I have today's schedule; two things open, four things closed. Tammy, can you hear me?

TAMMY: Yes, I can hear you. (*She starts setting up a shopping cart and suitcase, displaying her belongings to sell to passers-by*)

LEVINE: We're all together, for a change, let's polish up the last scene of *The Shanghai Gesture* for tonight. We also need to rehearse that dinner party scene and that's a must for later. Let's do that at one. You can come with me to the fashion show if you have something clean to wear. She pays thirty bucks. I've got a Jewish guy coming at three and I'd like you to be here. Tammy, don't peddle that junk when he gets here.

TAMMY: It's not junk, I use it myself.

LEVINE: And the show's at eight o'clock, and at seven-thirty there's a full press conference covering the bridge marathon, it could be our break. The bottom line is, if we make enough noise we're bound to attract the cameras, and we won't end up on the cutting room floor. We'll be sitting pretty by March. Okay, any questions? Good. Okay, please follow along from the middle of page one hundred eleven. Mother. Tammy. I want to work on that last scene where Mother Godam kills her daughter Poppy. Tammy, you're Poppy.

MOM: What kind of a name is that, Poppy?

LEVINE: Now Mother, this is the realization scene. Your sense of revenge has gotten out of your control. You thought you were going to get what you wanted by hurting Sir Guy Chartoris, but you got trapped and you end up hurting yourself, by killing your own daughter, Poppy. This is big tragedy, Mother.

TAMMY: Then I don't know why we can't do Gone with the Wind. At least it's a familiar story.

MOM: It's racist and sexist. Same as *Shanghai Gesture* is racist and sexist.

LEVINE: Mom, it's not racist and sexist. It has a very high consciousness. It was a hit in the twenties.

MOM: The teens.

LEVINE: Florence Reid virtually made her career with this scene.

TAMMY: Well then why can't I sing something?

MOM: You can, Tammy.

LEVINE: Just not right now, okay. Good. Good. Okay, let's walk through it, Mother. Tammy, you're Poppy. Places please, Mother.

TAMMY: Then why can't Poppy sing something?

LEVINE: Tammy, *The Shanghai Gesture* is a tragic story of revenge. The whole point is that Mother Godam is betrayed by Sir Guy Chartoris and sold into prostitution by him after he promised to marry her. She waits twenty years to get back at him and becomes a big madam at her own shop. You've got to admire that, hon' – a woman making it on her own in the twenties in a play.

MOM: The teens.

LEVINE: Then she holds a New Year's Eve party and Sir Guy is invited. Now that's the dinner party scene, Tammy.

MOM: He's not gonna kiss my hand. No man's gonna kiss my hand.

LEVINE: It's me, Ma, it's me. You used to let me kiss you all the time.

MOM: Well then, let's present *Medea*. Then you can kiss my hand. Hah hah hah.

LEVINE: If we did *Medea* you'd have to kill me for it, wouldn't you.

TAMMY: So, well, she's supposed to kill me instead? That's just fine, LeVine.

LEVINE: Don't worry, Tammy, she gets us both in the end. You'll remember that Sir Guy had two daughters, one with Mother Godam and one by that very wealthy English woman whom he married. Now earlier in the script, Mother Godam switched the two babies so that she raised Sir Guy's daughter, Lost Petal and her own daughter, Poppy Chartoris, was raised by Sir Guy in his lovely home with its lovely carpets. However, she became a dope fiend, that's you Tammy. (*She hangs Tammy a curtain with a Chinese New Year greeting attached to it.*)

TAMMY: But I don't want to play a dope fiend.

LEVINE: Look Tammy, Lucille Lortell played Poppy in the nineteen twenties and she's now a multi-millionaire with her own theater on Christopher Street, okay? (*Tammy begins to hand the curtain on a clothes line stretched across centre stage.*) Good, good. Now let's walk it through. Tammy, you're Poppy. Mother, I want to take it right at the cue for Poppy's entrance. Mother, I want to see you downstage center please. Tammy, you're backstage and we're gonna take it right at the cue for Poppy's entrance when Mother Godam is talking to Sir Guy, okay? Good, good. Standby please. Places.

(*Tammy takes her position behind the curtain. Mother centers herself in front of the curtain. LeVine stands off left*)

LEVINE: And, action!

(*Chinese instrumental music accompanies the scene.*

MOTHER GODAM/MOM: Now I will show China and the Chinese woman and clean my house.

POPPY/TAMMY: (*behind the curtain*) Let me go! Take your hands off me. I want my pipe.

SIR GUY CHARTORIS/LEVINE: (*joining Mother center*) Who was that?

MOTHER GODAM/MOM: Just another white woman who has found her way to my house on her own accord.

POPPY/TAMMY: (*entering*) Let me go! Take your hands off me. Let me go. (*Poppy and Sir Guy see each other*) Father!

SIR GUY CHARTORIS/LEVINE: Poppy!

MOTHER GODAM/MOM: (*shocked*) Father! Poppy! I, ya, ohhhhhh! (*Poppy and Mother Godam exit by walking behind the curtain*)

NARRATOR/LEVINE: Thus fate played one of the cruelest tricks and brought Mother Godam her own daughter, Poppy, back to her enmeshed in the glittering inequities of her own notorious house. In a revenge for which she had waited twenty years. Now the kaleidoscope of life spins very rapidly. In a tense tragic scene with Poppy, words heavy with hate are spoken.

Enter Mother Godam, strangling Poppy.

POPPY/TAMMY: Get your hands off me. Let me go. Take your filthy hands off me.

MOTHER GODAM/MOM: I made a vow, not to Lost Petal, but to the daughter of Mr. Blue Eyes and Miss Pink.

POPPY/TAMMY: (*crying and panicked*) Have you gone mad, you crazy old devil. You, my mother? My mother died when I was born. Oh, take you hands off me . . .

MOTHER GODAM/MOM: Cha Ka Nee Koya . . .

POPPY/TAMMY: Let me go . . .

MOTHER GODAM/MOM: (*strangling her more*) Keep my hands still. Cha Ka Nee Koyaaaa . . .

POPPY/TAMMY: No, don't kill me . . . don't kill me . . .

LeVine waves her hands to stop the action.

LEVINE: Cut, cut . . . Don't kill her that way, Ma. (*To Tammy*) Let me take your place here for a second. It's an impulsive gesture, an act of love and intimacy. It's anguish, Ma. Killing her is like killing yourself.

Tammy sees someone looking at her merchandise and walks off.

TAMMY: Hi, if you see something here you want, let me know . . .

To demonstrate what she means, LeVine positions herself as the Poppy character and places Mother Godam's hands on her neck.

LEVINE: You can see it in your body work. Grab her here, Ma. Put your arms around like this, and wrestle her down to the floor.

Mom starts to wrestle LeVine down to the floor.

LEVINE: Don't kill me, don't kill me. Very nice, Mom.

TAMMY: (*to the audience*) Oh don't worry, they know each other. That's really her daughter. I think she's just a little disappointed in the way she turned out. But don't you worry. I think any minute they'll just burst into song or somethin'. Wait a minute, oh my god that gives me a great idea. You hold on a second. I'll be right back. (*She crosses to center*) LeVine, oh, I have a great idea. Let me in there. Ohhh. Okay Mother, we're goin' to take it right from when I say: Don't kill me, don't kill me. Ohhh LeVine, you're gonna love this.

Tammy positions herself in front of Mom. Mom grabs her.

POPPY/TAMMY: Don't kill me, don't kill me. (*She starts singing a duet in the style of "True Love." She finishes the song in a romantic pose*) Wasn't that great, LeVine?

LEVINE: Well, it's not exactly what I had in mind, but thank you for sharing. Thank you very much, I think that's enough for today. Mom, you wanna help me out with some of these phone calls I have to make today? (*She takes the curtain off the line*)

MOM: What's the product today? Flesh junks? Sold to the junkman she won't last long! Heh-heh-heh!

LEVINE: No, these new General Foods coffee flavors, Ma. They're good.

TAMMY: They give you cancer.

LEVINE: They pay the rent.

MOM: Chu-a-chong, we don't pay rent.

TAMMY: (*to an imaginary customer*) Can I help you?

LeVine finds her clipboard with the telephone survey questions and makes her first call.

LEVINE: Hello? Mrs Jones? Madeleine LeVine, Data Development Corporation. Have you tried the General Foods Flavored Coffees? You did, good. And did your husband try them? He did. And is he head of the household, Mrs Jones? And does he make under 10,000 dollars? Does he make between 9,999 and 19,999 dollars? Between . . .

TAMMY: Oh that? That's an antique. I don't know how old it is, but it's old!

The bucket comes down. Mom pours another cup of coffee and sends the bucket back up.

MOM: (*up to the bridge*) How are you doing today my lost petal, my daughter? I know you've decided right now to be a part of that world. I'll visit you and you'll visit me. We're safe here, no one can see us, we're invisible. Don't worry, nothing can happen to hurt us. Only believers can see us and that doesn't mean they can even get to us. It's a trade you have to learn. We're safe. Be careful what you wish for, it may come true. I died once you see, I paid my dues. Survival is more than an instinct.

TAMMY: That? Well, that'll be twelve dollars. Oh, no, I don't think I could take less for them.

LeVine sits in the camper doorway and continues the telephone survey.

LEVINE: And did he complete grade school, some high school, high school, some college . . .

MOM: (*talking faster and faster*) I am your mother. I am the Hudson River, I am the bridge, I am the traffic. I am the government here, I am the police. That's what makes me invisible. I am your hope. I am the bluest skies you have ever seen. And water and food. I am big arms that hold you. I love you when you are unhappy, I love you the way you are. I laugh, I scream, I have to laugh.

Once when I was young, I went to a fair and saw a sign to see a fat lady for twenty-five cents. I gave the booth my money and walked into the tent to see my fat lady. It was a big tent, I was alone and there was a fat lady sitting in a big couch with her legs propped up on two stools and her arms supported by pillows. She was alone. I looked at her and she looked at me, she knew I had come to see her being fat. I ran out of the tent exhausted. I knew her, she was me, we were looking at each other. But I was tricked. The colors, the music, the lights, promised me entertainment and gave me more than that. I was right there at one with myself, me and that fat lady. I wish I was still there sometimes. I still remember the daylight seeping through the pinholes in the tent. I remember her fat was there overpowering me but I couldn't look at her. I love that fat lady. (*She begins to sing some of the lyrics from a song in the style of "I'm Gonna Be a Wheel One Day"*)

You have paid to see me. You will not get your money back. Your money does not pay me for my work. I work always. What circle do you move in? Do you have a bed to sleep in? And food? And a toilet? Do your friends? Do you have a need to share your life with others? Tell stories? Do you get paid for your stories? Do you get paid what you're worth for what you do? Am I worth five dollars (*or the price of a theater ticket*)?

Do you want more room to watch me? A bigger theater, more comfortable seats? Are you willing to pay for that or do you want to pay for a more comfortable show? I am a mother, a good mother, are you willing to pay to see a good lesbian mother?

My legs feel long and keep getting in my way. Do you want to see my legs? That's very expensive. I don't know if you have enough money to pay to see a good lesbian mother's legs.

I wear a ring for every time I see a fat lady, I wear beads for every time I cry. If I lost my beads and rings I would have my memories. If I sold my beads and rings I would have money to buy food. When I am rich I will buy my mother a house, a car, and a family. (*She sits in the chair*)

TAMMY: This? This is eight dollars. It belonged to my Aunt Edna. I wore it last year in a show. Yeah, I do shows. We had a show here last night, we have one tonight too. Oh I'm a singer really – Tammy, (*she laughs*) Tammy Whynot.

We live here – well for now anyhow. We're usually on the road and we just couldn't hold on to our apartments. Well I had one, I had a few really, but you know when you move around it's risky business. I had this one place, it was so cute. Little French doors, parquet floors. Well, I was hardly ever there and the landlord, he tried to prove that I wasn't me. Can you imagine? The real point was he wanted to double my rent – you know, the neighborhood was really coming along well, six hundred dollars and then besides all that I'd have to go to court to fight this man. Well –

And I also had this other place . . . it used to be a warehouse and now it's TriBeCa. But what I really want is MY OWN BUS . . . no not exactly a camper, a bus, you know like the kind that go every day to New Jersey but fixed up with chrome and maybe some purple air brush on the side. And everything inside. White shag carpet, an oval bed and oval mirrors. A refrigerator and freezer, a dinette suite.

You know, you could live in it, travel in it. Use it as a dressing room, if you wanted to. I have pictures here of some buses I've been dreaming of and hoping for. Would you like to see them? Oh no that's alright, I understand.

(That's why we're here really – our friend is up there on the bridge, in that living billboard contest. Scary, right? It's a contest for WUMH. If she stays up there the longest, she gets a lifetime supply of McDonalds, she gets to be in TV commercials, she wins a summer for two in East Hampton and and THE *BEST*, she's gonna win a mobile home. Well, not a real mobile home, no, not a BUS either. You know, like an R.V.)

That's a Recreational Vehicle. Something bigger than our van but not as big as a bus. (*Aside*) If you see anything you want, just tell me. (*Back to the previous customer*) So we're helping her to take care of all her – physical needs. And when she comes down she's gonna give US the mobile home. Then we'll do shows in . . . New Orleans maybe or . . . Oh okay. Don't you want to buy the bag? Oh okay.

(*To the new customer*) Hi, how you doin'? What a cute little accent you have. Where ya from? Russia? Oh how nice, you're here on vacation. Well how'd ya get here? Oh there's lost of places I escaped from too.

Yeah, I'm an actress, how did you know? I'm a singer really, oh, what's your name? Mr Rose Teacher. That's a pretty name for a man. Oh . . . Roy Sticher, I got an Uncle named Roy. Oh – you must be LeVine's friend, wait right here, Mister. I'll get her . . . (*she runs to the van*) LeVine, that old Jewish guy is here.

LEVINE: He's here early. All right, don't worry about it. You girls go get the skirt and I'll go get him.

TAMMY: Come on, Mother. We're going to have to do that Yiddish song. (*She runs to get the curtain. On the back of the curtain there are frilly curtains. Mom and Tammy wrap the curtain around them so that they appear to be wearing one giant, frilly, colorful skirt*)

LEVINE: Mr. Roy Sticher it's a pleasure to see ya'. It's been such a long time. You look so well. You know I was sorry to hear about your theater burning down. It was arson, wasn't it? Well we've been thinking about it and we really feel Yiddish theater is due for a revival and that's what we've . . . Your wife died? Oh God, when did that happen Mr. Roy Sticher? Well that's the time when you really throw yourself into your work isn't it?

Tammy and Mom are waiting with the giant skirt. LeVine continue to talk to Roy Sticher as Mom and Tammy squeeze close and LeVine joins them with Mom in the middle.

LEVINE: and we've been thinking about it and we really want to show the beauty of Yiddish in a context of something that everyone understands and that's why we've chosen *West Side Story (or appropriate musical)*, Mr. Roy Sticher. That ethnic flavor translates so well and you know Yiddish – everything sounds exactly like what it is, doesn't it? So why don't you sit right there and we'll show you what we've been working on. You know I think it has such a broad demographic base. Oh, Mr. Sticher, you're going to love it. Okay, is everyone set?

They are dressed in the giant skirt and start to sing and tap dance to the tune of a Broadway musical in the style of "America" from West Side Story *which has been translated into Yiddish.*

MOM: (*breaking out of the song*) I like the skirt idea but it's hard to move around in the middle. Besides trying to remember the words.

LEVINE: Don't you think the skirt adequately represents being bound together in the ghetto?

TAMMY: I think it looks great! *like dressing up*

MOM: Can't we just try it once without the skirt?

LEVINE: And it represents our alienation from the dance ...

TAMMY: (*noticing that they've abandoned their audience*) Roy, Roy, where you goin'? LeVine, you forgot all about Roy. (*There's silence as they look at each other*)

LEVINE: No, I didn't forget about Roy. It just so happens I'm the only one who knows how to tend an agent. Doesn't it? You don't bombard an agent with questions. You let them leave and they call you with an offer. Haven't you ever noticed that agents often leave in the middle of performances? It's not at all unusual. They call you with an offer ...

Roy is gone. Mom is resigned. Tammy is sad. LeVine is cool but defensive. They slowly remove the giant skirt. LeVine continues.

LEVINE: You know, his wife just died, he's not feeling particularly chit-chat ... Okay, good. I'd like to have a run through of *The Shanghai Gesture.*

Tammy slowly folds up the giant dress. Mom cleans up around her lounge chair.

LEVINE: Good, good. Tammy, I'd like to run through *The Shanghai Gesture.* Mother, I'd like to have a run through of *The Shanghai*

Gesture. Mother, I'd like to take it from right after before the horri-fied guests. Tammy. Mother, mother, I'd like to see you down stage center, please. Tammy, you're downstage left. (*She instructs Tammy to hang up the Chinese curtain*) And I'd like to take it from right after before the horrified guests. Okay places please . . .

Mother slowly moves into position in front of the curtain/blanket for The Shanghai Gesture.

LEVINE: . . . and stand-by and action.

Chinese instrumental music fades up.

MOTHER GODAM/MOM: Heh heh heh heh! You're all afraid of me! Shall I tell you why? Because you are LEECHES, LEECHES AND CONS.

SIR GUY CHARTORIS/LEVINE: Have that girl brought back quickly or there'll be trouble.

MOTHER GODAM/MOM: Take care, take care, Sir Guy Chartoris, remember when one brick in a building loosens, others loosen, too.

SIR GUY CHARTORIS/LEVINE: Do you threaten me?

MOTHER GODAM/MOM: . . . and down comes everything, thundering, splintering, crashing . . .

SIR GUY CHARTORIS/LEVINE: If Shanghai falls we'll take good care it falls on you!

MOTHER GODAM/MOM: You would risk to smash your own bones for a bloodtown girl?

SIR GUY CHARTORIS/LEVINE: I'll risk it, have that girl brought back, will you? Will you or will you not do as I order you to do?

MOTHER GODAM/MOM: No, I will not do as you order me to do.

SIR GUY CHARTORIS/LEVINE: Very well then, we'll see the finish here tonight of a very troublesome Chinese woman.

MOTHER GODAM/MOM: And the finish of a great foreign merchant who must now chew what he has bitten off. Now let all Shanghai here look its last on this man, as we have looked our last upon your Jewish friend, Mr. Roy Sticher. Perhaps we are not destined to fame and fortune in the Yiddish Theater, ha ha ha . . . .

Tammy and Mother laugh, then freeze as LeVine begins to defend herself.

LEVINE: (*addressing an unseen group of people*) I know what you're thinking. You're thinking I can't do my job. You think you've just seen someone on the stage that can't do their job. Well I can do my job. I can do this job and twenty other jobs. (*Soft-spoken*) I just left a job making 650 dollars a week. That's a lot of money. Do you make that much? I can act. You think I can't, but I can act. This show is very good. It's goin' to be on Broadway soon. I've got a very good agent who's interested. And, and I'm not going to tell you her name because you'll probably just go and steal my idea.(And I am feminine. I am. I'm not wearing a bra and I hold this up very well . . . My legs are very nice. Everyone has told me that . . . Get out. (*Screaming*) Get out! Take your stuff and yourself and just get out. (*Quiet*) I know what you're thinking. You think this woman's not normal. She's not normal, she's bitter and unhappy, (*excited*) and she's not playing with a full deck. Well I am normal, I drive a car. Just because I sit down on the floor of Grand Central Station does not mean I'm not normal. (*Quiet, getting upset*) I do that because my legs hurt. That's why I do that. It's practical. And I am talented. Didn't you hear that song I just sang? It was very good, and I am upwardly mobile. I've been asked to be married three times and one of the men was very well-to-do. And I am intuitive. I know what you're thinking. I know what you're thinking. I always know what you're thinking.)

Chinese music resumes.

MOTHER GODAM/MOM: (*coaxing LeVine back into the scene*) I think a Chinese woman helped you once, my friend.

SIR GUY CHARTORIS/LEVINE: Who are you, you yellow painted Jezebel?

MOTHER GODAM/MOM: Would you really like me to tell you who I am?

SIR GUY CHARTORIS/LEVINE: I would.

MOTHER GODAM/MOM: I was the princess of Tunko. My house the great house of the Chee-on-ko . . . my mother was a chieftain's daughter, my father a warrior king.

SIR GUY CHARTORIS/LEVINE: A king.

MOTHER GODAM/MOM: Ten thousand camels he had, and five thousand horses, and many many boxes of gold. Heh heh heh heh. Now my greatest pleasure is I too have many many many boxes of gold. Now do you know who I am? Look at me and tell me before them why *you may not order me*!

SIR GUY CHARTORIS/LEVINE: Who are you?

Tammy becomes bored and walks out of the rehearsal to behind the curtain.

MOTHER GODAM/MOM: Quick quick, the little love name you used to call me . . .

SIR GUY CHARTORIS/LEVINE: No no!

MOTHER GODAM/MOM: Hello, Mr. Blue eyes, are you not glad to meet again Miss Pink? Heh heh, those were the little love names we used to call each other. Miss Pink and Mr. Blue eyes.

SIR GUY CHARTORIS/LEVINE: You! You are that girl?

MOTHER GODAM/MOM: Ayee, that Manchu girl . . . .

LEVINE: Maybe we should take a break, I don't feel so good.

TAMMY: (*from behind the curtain*) LeVine, you just need somethin' t'eat. You don't eat too good.

MOM: What have we got . . . peanut butter? (*She takes the curtain down, revealing Tammy with peanut butter and crackers*)

TAMMY: And . . . we've got whole uncracked wheat crackers.

LEVINE: That's a contradiction in terms.

TAMMY: I'm hungry too . . . and I'm tired. I never felt so tired in my whole life. You know I'm not used to feelin' like this . . . I usually feel so positive and energetic all the time. I'm embarrassed to talk about it because I know what LeVine will think . . .

MOM: It doesn't matter what other people think.

They all sit to have a snack. The bucket descends.

TAMMY: It does matter what other people think, otherwise why do we keep showin' off our work to all these agents and producers all the time . . . LeVine keep your hands off my food.

MOM: Why don't you get your *own* cracker LeVine?

LEVINE: I always share my food with *you*, Mother.

MOM: I think we have hurt LeVine's feelings.

TAMMY: It's the same feelings. With LeVine you always end up hurting the same feelings over and over. Why don't you get yourself some new feelings, LeVine?

LEVINE: Because I live every day with the same people in the same van under the same bridge and I never get ANY privacy whatsoever. New feelings come when you get different mugs in your face in the morning instead of the same shit every day.

TAMMY: When we win our new mobile home we'll have lots of new feelings.

MOM: If we get it Tammy. IF.

TAMMY: What do you mean, Mother? Don't you believe she's gonna win it?

MOM: I try not to think about it too much. Could you please send some crackers up to Lost Petal?

TAMMY: *(putting a cracker in the bucket and sending it up)* How's that, Mom ... you talk to Lost Petal all the time ... we've been here for six weeks livin' like hobos and now you got the most worried look I ever say I saw on your face ... I bet you're just afraid of wishin' for it.

MOM: I am an ACTOR. I just want to do my work.

LEVINE: Gimme a bite of that, Tammy.

TAMMY: Why do we have to be so different all the time from what other people want and what other people think? I'm supposed to not care that I live in a van and don't have a bus, or running water or get to sing in concerts like I just bet I could, and I'm supposed to not care what anybody thinks about the fact that I live in a van with my crazy family not caring what anybody thinks.

LEVINE: Quit staring at me, Mother.

MOM: Chew your food, LeVine. You don't chew your food.

TAMMY: Don't you think she's gonna win that mobile home, LeVine? Tell me you're not hot for that mobile home.

LEVINE: If we don't win it we sure as hell can't pay for it.

MOM: We're paying for it now. These cold nights are the down-payments of our lifetime. After twenty years, after twenty years am I here to pay this debt to you ... henh henh henh HENH.

LEVINE: Someday everyone will know who we are and this will be just a memory.

MOM: Who is going to know us, LeVine, that will change our values into memories?

TAMMY: I one heard a preacher say, "Memories have great value."

LEVINE: Well that's a trite thing to say.

TAMMY: That's because LeVine's memories are of things that haven't happened yet. She buys her memories on credit with a charge card.

MOM: How many times do we have to sing for our supper?

LEVINE: You didn't sing for your peanut butter, Ma.

MOM: You'll have to sing for it, LeVine, since you picked it all from my cracker.

LEVINE: She can't sing for it, Ma, it sticks to the roof of her mouth.

MOM: Just like little Lost Petal sticks to the bridge and Tammy sticks to her dream and my tongue sticks in my throat whenever I try to perform that *Shanghai Gesture*. Let's try *Medea* instead.

TAMMY: LeVine says we can't make any money with *Medea*, Mom. She says we have to advertise ourselves.

MOM: The good stuff sells *itself*. The *shit* you have to advertise.

LEVINE: Then why are we sitting on a treestump eating elephant food, Mom?

TAMMY: You know, sometimes I don't know why we do any of the things we do. Sometimes I get so tired and discouraged I could just take this van and park it next to a river somewhere and stay there for the rest of my life.

LEVINE: Well, open your eyes hon', there's the van. There's the river.

MOM: Be careful what you wish for, it might come true.

TAMMY: I'm just so sick and tired and depressed. Sometimes I'm afraid we're just too far gone. I'm afraid we just slipped through a crack somewhere ...

Background piano music fades up.

TAMMY: ... and we're drifting out there, so far out there we'll never come back and nobody knows about us; nobody cares or even comes to see us. It's like we're living on the wrong side of the tracks. And I get so tired of waitin' for someone to bring us what we hav'ta have. I get so depressed when there's no toilet paper. I get tired of workin' for every lit'l thing we need. I get tired of peanut butter. I hate peanut butter! I hate seein' other people's pictures in *People* magazine. Then I get tired of tryin' to keep Mom's spirits up. I'm tired of sleepin' with LeVine. I love her but I don't understand her. I'm tired of feelin' the weight of the world; of trying to do something meaningful. I don't understand what that means. I'm tired of being friendly to people because I want them to buy my stuff. I don't even want to sell my stuff. I want to keep it for myself. I want to see it all lined up in a closet somewhere; in a nice big closet in the back of my bus. (*She puts on a sequined jacket from her stall*) And I'd be sittin' at my dressin' table and the countryside would be passin' us by and we'd be movin' and we'd be gettin' somewhere as we're driving down the road. Then we'd pull into a town ... pull up to the back of the Coliseum. I'd step off the bus and walk right backstage. I wouldn't even hav'ta go to the dressin' room, 'cause I'd have my bus. I'd hear the crowds clapping and cheering and callin' my name. (*The sound of a large audience*) And, and then, I'd see the lights dim. (*The lights dim, Tammy sits on the Coliseum*

roof. Red, blue, and spot lights fade up) And then I'd step out on
the stage into my spotlight. I'd feel the red and blue lights bounce
off my platinum wig and I'd see little specks of light like diamonds
reflectin' all over the auditorium from my sequin outfit. And I'd look
out over the crowd and then I'd raise my hands and I'd hear a hush
fall over the crowd ... (*The audience sounds fade out – her voice
is amplified with reverb*) ... and I'd say: Hi, how y'all doin' tonight?
I'm so happy to be here with y'all tonight. We've been travellin' all
over to get to you tonight. We've been in Tucson, we've been in St.
Louis and New Orleans. And I'm just so glad to be here with you
and we're goin' to have a wonderful time. You know how I know?
Because I love you so much. And because I love you so much I'm
gonna give this song right to you. (*Piano music begins. Tammy sings
a classic Tammy Wynette song in the style of "Your Good Girl Is
Gonna Go Bad"*)

Thank ya. Thank ya. I love you'all so-o much. (*She crosses to her
merchandise*) Oh hi, can I help you? Oh that? That's eight dollars. It
used to belong to my Aunt Edna. I wore it one time in a show. Oh
yeah. I do shows. I'm a singer. My name is Tammy. Tammy Whynot.
You do? You are? Maybe you could come see us tonight. We have a
brand new show. It's called *The Shanghai Gesture*. Oh, you can't?
Well maybe we could sing you a little song right now. Oh. Just me
and my group. Just us three women. Oh no, we're not feminists. Oh
no, we try not to do too much political stuff. We could even sing you
a song about a man. Could you just hold on ... I'll be right back.

LeVine, Mom, c'mon. There's this agent woman – maybe we could
sing her a song.

MOM: What will she do? Put us on Broadway? She will come in
here with her calculator and take us for a ride, and then we will
owe 6,000 dollars.

TAMMY: C'mon Mother, we're gonna sing "Sentimental Gentleman."
(*Or whatever song used in the following sequence*).

LEVINE: Who does she work for, Tammy?

TAMMY: Well now, I don't know. I think she books for some kind
of uh ... political organization or something.

MOM: Let's sing "True Love" like the old days.

TAMMY: No, Mother, "Sentimental Gentleman."

LEVINE: How about that Yiddish number? It's so well rehearsed.

TAMMY: No, LeVine. "Sentimental Gentleman."

MOM: I don't want to sing a song about a man.

Plate 5   Tammy Whynot and the Expectations
Photo: Donna Gray

TAMMY: I think she's looking for some tap dancing.

MOM: BUT.

LEVINE: Nothing like puttin' your best foot forward.

TAMMY: Put on your tap shoes.

MOM: This one time I will sing a song about a man.

They dress in matching white tuxedo jackets and tap shoes and stand in girl group formation while Tammy addresses the imaginary agent.

TAMMY: This is our group, Tammy Whynot and the Expectations.

The Women sing, a cappella, an embellished and highly spirited adaptation of "Sentimental Gentleman" or equivalent song from the 1940s that can be sung in close harmony, celebrates manhood and can be accompanied by some basic tap dancing.

TAMMY: Well, what'd you think? Oh, oh, that's all right. Sure, sure, we'll be right here. (*She yells in a weak voice*) Bye . . . we'll be right here.

Tammy is sad. Mom takes it in her stride, but shows signs of being let down. They sit down. LeVine is tense and tries to change the mood by singing a song in the style of "Something's Coming" from West Side Story. *She tries to belt it out with energy and animation. It is, however, a tired and weak rendition, both humorous and sad. In the middle of the song, LeVine strips off her clothes to reveal a long red gown and she lets her hair hang free. Lost Petal's bucket slowly gets lowered, ending LeVine's song.*

LEVINE: Look! A note!

TAMMY: Let me read it!

MOM: No, we'll each read it to ourselves.

LEVINE: No, I'll read it out loud and we'll play fill in the blank. Whoever gets the most words right gets the blue blanket tonight.

MOM: There's a blue blanket up above.

TAMMY: Spare me! She's had the blue blanket for a week now.

LEVINE: Okay, ya ready? Here goes. "Dear BLANK ...

MOM AND TAMMY: Girls!

LEVINE: Wrong. "Dear lovelies." Both of you get minus one.

TAMMY: We're going to get minus one – I'll kill her!

MOM: Lovelies. She's buttering us up.

LEVINE: "... I miss you. I never wrote so many BLANKS before."

TAMMY: Letters!

MOM: EPISTLES!

TAMMY: Checks!

LEVINE: Letters is right. Miss Blue Blanket is back to zero! And I continue: "... I've made my BLANK ..."

MOM: MONEY AND I'M GETTING OUT!

TAMMY: Bed!

LEVINE: Oh no, I'm sorry, you're both wrong. Mom is minus one, Tammy is a whopping minus five.

TAMMY: I am not minus five. I only guessed once last time.

LEVINE: Yeah, but you had minus four before that ...

TAMMY: Don't you get a positive number when you add two negative numbers?

LEVINE: No, you're thinking of multiplication.

TAMMY: They're all the same anyway. Keep reading. Wait. What's the blank in there?

LEVINE: Mind, Tammy. "I've made up my mind and I'm comin' down. I know you will be very BLANK with me."

TAMMY: (*screaming*) Pissed off!

MOM: Patient.

LEVINE: (*quickly*) I'm sorry. Both of you are wrong. The word is angry.

TAMMY: (*loud, excited*) What's the difference between pissed off and angry?

LEVINE: You've got a point there. You're back to minus four. I continue . . . "There's a woman up here who I've come to like very much. She and I BLANK deeply for one another.

MOM AND TAMMY: CARE!!!

LEVINE: Right, Mom's back to zero, Tammy's at minus three. "We have together come to realize the money, the commercials and car mean less to us than BLANK . . ."

TAMMY: SEX!

MOM: Show business!

LEVINE: Sorry, you're both wrong, the answer is love. Mom, you're minus one. Tammy you're minus four once again, dear. I continue – "This woman has put me in touch with a strong desire. I have to settle down and it just so happens she has just bought herself a new co-op apartment with a doorman, a washer-dryer, a sunroof and BLANKETY BLANK BLANK." Now this one's a multiple word phrase. You get partial credit for partial right answers.

TAMMY: You mean partial penalty for partially wrong answers.

MOM: Don't be so negative.

TAMMY: Well it seems that all we get is minus this and minus that.

MOM: <u>Life imitates art.</u>

LEVINE: Do I have any submissions?

TAMMY: Read it again?

LEVINE: Okay, listen carefully. This is worth ten points. The entire game may hinge on it. "This woman has put me in touch with a strong desire. I have to settle down and it just so happens that she has just bought herself a new co-op apartment with a doorman, a washer-dryer, a sunroof and BLANKETY BLANK BLANK."

TAMMY: A formica dinette suite.

MOM: A color TV!

LEVINE: Mom is right!! A Betamax video cassette recorder with full four color and time memory! I continue: Mom you're seven. Tammy you're minus five again. I'm sorry, hon'. Here we go – "I understand that you are my closest BLANK."

MOM: Competitors!

TAMMY: I don't want to play anymore.

LEVINE: No, I'm sorry. A minus one gives you a plus six. The answer is friends. "I know you, my closest friends, have stood by me since day one of this marathon, and have made it possible for me to learn as much as I have and to come for the first time into a full understanding of my own moral BLANK!"

MOM: Decrepitude!

TAMMY: Filth!

LEVINE: I'm sorry, both of you are wrong. The answer is values.

Pause.

TAMMY: (*sad*) So she's comin' down and we don't win a mobile home.

MOM: (*matter-of-fact*) No.

TAMMY: We don't win nothin'.

MOM: No.

TAMMY: We wasted all this time for nothin'.

LEVINE: No, it was not for nothing, Tammy, we just have one less iron in the fire, that's all. It's not a tragedy. Now gather round please. Get your costumes, your props. We have a show in twenty minutes, hon'.

TAMMY: (*choking back tears*) You mean we're gonna go ahead and do the show just like nothin' happened?

LEVINE: (*softly*) Yes . . . yes. (*She coaxes Tammy to hang the curtain, which she does*)

TAMMY: It's not fair. It's just not fair. We have nothin'. We have absolutely nothin'. It's like havin' a job and not gettin' your pay.

MOM: We got our pay. The sense to do what we want in the first place instead of waiting around for a bonus prize at the end of a

Plate 6   Performance of *The Shanghai Gesture*
Photo: Eva Weiss

stupid game show. And Lost Petal is out of the range from Concorde planes.

TAMMY: (*crying*) Oh, I hate Lost Petal! (*She goes behind the curtain. Mom and Tammy change into highly colorful and theatrical gowns from different periods. LeVine is still in her long red gown. The following scene is done from behind the curtain*)

LEVINE: Why do you call her Lost Petal, Mom? She always gets exactly what she wants.

MOM: Because she pays her soul for it.

LEVINE: Oh, really. What's your soul worth if it's always too high a price to pay for anything, Mom?

TAMMY: I could have been a soul singer if I didn't get messed up waitin' for everybody else to keep their promises.

MOM: LeVine, wash the peanut butter off your skirt before the show.

TAMMY: So what are we goin' to do now, LeVine? You're the big producer. Just what in the hell are we gonna do now?

LEVINE: (*moving from cool to upset*) First thing I'm gonna do is perform *The Shanghai Gesture*! Then I'm gonna wash my hair. Then I'm going down to the city desk and get our story in the human interest section. Then I'm gonna come back and I'm gonna do my laundry, then I'm gonna sit by the phone and wait for it to ring with an offer.

MOM: First you wash your dirty laundry in public, then you wash it in private. Relax, LeVine, you run around too much.

LEVINE: (*coming from behind the curtain*) Okay, I think this is it. Tammy, get out in front of the curtain. Stand by everybody. Places please! Tammy we're gonna go on a count of five. All right, stand by. Five-four-three-two-one and action.

Music and the performance of The Shanghai Gesture *begin. LeVine stands in front of the curtain. Tammy stands off to her left holding a gong. Mom waits behind the curtain. Tammy hits the gong, and Chinese music fades up.*

NARRATOR/LEVINE: She knows the secrets of all China. She knows also the tongue is an ax for the neck. But never in her life has she parted with her secrets for the joy of telling. That's why she is necessary for the government. That is why the police use her, protect her and dread her. That is Mother Godam.

Tammy rings the gong. Mother Godam enters from behind the curtain with a Chinese pin cushion/sewing box on her head as a hat. This is the performance for which they have been rehearsing.

SIR GUY CHARTORIS/LEVINE: Mother Godam!

MOTHER GODAM/MOM: I am honored to welcome Sir Guy Chartoris to my house. (*She bows, removing the lid from the sewing box as if tipping a hat*)

SIR GUY CHARTORIS/LEVINE: It is a far greater honor for Sir Guy Chartoris at last to be welcome by Mother . . . Mother . . .

MOTHER GODAM/MOM: GODAM . . . you have not heard the name? Are you afraid to say it?

SIR GUY CHARTORIS/LEVINE: Hitherto we . . .

MOTHER GODAM/MOM: Hitherto we smiled with half our faces . . .

SIR GUY CHARTORIS/LEVINE: And now??

MOTHER GODAM/MOM: And now you kiss my hand.

SIR GUY CHARTORIS/LEVINE: Now I kiss your hand. What charming little hands you have.

MOTHER GODAM/MOM: You think so?

SIR GUY CHARTORIS/LEVINE: Yes. Your face is an enigma. What are you thinking, Mother Godam?

MOTHER GODAM/MOM: I am thinking that our meeting is like the rush of two big storms . . . one from the East . . . one from the West . . . racing up from the inferno to a meeting. Heh heh heh. You know . . . I think we are going to like each other . . . very much. Heh heh heh HAYNH!

Tammy enters gonging

MOTHER GODAM/MOM: Ooo dee pah tree, the greeting of the New Year to all of you, and welcome to my home. You know this is the Chinese New Year, this is the day in China to pay all debts, big, little, great or small, you pay yours, I pay mine. Mine to you, Sir Guy, yours to me.

SIR GUY CHARTORIS/LEVINE: Mine to you??? Surely there's no outstanding debt between us, is there?

MOTHER GODAM/MOM: No.

SIR GUY CHARTORIS/LEVINE: If there should be, tell me.

MOTHER GODAM/MOM: Oh, it is only a figure of my speech. For many years I have owed a debt, tonight I will pay it. That is all, heh heh heh.

Tammy gongs

SIR GUY CHARTORIS/LEVINE: The very look, the very laugh you had last night at the opera.

MOTHER GODAM/MOM: Ah yes, the Madame Butterfly, poor papillon, a man forsakes her and she kills herself. How stupid. How could I have forgotten? She was Japanese.

SIR GUY CHARTORIS/LEVINE: What is the Chinese woman's way?

MOTHER GODAM/MOM: Ah she would wait I think for many years. Everything would go . . . and a lingering death . . . a slicing-off process. A little bit cut off each day and the raw edge left to be sliced again the next day. But these things alone would die . . . the woman . . . no . . . what is your opinion, Sir Guy Chartoris?

SIR GUY CHARTORIS/LEVINE: I am not an authority on Chinese women.

MOTHER GODAM/MOM: No? And yet you have lived in China so many years.

SIR GUY CHARTORIS/LEVINE: Nearly thirty.

MOTHER GODAM/MOM: In spite of the many years you have lived here you still know nothing of Chinese ways. Chinese women. You will learn. Ha ha ha ha ha ha ha ha. (*Tammy gongs*) Tonight my comic spirit runs fast along and now for your entertainment my *pièce de resistance*. Now I will show you China and the Chinese woman. Bring in the junkmen.

TAMMY: BRING IN THE JUNKMEN! (*She gongs*)

SIR GUY CHARTORIS/LEVINE: A naked girl on a tray! What does this mean?

MOTHER GODAM/MOM: It means tonight I hold an auction sale. Tonight I sell this girl as a flesh junk to those many junkmen yonder; they have come to bid for her.

SIR GUY CHARTORIS/LEVINE: The girl is white, how dare you? We'll have the law in there in half a moment if you don't stop.

MOTHER GODAM/MOM: Heh heh heh HAYNH! The law! I am the law! Here I am the government. I am the police. Here. Heh. You have all been asked here for a purpose and here you will stay. Until I am through with you. Now you junkmen, how much will you bid for this girl?

NARRATOR/LEVINE: Before the horrified guests Mother Godam auctions off the girl Lost Petal to the highest bidder among the frantic junkmen. Finally the girl is taken away and the noise subsides. The guests sit frozen in their seats as Mother Godam says:

MOTHER GODAM/MOM: I'M GONNA BE A WHEEL ONE DAY. (*She sings this song or one similar with the help of LeVine and Tammy, pretending she's James Brown, throwing her cape around her. The song finishes and Mother Godam says, exhausted:*) Let's do *Medea*.

TAMMY: I want to go to New Orleans.

LEVINE: We can't do *Medea* in New Orleans.

MOM: We can do *Medea* anywhere we please. We can do it in Shanghai if we please.

TAMMY: You mean in the middle of the play all of a sudden we do *Medea*?

LEVINE: Interesting montage concept, Ma.

TAMMY: Is there any music in *Medea*?

LEVINE: We can put it to music, Tammy.

A medley of earlier songs fades up.

TAMMY: Oh Mother, could we go to New Orleans, please?

MOM: Ask LeVine. She keeps the time.

LEVINE: Mom, does the van still work?

MOM: We'll have to remind it of its purpose. It's been thinking it's Bleecker Court Co-op Apartments.

TAMMY: Wouldn't it be nice for a while, please LeVine.

LEVINE: Yes, it would be quite nice to go to New Orleans.

MOM: Let's pack up.

The women start loading things into the camper. Tammy notices someone at her sale. She walks toward them.

TAMMY: Can I help you? (*An imaginary customer refers to the suit coat that LeVine has thrown off during her song*) Yeah. Well sure, she doesn't care much about that one. Hold on just a second, she was only modeling it, really. It was here on this table just a second ago. She put it on cause she took a little chill. Looks like rain soon. She's got plenty of her own. Hold on ... LeVine, that lady wants to buy your suit. She's loaded ... she'll give us twenty dollars. Even fifty I bet. I'll tell her it's an antique.

LEVINE: (*offended at the request*) She wants to buy my clothes, my only clothes?

TAMMY: Yeah, c'mon LeVine. Money for travellin'.

LEVINE: What'll I wear to work?

TAMMY: Oh screw, LeVine, nobody can see your clothes on the phone.

MOM: (*giving her ring to Tammy*) Throw this in as a bonus, tell her for an extra five the junkmen will love it.

LEVINE: You're a real Mother of Pearls, Mom.

MOM: I am a mother, a good mother. That's all.

TAMMY: She's thinking it over.

MOM: (*to LeVine*) You know that part where she's telling off that Guy Charter-Bus?

LEVINE: Chartoris, Mom.

MOM: ... and she talks about hate helping her survive ... that's a monologue worthy of *Medea*.

MOTHER GODAM/MOM: Into the nasty entrails of the China Sea he sold me. On a junk with giggling hopeless girls I went fastened under the battened hatch of a floating catchall for all the pimps the land spews out! That's how Mr. Blue Eyes tried to do away with Miss Pink. Sold to the junkman she won't last long!

A new port everyday and for her all the coolies screech and the gang men yell when the flesh junk comes sliding in from greasy seas. Brown men black men yellow men white men how they curse and fight and how those women scream and cry for every girl there's men, many men, think of it, and soon the women die.

Mom's monologue falls into a rhythm with Tammy and LeVine's dialogue.

TAMMY: Ouu! *Medea* in New Orleans, we'll have people standin' at the end – standin' and clappin' like a standin' ovation.

MOTHER GODAM/MOM: Hate helped me and I survived.

LEVINE: I'll write an article.

MOTHER GODAM/MOM: Rickshaw men of Nagasaki I survived.

LEVINE: I'll send it to John Perrone in New Orleans at the Ledger. We'll get some advance publicity for this thing.

MOTHER GODAM/MOM: Coolies from Papua.

TAMMY: (*to a new customer*) Can I help you?

MOTHER GODAM/MOM: Nugget men from New South Wales.

TAMMY: Why yes it's for sale.

MOTHER GODAM/MOM: I survived.

TAMMY: Oh sure, we just replaced the fan pump and put in a new water belt. All new and fit as a fiddle.

MOTHER GODAM/MOM: Red hot sulphur burned into my naked back to make my tired body gay.

TAMMY: You hold on a minute.

MOTHER GODAM/MOM: I survived.

LEVINE: Mom keep your throat open, hon'. Let the bitterness flow right out.

MOTHER GODAM/MOM: The soles of my feet slit open and pebbles sewn inside to keep me from running away.

TAMMY: LeVine!

LEVINE: (*reading from a clipboard*) Tammy, how does this sound: a troupe of actors got tricked into the American dream.

TAMMY: Some man out there wants to buy our van.

LEVINE: How much is he offering?

MOM: Tell him no! We're going to New Orleans. I did not die, no, I lived.

LEVINE: (*to Tammy*) We're going to New Orleans.

TAMMY: We're going to New Orleans!

MOTHER GODAM/MOM: And here I am after twenty years, after twenty years am I my dear to pay this debt to you.

TAMMY: (*to the customer*) I'm sorry but we changed our minds.

MOTHER GODAM/MOM: But we will let that pass for the moment I wish you all adieu you can go wherever you like there will be no more dinner. I very wisely did not order anything beyond the fish, I was quite certain there would be no further appetite. So I have saved myself entree roast and sweets ... HEH HEH clever these Chinese. Adieu bon nuit, bonsoir, bonsoir ... bon nuit ... bon nuit ... (*The medley of music returns. The lights fade out.*)

THE END

LITTLE WOMEN

The Tragedy

**DEB MARGOLIN, PEGGY SHAW,
LOIS WEAVER**

Conceived and directed by Lois Weaver
Scripted by Deb Margolin
With additional text by Peggy Shaw, Lois Weaver and
Louisa May Alcott
Performed by Deb Margolin, Peggy Shaw and Lois Weaver
Set by Peggy Shaw
Lights by Joni Wong
Costumes by Susan Young
Choreography by Stormy Brandenberger

Originally produced in spring 1988 at WOW Theatre,
59 E. 4th Street, New York

CHARACTERS

Khurve, the sensualist who also plays Amy (Deborah Margolin)

Louisa, the writer who also plays Jo (Lois Weaver)

Hilarious, the moralist who also plays Meg (Peggy Shaw)

The stage is bare except for three silk, four-foot-wide banners suspended from the floor to the ceiling. They are widely spaced to create entrances between them. As the audience arrives the three performers are in the auditorium greeting people they know and introducing themselves to those they don't. They are dressed in dressing gowns and out of character. The show begins as Louisa crosses center stage and begins to address the audience.

LOUISA: (*crossing onto the stage from the audience to center stage*): Someone said to us, you should do *Little Women*. So we thought we'd give it a try. And then we got interested in Louisa May Alcott, and her work and her life, and all of the mystery that surrounded that. And then we got interested in censorship, and pornography, and morality as it was represented by set design during the Italian Renaissance. And then we got interested in burlesque as a style. And then we got interested in sex. (*In an announcer's voice*) For those of you who care for your immortal souls; those of you who are concerned with family values; those of you who represent the mayor's office on the preservation of public decency; all of you vice crusaders, self-appointed vigilantes, and . . . drama critics: this is not a theatre, it's a hall, and this is not a show, it's a concert, a lecture on the life and work of Louisa May Alcott; a dissertation on the making of scenes and machines during the Italian Renaissance, and we are here for your literary entertainment.

HILARIOUS: "Hit it, Maestro!"

The stage is in blackout and piano music is heard. As the lights fade up a large umbrella with a sheet of silk attached to its tips, covering the three performers underneath except for their bare feet, begins to move from behind the silk banners and to progress toward center stage. This creates the effect of a small mobile carnival tent or an extraterrestrial creature. Once center stage the three performers remain under the "tent" and enact a scene from the book Little Women.

LOUISA/JO: It's no use! I'm stuck. Can't write a word.

HILARIOUS/MEG: Jo! You're scratching out everything you've written today.

LOUISA/JO: Can't help it. It's not worth reading. If Father were here, he'd tell me to throw it on the fire.

HILARIOUS/MEG: Put it away for a while, Jo dear, and give your mind a rest. You've been working over it all day.

LOUISA/JO: I know it. And nothing to show for it. Oh dear! Sometimes I'm afraid I'll never learn to be a writer.

HILARIOUS/MEG: Oh, yes you will! One of these days, you'll write a great book. And people will read it all over the world. And you'll be very famous. And very rich!

KHURVE/AMY: Pre-sum-tu-ously rich!

LOUISA/JO: (*laughing*) Well, I wish it would happen right this minute, then – so we could all give presents for Christmas.

KHURVE/AMY: So do I! Christmas won't be Christmas without any presents.

HILARIOUS/MEG: Well, Mother thinks we ought not to spend our money for pleasure, when our men are suffering so in the army.

LOUISA/JO: Christopher Columbus, Meg! The little money we have wouldn't do the army any good. Let's each buy what we want, and have a little fun! I'm sure we've worked hard enough to earn it.

HILARIOUS/MEG: I know I do, teaching those tiresome children all day, when I'm longing to enjoy myself at home.

LOUISA/JO: You don't have half such a time as I do, with Aunt March. How would you like to be shut up for hours with a nervous, fussy old lady?

KHURVE/AMY: I don't believe any of you suffer as I do, for you don't have to go to school with impertinent girls who laugh at your dresses and – label your father if he isn't rich.

LOUISA/JO: (*laughing*) If you mean libel, Amy, I'd say so, and not talk about labels, as if Papa were a pickle bottle.

KHURVE/AMY: (*with dignity*) I know what I mean, and you needn't be so statistical about it, Jo March. It's proper to use good words, and improve your vocabillary. Don't whistle, Jo. It's so boyish.

LOUISA/JO: That's why I do it.

KHURVE/AMY: I detest rude, unlady-like girls.

LOUISA/JO: And I hate affected, niminy-piminy chits!

Silence. Three sets of binoculars suddenly come shooting out through the gaps between the umbrella and the silk of the "tent." As they

Plate 7   Arriving in Heaven
Photo: Jean Frasier

*survey the audience we hear expressions like: "OH WOW!" And
"LOOK AT THAT ONE! SHIT!" and "SOME KNOCKERS!
LOOK AT THE TITS ON THAT ONE" etc. This builds in excite-
ment until the binoculars draw back from the gaps and the umbrella
tent is tossed backwards over the shoulders of the performers
revealing three completely naked bodies. Blackout.*

KHURVE: Hey wait a minute! Let's take that back, I want to see
that again.

*The lights come back up and go out again. We hear voices in the
blackout.*

KHURVE: Hm . . . Just what I thought. MM hm.

LOUISA: The show dealt with a subject usually discussed only in
medical journals.

HILARIOUS: The police should forbid on the stage what they forbid
on the street.

KHURVE: Looks like burlesque is going the way of all flesh.

*There is a fanfare followed by heavenly music. Lights up. Three suit-
cases are thrown on stage from behind the silk banners followed by
Louisa, Khurve and Hilarious dressed in hospital gowns with angel
wings attached to their backs. They tumble onto the stage and slowly
begin to sit up.*

Plate 8   Left to right: Hilarious, Louisa and Khurve survey the audience
Photo: Amy Meadow

LOUISA: I've been struck!

HILARIOUS AND KHURVE: (*realizing they are not alone*) Struck?

They all spin around and discover their wings and each other for the first time.

LOUISA: Excuse me . . . hee . . . heee

Laughter – silence.

ALL: I saw a horse!

Laughter – silence.

HILARIOUS AND KHURVE: (*both start to speak at once and then refer to each other*) You first!

LOUISA: Me?

Silence.

HILARIOUS: A horse with wings.

LOUISA: Yes, I noticed!

KHURVE: It was . . .

LOUISA: Brown . . .

HILARIOUS: White . . .

LOUISA: Roan ... like the pony he kept in that yard where the morning glories grew on the sides ...

Silence.

KHURVE: Someone was sitting ...

HILARIOUS: Hair like a cloud ...

KHURVE: Smoke!

LOUISA: Like a puff of smoke!

HILARIOUS: Her arms were feathered!

KHURVE: Wings!

LOUISA: They must have been wings!

KHURVE: I don't think so at all.

LOUISA: Why, I saw with my own two eyes ...

KHURVE: It was one of them new sweaters ...

HILARIOUS: A sweater ...

LOUISA: A flying sweater!

HILARIOUS: I'm sweating!

KHURVE: I'm flying!

Laughter – silence.

LOUISA: I'm thinking.

HILARIOUS: (*to Louisa*) Can I help you?

KHURVE: With what?

LOUISA: Thank you!

HILARIOUS: Can you stand?

KHURVE: What?

LOUISA: Stand. Can you stand?

KHURVE: Stand what?

LOUISA: I'm thinking ... I think I've been struck!

KHURVE: You look very nice.

LOUISA: Thank you.

HILARIOUS: You both look very nice.

LOUISA AND KHURVE: Thank you.

LOUISA: (*to Hilarious*) You also look ... very ... you look like ... you look very ... very much like me, actually ...

KHURVE: Oh hon, I really don't see that ...

LOUISA: Not like me ... no not really at all ... you both look ... really ... like ... thoughts! You both look like thoughts!

HILARIOUS: Thank you.

KHURVE: Wait. Wait. Just wait a second. Dearie? We look like thoughts?

LOUISA: Yes. You look like thoughts. You look ...well ... you look like the *process* ... of thinking ...

KHURVE: What are you talking about?

HILARIOUS: Where is this going?

LOUISA: Why are you both so ...

ALL: *WHERE ARE WE?*

Silence.

LOUISA: I guess it really doesn't matter very much.

KHURVE: What do you mean it doesn't matter very much? How can we order in if we don't know where we are?

HILARIOUS: We're in Hell!

KHURVE: We're in Heaven!

ALL: We're in *shock*! (*They stand up, finally*)

LOUISA: What's important here ... of the essence, in fact ... is that we're together.

KHURVE: Do you think that means something?

HILARIOUS: Chinese food.

KHURVE: That sounds fine.

HILARIOUS: Not even Chinese food can help us at a moment like this ...

A muslin banner with a Renaissance drawing of the devil and the word HELL across the top begins to unroll from the floor and ascend to ceiling, creating another hanging banner stage left. It should have the effect of appearing suddenly from under the floor of the theatre.

IN UNISON:

HILARIOUS: The Lord is my shepherd, I shall not want.
He maketh me to lie down in green pastures
He leadeth me beside the still waters
He restoreth my soul.

KHURVE: I'm sure you've heard the story of Adam and Eve
When Adam was tempted by an apple, I believe,
But between me and you, that rumor is vicious
Adam was tempted all right, but not by a golden delicious.

LOUISA: The Marchs' sitting room, several weeks later. The Christmas decorations have been removed. Meg is at the writing desk, Amy at the fireplace, with her drawing-board; and Beth at the window, looking out anxiously. It is early afternoon.

Silence. A muslin banner with a Renaissance drawing of an angel and the word HEAVEN across the top drops from the ceiling, creating another banner stage right. It is accompanied by celestial music and shrieks of surprise and happiness from the characters.

HILARIOUS: Praise the Lord!

They spring apart.

KHURVE: Pardon?

HILARIOUS: Praise the Lord! The kingdom of Heaven belongs to the righteous!

KHURVE: No it doesn't!

LOUISA: She speaks metaphorically!

HILARIOUS: No I'm not!

LOUISA: Yes you are!

HILARIOUS: (*pointing to Heaven*) What's that, then?

KHURVE: How do you know what other people think?

LOUISA: I'm the writer!

KHURVE: Who gives a shit?

HILARIOUS: Look who they let in here!

KHURVE: Fuckin' A! (*She laughs happily*)

HILARIOUS: I have preached the word of God and now I am the lamb of God!

KHURVE: I starred! I absolutely starred! I make love movies. All those love movies, I'm the star.

HILARIOUS: The black crook dancer . . .

LOUISA: Just like I pictured them! They're perfect! Perfect! (*To the audience*) Can you see the conflict? Only it's not really a conflict. We hang the hammock of our lives between the trees of our inner opposites! If only society weren't so organized against the truth.

HILARIOUS: If only the Devil were laid to rest!

KHURVE: If only my hairdresser were here!

As Carnival Music comes up the three characters go for their respective suitcases. They realize they have the wrong ones and proceed with a slapstick dance of switching suitcases until they manage to get the right ones. The dance continues as they go backstage, throw off their angel wings, and each enters naked with a wooden cutout of a cloud painted with chapter headings and illustrations from Nicola Sabattini's manual for Constructing Theatrical Scenes and Machines (1638). *The clouds are just large enough to cover the characters' vital parts. At the end of the music they drop the clouds, revealing again their nakedness. Blackout. Lights come up slowly revealing Louisa holding a cloud labeled "CHAPTER V: HOW TO CHANGE SCENERY" accompanied by the appropriate illustration. She hangs the cloud on a hook above her head. (This placing of clouds with chapter headings and illustrations will continue throughout the performance until the clouds occupy roughly the equivalent positions found on a stage employing Italian Renaissance scenery.)*

Louisa is wearing a see-through tunic with strategically placed fig leaves. After some embarrassment, she yells "HIT IT MAESTRO!" and strip music in the style of David Rose's "The Stripper" begins playing and Louisa begins to dress in nineteenth-century undergarments using the dressing gestures as if she were undressing in a striptease. As she completes the costume of bloomers, hoop petticoat and bodice with hat and gloves, she moves centerstage.

LOUISA: (*standing at center stage, addressing the audience*) I am what remains of Louisa May Alcott. My life, my life is a play for two characters, and since I chose to remain unmarried, I play both parts. My life is a play for two characters, written by two hands, a portrait, in fact, of two hands drawing each other. Did you know that in my later life I taught myself to write with my left hand, so that I could stay at my desk twice as long and produce twice as much? And I found to my delight and amazement that my left hand wrote in a voice more intimate, more seductive, more passionate . . . more culturally marginal than my right hand. My right hand . . . oh, you know my right hand. This is the hand that supports my family, the hand that Jo sprang from, and *all* the little women, my right hand. And what if they might meet someday, in an earthy paradise, a garden, perhaps. (*During this section of the monologue she uses the appropriate hand to indicate each voice*) The right hand of reason would wait as (*she gestures with the left hand*) romance approaches. And she (*right hand*) would say: I know you, you have whispered through my chambers. You have disguised yourself in the smell of my geraniums, you have cloaked yourself in my morning glories, you lured me into this garden. And she (*left hand*) would say: (*She laughs*) and far over the garden wall! For my aspirations far outstep the bounds of Victorian propriety. Frost comes last to those who bloom the highest. And she (*right*) would say: well, surely you're talking about *my* success as the celebrated author of children's literature! She (*left*) would say: if you're talking about *Little Women*, I never wanted to write it! I thought it was dull and not a bit sensational! And she (*right*) would say: but it was *the* American female myth. And she (*left*) would say: I hated writing moral pap for the young. And she (*right*) would say: but there is beauty in those themes of sweet self-denial. And she (*left*) would say: I was drawn to more earthquakey and volcanic themes. I wanted to be the sharp-tongued master of racy, unladylike American vernacular. And she (*right*) would say: but I was always known for my womanly goodness! And she (*left*) would say: I wanted to see one dark mind shape another, I wanted to create a character seductive, viperish, manipulating, who wins even as she loses. Oh, but what would my own dear father think of me, if I set folks doing the things I longed to see my people do? And she (*right*) would say: But I was always ... And she (*left*) would say: the wretched victim of the respectable traditions of Concord. And she (*right*) would say: well known as the children's friend. And she (*left*) would say: (*laughing*) I sold my children! And she (*right*) would say: you never married! Even your Jo ... And she (*left*) would say: oh, I would rather be a free spinster and paddle my own canoe! Liberty is a better husband than love to many of us. And she (*right*) would say: well! And she (*left*) would say: I am more than half persuaded that I am a man's soul put by some freak of nature into a woman's body, for I have fallen in love so many times in my life with so many pretty girls and never once with any man. Suddenly the garden grows silent. (*Now she gestures with both hands*) We hear things, larks, finches. Two clouds part, blue skies shine through. (*Hilarious, carrying a music stand and dressed in a brown suit, white shirt, tie and straw boater suggesting a preacher or side show barker, enters and crosses to slightly upstage right of Louisa, as Khurve, dressed in a flowing kimono with a boa, enters from behind a banner and stands upstage left. Thus, the two frame Louisa*) The right hand of reason turns to go, as the left hand, the lover, the counter part says: now, at last I have found you. And she would say: excuse me? .. and she would say: it is you that I have ... and she would say: Madam .. And she would say: waited for ... And she would say: Madam please ... And she would say:

I throw myself at your feet ... And she would say: I beg your pardon? ... And she would say: this is the thing I have searched for, the moment I have waited for ... And she would say: I cannot ... And she would say: the longing I have longed for ... and she would say: I ... I ... And she would say: you ... you ...

The end of this scene is an attempted seduction of the right hand by the left while the conflict is represented physically by Hilarious on the right and Khurve on the left. The right hand keeps refusing until Hilarious interrupts Louisa with kazoo playing and crosses center stage with her suitcase, music stand and cloud labeled "Chapter VI: HOW TO CHANGE SCENERY BY ANOTHER METHOD." She continues to play the kazoo until she hangs her cloud stage left and sets her music center stage for her sermon. Louisa curtsies and exits. Khurve moves upstage left and sits on a stool and watches as Hilarious delivers her monologue.

HILARIOUS: (*at the center, loudly*) Hold it! Hold it! Hold it! Hear ye! Hear ye! Hear ye! (*A bell rings*) Don't miss it! You're missing nine-tenths of what you were born for! (*She crosses the stage into the audience and passes out slips of paper with little sayings printed on them, such as "Clothes Make the Man," and speaks in a gentler voice while in the audience*) Hello, sweetheart, don't be afraid. Aren't you a little darling! It's nice to see you tonight! (*She crosses back to center stage, speaking loudly*) Step right up, step right up! Let us be in Heaven together! How do you like this? Hilarious B. Hooves, that's my name! Hilarious, my given name, named after my first mother. Of course, we all have only one mother, the mother of God! (*She pulls a small statue of the Virgin Mary from her pocket and displays it*) We kill, we kill. We kill one by one over the rooftops. We kill for love! (*She crosses again into the audience, passing out slips of paper, ad-libbing to audience, then returns to center stage*) Hear ye! Hear ye! Hear ye! I am talking about the truth! Like my mother (*she shows the statue again*), and the mother of us all, I have an open throat. Please stand back, I spit when I talk! This morning, with my voice lowered by morning, I started my daily rituals, and in my thoughts formed words that giggled inside me. Stand back please, I spit when I talk! Oh, that I could share with you, so early in the day, in trying to adjust my shoulders and put the swing back in my hips that will enable our communion, and I ask the Lord, dear God, to give me the ability to rock back and forth. I ask the Lord, dear God, to enable me to win your love that you will be attracted to my truth. And I ask the Lord, dear God, to help me lead you to that gray area. That area we don't work very hard to understand. That area somewhere between the night and the dawn, somewhere between our hearts and our thighs. Just look at this! Chinese food cannot help us at a moment like this, oh my hearers! When we seek that holy and sacred place we all want to understand . . . (*she looks at Khurve*) the body! Before we bow our heads in facts, one thought: if you should happen to go around the corner to Hell mixed up in the rip and roar, men in little holes are ready to sell you tickets of wrath to go in and see the black crook dance and the hips that jiggle with nothing to wear. Obliging drivers are willing and offering to take you where the brass bands play and to where fortunes amount to nothing under the flesh. Hear their screams! (*She crosses down into the audience, throwing the slips of paper into the air*) Take it! Take it! Take my happiness and spread it like the seed of the twelve tribes of Israel! Do not defend the fact anymore. If I wanted to be liked I wouldn't hang around this place! Jesus had only three friends and one of them killed him. You mistake the fact for an actor! You mistake the Lord for an actor upon the stage! You go home to your salacious couches! You don't see the future! You don't see the whole thing! Let us pray! Every head bowed, every eye closed. (*She kneels on one knee and sings in an earnest voice*) Jesus wants me for a sunbeam, sunbeam, sunbeam. Jesus wants you for a sunbeam to shine for him each day. (*During this Khurve has crossed to stage left, where she gets a suitcase, then she crosses to right center. She takes from the suitcase a very large fake rock and begins slowly and laboriously to cross toward Hilarious*) Guide us in that area where we wander, or are tempted to wander, our own body. Guide as at a price that is lower than our cost, as we are especially anxious at our conditions. Temptations try us over. Our flesh is weak. But thou art with us in that area, that gray area between the night and the dawn, between the facts and the truth, between our hearts and our thighs. Oh, Lord, let them who are without sin cast the first stone.

Khurve has reached Hilarious at this point and heaves the fake rock at her head, and "birdie" noises announce its effect on Hilarious. When she comes to, she introduces Khurve in the style of a burlesque showman

HILARIOUS: Ladies and Gentlemen . . . (*she gestures towards Khurve*)

Having removed her kimono to reveal a skimpy red showgirl costume, Khurve places her cloud labeled "CHAPTER VII: THE THIRD METHOD OF CHANGING SCENERY," poses between banners and sings accompanied by piano music. She points to and touches parts of her body suggestively while singing a classic burlesque number in the style of "Adam and Eve" by Gypsy Rose Lee.

KHURVE: (*at center, addressing the audience*) Well, I haven't done that one in a long, long, long time. They didn't like that one at all, oh no, those big, strong pencils and padlocks. They used to sit in the music hall with their seersucker knees up on the seat in front of them, writing so fast with their pencils you woulda thought they were lunatics conducting an orchestra. And then they'd close down the hall with a padlock. But not right then. They'd do it the next day, or in the middle of the night. Like it was their big secret. Oh yes, every time, it was the same big secret. And such a *small* padlock for such a *big* door. (*She gestures*) It was this big. Pencils and padlocks, we used to call it. Oh, they hated that one 'cause it was from the Bible! You know, Adam and Eve, the snake and the apple, it was from the old Bible, you know the very first original one. Pencils and padlocks. Well, they came to uphold decency. But not till after they watched every act in the show first! Sure, it's fine to close me down after you've seen my act fifty times! They came to defend God and country! From me! From little ol' me! Doesn't say much for God, now does it? No offense, honey (*indicating her arrival in Heaven*)! But I won something. I feel like I won a great, big sweepstake, or something. I pinned the tail on the donkey and they took me too. Hannah, my mother, said "Pretty is as pretty does. Beauty never lies," Hannah says. I'm a little ball of trouble and pretty as a church. Everybody loves to play, only I did that for a living. I'd play lots of things. And there's nothing wrong with that, as you can see quite plainly. There's nothing wrong with that. People look at me and they do that. Leastwise, they *did* that. Let's see, does it work up here? Look at me. Now put your hand in your pocket. Does it work up here? Does it work up here? Mind me. Mind me. Does it work up here? Pretty is as pretty does, my mother Hannah used to say. She doesn't even know I'm up here. I want to show my mother. Hannah! Hannah! I won something! Hey Hannah, I won something! (*Louisa enters with a fake camera. Khurve takes a pose*) Oh, honey, I can't get up. This is my deathbed. (*She takes another pose*) Call the doctor quick! En arrive. En arrive.

HILARIOUS/MEG: (*entering and dragging her away from her picture-taking*) Really, Jo, you are old enough to leave off your boyish tricks, and behave better. It didn't matter so much when you were a little girl, but now you are so tall, and turn up your hair, you should remember that you are a young lady.

LOUISA/JO: I'm not a young lady! And if turning up my hair makes me one I'll wear it in two tails until I'm twenty! It's bad enough to be a girl anyway, when I like boys' games and work and manners. It's worse than ever now, for I'm dying to go to the war and fight with Papa, and I can only stay at home and knit, like a poky old woman! There is so much to do about the play tomorrow night.

KHURVE/AMY: (*in a tone of exasperation*) That play!

HILARIOUS/MEG: Now listen, Jo. I don't mean to act any more, after this time. I'm getting too old for such things.

LOUISA/JO: Oh, you can't stop, Meg. Come here, Amy, and do the fainting scene, for you're as stiff as a poker in that.

KHURVE/AMY: I can't help, Jo. I never saw anyone faint, and I don't choose to make myself all black and blue, tumbling down flat, as you do. If I can go down easily, I'll drop. If I can't, I shall fall into a chair and be graceful. I don't care if Hugo does come at me with a pistol.

LOUISA/JO: Well, do it this way. Clasp your hands in front of you – so. And then stagger across the room, crying frantically (*she becomes very dramatic*) "Roderigo! Roderigo! Save me! Save me!" (*She utters a wild scream, and falls down in a heap on the floor. Meg applauds*) . . . Now come on, Amy. You do it!

KHURVE/AMY: (*looking like a martyr*) Oh dear! (*She sticks her hands out stiffly before her, and stumbles across the stage giving a feeble imitation of Jo's performance*) Roderigo! Roderigo! Save me, save me!

LOUISA/JO: Scream, Amy! Scream!

KHURVE/AMY: Owwww! (*She moans as if having an orgasm and then drops daintily down into the chair. Meg and Jo laugh*)

LOUISA/JO: It's no use. Do your best when the time comes, and if the audience laughs, don't blame me.

Blackout.

KHURVE: (*in the blackout*) Excuse me. Could you roll that back? I'd like to see that again. (*Lights up. They all faint. Blackout*)

HILARIOUS: (*in the blackout*) How would you like to be the third girl on, in the Pickle Persuader Bit?

KHURVE: Me? In the Pickle Persuader Bit?

HILARIOUS: First, you cross stage center, with a yackety-yak. Then you do the double clinch and put the newspaper bit under your neck. Then we segue into the fairy godmother finish. I get the seltzer water in the pants.

KHURVE: When do I get to rehearse?

HILARIOUS: You just did, honey.

Lights up to reveal a large cloud labeled "CHAPTER XXXIV: HOW TO MAKE DOLPHINS AND OTHER SEA MONSTERS APPEAR TO SPOUT WATER WHILE SWIMMING," which moves from right to left center. Khurve, Louisa and Hilarious emerge from behind the cloud with cameras pointed at the audience, and begin to sing while taking pictures. The cameras are water guns which squirt water at the audience)

ALL: (*singing in harmony to a made-up tune in the style of a nursery rhyme*)

> Watch the birdie
> We'll take a candid camera shot

Watch the birdie
Come on and give it all you got
Watch the birdie

Louisa and Khurve cross into the audience; Khurve is placed into an audience member's lap in preparation for the "Pieta" images.

Just let me see your pretty smile and hold it.

HILARIOUS: Michaelangelo's "Pieta" on tour of the Midwest!

ALL: (*singing*) Hold it!

HILARIOUS: Top government official dies in the arms of his male lover!

ALL: (*singing*) Hold it!

HILARIOUS: Woman in occupied country mourns over her dead children as soldiers renew conflict in the area!

ALL: (*singing, all three again on stage*) Watch the birdie

Watch the birdie
We'll take a candid camera shot
Watch the birdie
Come on and give it all you got
Just let me see your pretty smile and hold it.

Louisa brings an audience member on stage for the "Handcuffs" captions.

HILARIOUS: Mae West spends ten days in Women's House of detention following lewd portrayal of sex acts on the Broadway stage!

ALL: (*singing*) Hold it!

HILARIOUS: Feminist makes citizen's arrest at S/M club, citing pro-bondage feminists as "FASCISTS."

ALL: (*singing*) Hold it!

HILARIOUS: The law recognizes the fact that many people must be protected from their very selves!

ALL: (*singing*) Hold it!

LOUISA: (*to an audience member*) You want it! You want it real bad! Say it! Say it! (*The audience member says "Yeah, I want it," and is guided back to seat*)

ALL: (*singing*) Hold it!

They all sing the refrain while Louisa brings another audience member on stage, making her kneel for the "Supplicant" captions.

HILARIOUS: Princess Diana comforts the young Prince Henry as he scraped his knee during a game of punchball!

ALL: (*singing*) Hold it!

HILARIOUS: The Pope visited Solidarity headquarters and conducted mass for nearly fourteen thousand members!

ALL: (*singing*) Hold it!

HILARIOUS: Television evangelist begs forgiveness after night in house of prostitution!

ALL: (*singing*) Hold it!

HILARIOUS: Pretty nearly the most nauseating feature of the evening was the laughter of the audience! (*They look at the audience*)

They all sing the refrain, and strike poses for the "Sex Image" captions.

HILARIOUS: Miss Universe of last year crowned a new Miss Universe in ceremony in Las Vegas last night!

ALL: (*singing*) Hold it!

LOUISA: Well-known author of children's literature found running naked in the woods near Walden Pond!

KHURVE: It's safe to say that nearly one-third of the first night house never understood what it was all about.

ALL: (*singing*) Hold it!

ALL: (*singing*) Watch the birdie

> We'll take a candid camera shot
> Watch the birdie
> Come on and give it all you got
> Watch the birdie
> Just let me see your pretty smile and hold it
> Hold it. Hold it.

The song's end finds Khurve and Hilarious positioned in the audience, where they remain throughout the next exchange which is a scene from Little Women.

HILARIOUS/MEG: I hope nothing's happened to Jo. You know how Jo hates to ask a favor of anyone – and particularly Aunt March.

KHURVE/AMY: Well, when your father is sick in the hospital, and your mother has to go to Washington and take care of him, and she needs money to stay there, it's time to come down off your high horse, and ask a favor.

HILARIOUS/MEG: Jo did, my dear. As soon as we read Marmee's letter, she put her pride in her pocket, and went straight to Aunt

March. I wanted to go, but Jo wouldn't hear it. She said it was the man of this family, and it was her business to provide for us.

KHURVE/AMY: What if Aunt March won't give her the money?

HILARIOUS/MEG: Amy, don't mention such a thing!

KHURVE/AMY: Well, Jo has a very unfortunate way with her.

HILARIOUS/MEG: You're out of sorts today, Amy.

KHURVE/AMY: Well, who wouldn't be? Last night Laurie came over to take Jo to the theatre, and it was a play I particularly wanted to see. And I asked Jo to take me, and offered to pay my own way, out of my rag money. And she wouldn't take me.

HILARIOUS/MEG: It wouldn't have been polite for you to go when you weren't invited.

KHURVE/AMY: If Jo had just taken a little trouble, I might have been invited.

HILARIOUS/MEG: You shouldn't have been angry with Jo about that, Amy.

KHURVE/AMY: I was angry with her. And still am! So there! ... There she is!

Louisa enters pulling a large cloud labeled: "CHAPTER XXXV: HOW TO PRODUCE A CONSTANTLY FLOWING RIVER" on stage with a rope, giving the impression she has been working very hard

HILARIOUS/MEG: Jo, dear!

LOUISA/JO: Hello, everybody!

HILARIOUS/MEG: Jo, we've been worried about you. Have you had a bad time?

KHURVE/AMY: Did you get the money?

LOUISA/JO: There! Never say this family doesn't have a bread winner! (*She trips and falls and loses her wig and hat, exposing the performer's real hair*)

HILARIOUS/MEG: Your hair! You've cut your beautiful hair!

KHURVE/AMY: Jo! How could you? Your one beauty!

HILARIOUS/MEG: Jo, darling, you're magnificent!

KHURVE/AMY: Didn't you feel dreadfully when the first cut came? (*She voices disgust at having to continue with the script*)

LOUISA: What's the matter?

KHURVE: Nothing.

LOUISA: We were in the middle of a scene.

KHURVE: Yeah, well I didn't like it.

LOUISA: I was under the impression that you were an actress by profession.

KHURVE: How did you know? Do you know my mother? Or have you see my movies?

HILARIOUS: She doesn't have to see your movies to know your mother. No. I mean she doesn't have to see your mother to know your movie. No. I mean she doesn't have to know your movies or see your mother to know what kind of woman you seem to be.

KHURVE: What is that supposed to mean?

HILARIOUS: I think Shakespeare said it very well: "God hath given you one face and you make yourselves another. You jig, you amble, and you lisp . . ."

KHURVE: I foxtrot and I jitterbug but the rest I don't know *squat* about it . . .

LOUISA: Don't you think now that we're in Heaven we should try to get along?

HILARIOUS: This is more like HELL than Heaven! I don't understand the Heaven where *you* are.

LOUISA: That's very lyrical, Hilarious. (*She sings*) I don't understand! The Heaven where you are . . .

HILARIOUS: (*kneeling and praying loudly*) Almighty God! In your infinite wisdom please show me the reason why these amoral women . . .

KHURVE: There's no reason to pray, we're already up here.

HILARIOUS: . . . have achieved the stature of your grace . . . I have devoted my earthly life to gestures of grace and then I pass on and these are my deserts . . .

KHURVE: Desserts?

LOUISA: Deserts in the sense of getting what one deserves. Fate or destiny is a constant theme in human history. As a writer I tried to separate destiny from the concepts of good and evil.

KHURVE: Oh honey, what a relief.

LOUISA: (*spluttering with feeling and enthusiasm*) . . . so that I could capture character . . . and character is beyond judgement . . .

KHURVE: (*to Hilarious*) Hey, look! She spits when she talks also! Did you see that! She spits when she talks!

LOUISA: . . . and that is the essence of righteousness to me . . . allowing character without judgement . . . I felt like God when writing . . . I had the fates of these people in my hands . . . and I treated them kindly and simply . . . and my readers wanted more cruelty from me but I frustrated them with kindness. I worried, oh God, I was up many nights . . . those candles on plates I used, burnt down one after another in a row along the window . . . it was that struggle between what my dear readers wanted and what I myself believed . . . like being in middle management. The whole struggle . . . you know . . .

KHURVE: I was into that too really . . . pretending to be people. It's Hilarity I don't get. Why do they let Hilarity in here?

HILARIOUS: Hilarious. Hilarious . . . Didn't you learn any Latin?

KHURVE: No, but I French pretty good . . .

HILARIOUS: I am displaced . . . I am disgraced . . . I am disgusted . . . I am shocked . . . To have God on my right and this hussy on my left . . .

KHURVE: Who is on your right?

HILARIOUS: God. God. God! I could have had many lovers. But I turned the corner. I had my human nature in one pocket and the will of God in the other.

LOUISA: What *is* the will of God?

KHURVE: The will! The will! It's when someone dies and they say in a piece of paper who gets their stuff.

HILARIOUS: . . . it's easier to see the will of God than to act on it! The woman in the church with the silk scarf! I let her go! After one song I knew every shadow of the blue of her eye and I let her go! And my mother's brother's secrets! I never told them! And I killed a suffering animal! I hate blood! I crushed its head with a rock! And I believed all the things I said to people! I believed I would go to Heaven and that the heavenly kingdom was the kingdom of God and the kingdom of Jesus Christ his one and only son! I believed that! I believed that! And I was a liar! And here I am in Heaven! And the reason I was a liar was that I believed that Heaven was heavenly! And I haven't seen God yet! And all I've seen is some heathen pagan bookworm and a strumpet! I just can't understand.

KHURVE: Me? You can't understand me? I think you understand real well. I got nothin' to apologize for. I never made no deals. I did what I did and I never asked nothin' and I never tried to hide from anyone anything. Me and my mother were real close and I made my movies and that's it. No, that's not really it, I did live shows for a while too. But they were behind a wall with peepholes and no one ever touched me, not once, never. And I can dance, too! And there's nothing wrong with that! People like other people's bodies and that's just a fact of life and that's it that's that, final, period, that's it. And I was just one of those people that let you see their body. Period. The desire to see other people's bodies is built in. That's it. It's built in! I didn't make it up! Now that's evil! To think you made it up! Or to think you can *un*make it up! Or tell people it's evil! *That's* evil! I just showed my body to people who wanted to see it! Period! That's it! Period!

LOUISA: Suddenly the garden grows quiet. We hear things. Larks. Finches. Two clouds part. Some blue sky shines through. And the right hand of reason turns to go as the left hand, the lover, the counterpart, says . . .

KHURVE: Now, at last I've found you. (*She starts back to the stage*)

LOUISA: And she would say . . .

HILARIOUS: Excuse me? (*She heads back to the stage*)

LOUISA: And she would say . . .

KHURVE: It is you that I have.

LOUISA: And she would say . . .

HILARIOUS: Madam . . .

LOUISA: And she would say . . .

KHURVE: . . . waited for

LOUISA: And she would say . . .

HILARIOUS: Madam, please . . .

LOUISA: And she would say . . .

KHURVE: I throw myself at your feet.

LOUISA: And she would say . . .

HILARIOUS: I beg your pardon.

LOUISA: And she would say . . .

KHURVE: This is the thing I have waited for, the moment I've searched for.

LOUISA: And she would say . . .

HILARIOUS: I cannot.

LOUISA: And she would say . . .

KHURVE: The longing I have longed for.

LOUISA: And she would say . . .

HILARIOUS: I ... I ...

LOUISA: And she would say ...

KHURVE: You ... you ...

Hilarious and Khurve have come face to face centerstage on either side of Louisa.

LOUISA: Hit it, Maestro! (*She exits, leaving them to get on with it*)

Vaudeville music. Hilarious and Khurve do a bizarre preacher/prostitute seduction dance in which they burlesque sexual positions.

LOUISA: (*interrupting the most explicit sexual position*) Hold the music! (*The music stops. Hilarious and Khurve freeze*)

LOUISA/JO: Has anyone seen my book? The one with my new story. The one we all thought was good enough to sell? I left it on my bureau last night when I went to the theater.

HILARIOUS/MEG: Maybe it's in the attic with your other manuscripts.

LOUISA/JO: No it isn't. *She's* got it.

KHURVE/AMY: Why, I have not!

HILARIOUS/MEG: Now, Jo!

LOUISA/JO: And you needn't take her part, Meg March. The last time, she turned my bureau drawer upside down on the floor.

KHURVE/AMY: I haven't got your old book.

LOUISA/JO: Well you know something about it, and you'd better tell at once or I'll make you!

KHURVE/AMY: Scold as much as you like, you'll never get your silly old story again.

LOUISA/JO: Why not?

KHURVE/AMY: I burnt it up.

HILARIOUS/MEG: Amy!

LOUISA/JO: What, my little book I was so fond of and worked over and meant to finish before Father got home? Have you really burnt it up?

KHURVE/AMY: Yes I did. I told you I'd make you pay for not letting me go to the theater with you and Laurie and I have, so there!

LOUISA/JO: You wicked, wicked girl, I never can write it again and I'll never forgive you as long as I live! (*She exits*)

HILARIOUS: (*trying to save the scene*) Hit it, Maestro!

They continue the dance. Khurve exits, satisfied at end of dance.

HILARIOUS: (*standing and dusting herself off*) This is the foulest perversion of sex ever attempted by theater baiters for dirty dollars.

LOUISA/JO: Oh Meg! What shall I do? It seems as if I could do anything when I'm in a passion. I've never eaten any meat and I'm still cross and irritable. I'm afraid I shall do something dreadful someday and spoil my life and make everybody hate me. Oh Meg! Help me!

HILARIOUS/MEG: Jo, dear, we all have our temptations, and it often takes us all our lives to conquer them. You think your temper is the worst in the world, but mine used to be just like it.

LOUISA/JO: Yours, Meg? Why, you are never angry!

HILARIOUS/MEG: I've been trying to cure it for many years, and have only succeeded in controlling it. I am angry nearly every day of my life, Jo; but I have learned not to show it.

LOUISA/JO: Tell me how you do it, Meg dear.

HILARIOUS/MEG: I've learned to check the hasty words that rise to my lips, and when I feel they mean to break out against my will, I just go away a minute and give myself a little shake for being so weak and wicked.

Hilarious exits and Louisa turns to the audience and walks downstage.

LOUISA/JO: Are there any questions?

LOUISA: Any questions? (*She asks for and answers questions from the audience during the course of the monologue. She must attempt to answer the questions as truthfully as possible either as the character of Louisa or as the performer herself. She is down stage center*) Any other questions? (*She bends and begins to untie her left shoe*) I guess I'm really not too interested in your questions, I am far more interested in my own. Oh, I know that is dreadfully selfish. Dreadfully selfish for a woman, so are there any questions? I am so glad you liked *Little Women,* and your daughter Jenny loved it, it changed her life. It gave her everything she needed to carry in the suitcase of her memory on her journey toward womanhood. That is wondrous. You know, I never really wanted to be a literary nursemaid. (*She bends to remove the shoe*) I plodded away, but I didn't enjoy such things, perhaps I should wear my shoe on my nose. Here. (*She balances the shoe on her face momentarily, then removes it*) How do you like it? This shoe is *Little Women.* And what if I were known for wearing my shoe on my nose? Would I go to the market that way? Should I spend the rest of my life being loved for that part of myself that I despise? (*To the audience*) Is there another question? (*She responds to a real or imaginary question with this answer*) Those necessity stories? The potboilers, the thrillers, that wasn't me, that was someone else. I never swung in a tree. What would I be doing in a tree? I'm a dutiful daughter, I'm not the writer of purple passages and scarlet motifs. I have never imagined hashish between the sensuous and painted lips of a lurid heroine. That was someone else. That was A.M. Bernard. He – she – lived over there in that insatiable, demon place of success. Oh yes, *she* was successful! She was not a hypocrite! She raged at servitude! She dizzied at the prospect of eternal pretense and repression! She swung from trees with pen in one hand and opium in the other. She was a woman to be respected! She was not a woman to be afraid of! I am afraid my shoe has slipped off my nose. Perhaps I'd better take another question. (*Pause*) Is there another question? (*Pause*) Oh, yes, I am a woman's woman. I mean, a woman's rights woman. I was a feminist. I longed to see a war. But since I was a woman and I could not fight, I had to content myself with working for those who did. I nursed four hundred fathers by the light of a kerosene lantern. I nursed the wounds of four hundred men who had what I had not: Power! I nursed the bodies of four hundred men, four hundred *men's* bodies, whose touch froze me and whose kisses covered my nose like a shoe. (*She balances the shoe on her face briefly, until it falls and she retrieves it*) And they screamed with pain. But what is their pain when compared to mine? What is the wound of a gun or a sword compared to the other wounds, the lie, the lies of the *Little Women*? I'm afraid my shoe has slipped off my nose. And I must go in now and knit. (*She crosses up stage and right*) Oh, I know there is a war afoot, but I must go in and knit, because war is not for women unless it's the war within. Is there one more question? (*Pause*) Thank you. (*She curtsies and exits*)

Carnival music begins a burlesque dance sequence bringing four more clouds into place. Hilarious enters with a cloud: HOW TO DIVIDE SKY INTO SECTIONS and, as she exits, runs into Khurve wearing large fake tits and ass. As Khurve exits she runs into Louisa carrying a cloud labeled: "CHAPTER XXXVIII: HOW GRADUALLY TO COVER PART OF THE SKY WITH CLOUDS."

KHURVE: You know I'm the kind of girl who climbed the ladder of success.

LOUISA: How?

KHURVE: Wrong by wrong.

This farcical dance of entrances and exits builds until Khurve and Hilarious notice Louisa with a suitcase in hand, crossing the stage with the intent to leave the theatre.

HILARIOUS: STOP THE MUSIC! What's going on?

LOUISA: I'm leaving.

KHURVE: What about us?

LOUISA: I don't like you anymore.

HILARIOUS: You don't *like* us?

LOUISA: Well . . . I don't like *living* with you.

KHURVE: Oh, get over it sweetie. That's like saying you don't like living with your legs.

LOUISA: My legs are none of your business!

KHURVE AND HILARIOUS: Oh no?

Hilarious and Khurve dive under Louisa's skirt. She lifts it, revealing them in a sexual position. Blackout.

KHURVE: Could you roll that back please? I'd like to see that again.

Lights up. Louisa lifts her skirt again, revealing them in reversed positions.

LOUISA: Hit it, Maestro!

Hilarious leaves to get a cloud. Louisa is packing.

KHURVE: I used to be terribly ashamed of the way I lived.

LOUISA: Did you reform?

KHURVE: No.

LOUISA: So what happened?

KHURVE: I'm not ashamed anymore.

Khurve leaves. Hilarious comes out with the cloud, labeled: "CHAPTER XLII: HOW TO COVER PART OF THE SKY, BEGINNING WITH A SMALL CLOUD THAT BECOMES LARGER AND LARGER AND CONTINUALLY CHANGES ITS COLOR," catches Louisa's hand before it hits the suitcase, they swing around, then Louisa grabs Hilarious's breast and is shocked. Khurve enters and sees Louisa with her hands on Hilarious's breasts.

KHURVE: Stop the music!

LOUISA: I gotta get out of here.

KHURVE: You can't leave. This is Heaven.

HILARIOUS: It's Hell.

LOUISA: It's the togetherness I can't stand.

HILARIOUS: You can't leave, you're dead.

LOUISA: I'm a writer!

KHURVE: So you're a dead writer!

LOUISA: I'm going!

HILARIOUS: Don't go! You're welcome!

KHURVE: Thank you!

HILARIOUS: You're welcome!

KHURVE: You said that already!

HILARIOUS: Right. Thank you.

KHURVE: You're welcome!

HILARIOUS: No, *you* are welcome.

KHURVE: Oh, thank you!

HILARIOUS: You're welcome!

LOUISA: Hit it, Maestro!

Hilarious goes to get a cloud labeled: "CHAPTER XLIII: HOW TO MAKE A CLOUD DESCEND PERPENDICULARLY WITH PERSONS IN IT." Khurve starts to leave, but turns and looks at the spot where Louisa was standing. Louisa, leaving, moves down into the House.

KHURVE: I wrote this show myself. It's the story of a girl who lost her reputation . . . but never missed it!

HILARIOUS: (*entering*) She *did* miss it! She missed it terribly!

LOUISA: I wrote this show!

KHURVE: You wrote that *book*!

LOUISA: I want to write a different book!

KHURVE AND HILARIOUS: What shall we do?

LOUISA: Do what you want.

KHURVE: (*to Hilarious*) What do we want?

HILARIOUS: We want her to stay.

LOUISA: That's not what you want.

KHURVE: How do you know what everybody thinks?

LOUISA: Because I'm the writer.

HILARIOUS: Stay.

LOUISA: Don't push me.

KHURVE: We're doing what we want.

LOUISA: Oh please . . . let me *think*.

HILARIOUS: Thoughts . . .

KHURVE: We both look like thoughts!

LOUISA: (*mad*) You look like the *process* of thinking!

HILARIOUS: What are you talking about?

LOUISA: Why are you both so . . .

Khurve and Hilarious turn to exit but Hilarious turns back and crosses downstage left of Louisa and stands among the clouds delivering the following monologue as Louisa watches.

HILARIOUS: I came home to go to Amy's wedding. I loved Amy so much, and my mother must have seen that in me while I was getting dressed. I let myself take forever getting dressed to watch Amy get married. My mother saw my love. She loved me, my mother. I put on a white suit, beautiful tailored white, as if Amy was going to marry *me*, and my mother watched me. I dressed in my mother's memories. I could tell, because she told me how handsome I looked in my suit, and she smiled that smile of memory. Then I put on my gold cufflinks and tiepin, and I was my father. I looked just like my father, she said, and she remembered him. And then I shined my shoes, and her smile got even deeper, and I looked just like my father she said, and then I put on my white Panama hat. I think she wanted me to kiss her hand . . . and all of a sudden the spell was broken . . . I turned from her to leave for the wedding and her face fell and she forgot that I was her lover and she said, I hope you don't think you're going out dressed like that?

LOUISA: (*to the audience*) Any questions?

Hilarious crosses to Louisa and sings the following song and leads her in a dance of Victorian romance.

HILARIOUS: I can see through you, do you want to take a chance
I can outdo you, through the action of romance
I'm even better in a moment of despair
I even get my heart all tangled in your hair

Do you still want me?
I'm sick of waiting.
I will outdo you.
I will come to you.
I'm a bit lovely.
You'll recognize me.

If you can stand it, I will touch your arm like this.
At your command I'll turn and ask you for a kiss.
There is a saying that I make the time stand still.
I won't be playing when you go against your will.

Do you still want me?
It will not last long.

I'm sick of waiting.
I'm more than gorgeous.
How can you stand it,
You'll recognize me.

Your heart is beating hard, I see the drops of sweat.
Your part is fleeting, I can see that's what you get.
You're hesitating, moving to the side of right.
I won't be waiting once I've lost you from my sight.

You're an asshole
You really blew it.
I'm changing shape now.
I was a vision.
Now I'm just vapor.
I'm disappeared now.

At the end of the dance Hilarious exits and leaves Louisa, a bit shaken, on stage right.

LOUISA: (*to the audience*) I'd like to sit down . . . (*She looks around for a place to rest*) I'd like to sit down. (*A swing on a white silk rope descends from the ceiling. Louisa walks over and sits*) So this is Heaven. Oh, it feels so nice to give my weight to the earth as it passes through a chair or through the grass, or . . . even gravity itself! The way the earth has of not letting me go . . . as though I'm greatly beloved!

KHURVE: (*enters and stands behind Louisa on the swing*) You see me. Come on, admit it. You see me. Look. Look at this. Look at me. Don't sit next to me without looking at me.

LOUISA: I used to love to sit, I used to wander. I had wanderlust . . . oh . . .

KHURVE: I'm like a tract of land, I want you to look, I want you to look at me, buy me, look at me, build on me, mine and shave me. Make a house on me and bury your dead . . .

LOUISA: Children are so funny.

KHURVE: All the way in me.

LOUISA: I used to have a path I followed, always the same path. It went to a spring. I used to wait till it was almost dark and follow this well-known path, as if it were the very first time. I rehearse my surprises you know . . . ha ha ha . . . And then I'd get there, to the spring! It came as a great and delicious shock every day of my life to see it there like it waited for me . . . it had no other friends but me. And I reached my hands into that spring and it was so cold, oh my god so cold. On the hottest day it was snow in motion. It was almost a person ... someone waiting for me ... There's someone next to me ...

KHURVE: I'm talking to you.

LOUISA: Someone waiting for me ...

KHURVE: I'm talking to you in heartbeat.

LOUISA: There's someone sitting next to me.

KHURVE: I'm talking heartbeat to you.

LOUISA: Who are you?

KHURVE: You see me.

LOUISA: Who are you?

KHURVE: You see me.

LOUISA: What do you want?

KHURVE: You want me.

LOUISA: It was just a fantasy but how real it seemed ... children are so funny.

KHURVE: Don't act like you don't see me. I come. I come.

LOUISA: Someone sitting next to me ...

KHURVE: Did you know I come?

LOUISA: Facing whatever way I faced. If I faced the mountain, she faced the mountain.

KHURVE: This is what I am, and I want it that way.

LOUISA: If I faced town, she faced town.

KHURVE: Look at me.

LOUISA: If I laid down and faced the sun ... she lay down next to me.

KHURVE: Why won't you talk about it?

LOUISA: So I never saw her, I couldn't see her.

KHURVE: Look! Look what a lover I am. You want me ... say it!

LOUISA: I find communion through understanding. I find these springs in my mind, full of surprises. Manageable surprises.

KHURVE: I'm getting fat like the earth, who's fatter than me. She's a huge fat lady with fat thighs made of water.

LOUISA: The spring was a manageable surprise. It was drinkable.

KHURVE: And the fatter I get the tighter she holds me.

LOUISA: I would have liked to turn her.

KHURVE: She wants me back.

LOUISA: I would have liked to turn her.

KHURVE: She wants me back.

LOUISA: This friend of mine . . . but after you sit . . .

KHURVE: I'm getting big . . .

LOUISA: Side by side . . .

KHURVE: I'm overwhelming . . .

LOUISA: . . . for so many years as a child . . .

KHURVE: I'm going to overwhelm you . . .

LOUISA: It's hard to face someone . . .

KHURVE: Look over here . . . I'm huge . . . my thighs won't close . . .

LOUISA: But I love them, I love my gardening, my reading, my work.

KHURVE: Flies are buzzing around my twat. You see me.

LOUISA: And this companion . . .

KHURVE: You see me . . . Talk to me . . . Don't say no to me . . .

LOUISA: She's . . .

KHURVE: Don't say no to me!

LOUISA: She's . . .

Hilarious enters and kneels at Louisa's feet as if proposing.

HILARIOUS: (*stepping upstage of Louisa and Khurve in the swing so that they are all framed by the rope*) The ball rolls round and round and where it stops is of no concern to me! Because I'm not playing by the rules, as I'm not included in the rewards. I'm not the one you think I am. I sparkle in your eyes for a moment before you condemn me to a pit not realizing that by doing so you will never see me again for eternity. Include me in your will of dreams. Take me with you as you fly to desire and your breasts are finally yours and your tears are your tears of your own joy and not of others. Reach forward as far as you can and try and touch me. Through me you can rock and roll. Through me you can see the supper table spread with delicacies from every country and tea and flesh and all that we can afford. Touch me without your face covered by your fingers, without the shame of champagne and burgundy, without the shame of the players who put down less than they take up. You will be awarded with my desire. You will be awarded with affections without attachments. I'm going through all the red lights. It'll be your pleasure to come with me. And there's no danger, because I own the amusement park, and I'm letting you in for free!

Blackout. Lights come up on the three characters still framed by the swing. Louisa swings with abandon while Hilarious and Khurve strike poses and sing a burlesque song in the style of Mae West's "That's All, Brother, That's All." At the end of the song Khurve is crossing the stage with a suitcase as if to leave the theatre.

LOUISA: (*to Khurve*) Where did you get that suitcase?

HILARIOUS: That's not your suitcase!

LOUISA: Yours was green.

HILARIOUS: It was plaid.

KHURVE: How do you know?

HILARIOUS: I saw it.

LOUISA: I'm the writer!

HILARIOUS: Why do you keep saying you're the writer?

KHURVE: Who cares?

HILARIOUS: You stole that suitcase!

LOUISA: I care!

KHURVE: I did not!

LOUISA: I created you!

HILARIOUS: What?

KHURVE: I took it but I didn't steal it!

LOUISA: I said I created you!

HILARIOUS: Did you hear that?

KHURVE: There are plenty of them!

LOUISA: *You*! (*she grabs Hilarious by her collar*) I was awake all night over! But *you* (*she grabs Khurve's hand on the suitcase handle*) just came to me quickly in the afternoon!

HILARIOUS: God!

LOUISA: Where?

KHURVE: Dunno.

Fade to blackout.

THE END

BELLE REPRIEVE

A Collaboration

BETTE BOURNE, PAUL SHAW, PEGGY SHAW, LOIS WEAVER

Directed by Lois Weaver
Sets designed by Nancy Bardawil and Matthew Owen
Costumes designed by Susan Young
Music composed and directed by Laka Daisical and Phil Booth
Lighting designed by Liz Poulter

Originally produced on January 8, 1991, at The Drill Hall Arts Centre, London. Produced in association with The Club at La MaMa E.T.C., New York, and opened at La MaMa on February 14, 1991. Lighting for the New York production was designed by Howard Thies.

Copyright: Bourne, Shaw, Shaw, Weaver, 1991

"I'm a Man" by Elias McDaniel. Copyright © 1955 Arc Music Corporation, by permission of Tristan Music Ltd
"Running Wild" by Joe Grey, Leo Wood and A. Harrington Gibbs. Copyright © 1950 (renewed) Leo Feist Inc., by permission of EMI Feist Catalog Inc.
"Sweet Little Angel" was written by Lucille Bogan
"Pushover" by Billy Davis and Tony Clark. Copyright © 1963 Chevis Publishing Corporation, used by permission
"I Love My Art" was written by Edward Clark

ORIGINAL SONGS

"Under the Covers," words by Peggy Shaw and Paul Shaw, music by Phil Booth
"Bautiful Dream," words and music by Phil Booth
"The Fairy Song," words and music by Paul Shaw

CHARACTERS

MITCH, a fairy disguised as a man (Paul Shaw)
STELLA, a woman disguised as a woman (Lois Weaver)
STANLEY, a butch lesbian (Peggy Shaw)
BLANCHE, a man in a dress (Bette Bourne)

An empty stage. The backdrop is a scrim painted to resemble the interior of a 1940s New Orleans apartment. There are three high-tension wires strung across the stage. Throughout the play, various painted cloth curtains are pulled across these wires to denote a change in scenery or mood.

Four o'clock in the morning.

ACT I

Mitch is wheeling three large boxes onstage with a handtruck. One is designed to resemble a steamer truck. The second is square, large enough to hold an actor, and shaped to resemble a card table, which it becomes in later scenes. The third is tall, rectangular, and large enough to hold another actor. It is turned on its back to represent a bathtub in the second act.

MITCH: Inside this box it's four o'clock in the morning. I know that sounds incredible but it's true. I know because it's *my* four o'clock in the morning. Every time it comes around, I put it in this box. I've been doing it for years now. At four o'clock in the morning, the thread that holds us to the earth is at its most slender, and all the creatures that never see sunlight come out to make mincemeat of well-laid plans. So you can imagine what it's like in there. If you listen closely you can hear them shuffling about, like the sound of rain or chittering birds. It reminds me of a soundtrack, the beginning of a movie ... (*Stella appears drinking a Coke behind the scrim*) a clean slate. Darkness all around. Small sounds that give a taste of an atmosphere, a head turning, a body lit from behind, shadows in a dark, tiled hallway, a blues piano. (*Pianist strikes a match and begins to play the blues*)

STELLA: (*Moving to center from behind the scrim, still drinking the Coke*) Is there something you want? What can I do for you? Do you know who I am, what I feel, how I think? You want my body. My soul, my food, my bed, my skin, my hands? You want to touch me, hold me, lick me, smell me, eat me, have me? You think you need a little more time to decide? Well, you've got a little over an hour to have your fill. Meanwhile ... (*Mitch enters with the last box, swatting bugs*) I'm surprised there aren't more bugs out this time of year. All the ones that are out seem to be buzzing around my head.

MITCH: No, there's plenty for both of us. Don't feel singled out.

STELLA: I think it's 'cuz I eat so much sugar that they're attracted to me. Sugar in my blood. And my veins are close to the surface.

MITCH: You know that they excrete something to digest your blood, that's why they leave that bump on your skin.

STELLA: I always worry that they carry things with them, transferring them from person to person.

MITCH: That's an old wives' tale. This country has no tradition of disease being spread by mosquitoes. You're mistaken.

STELLA: Well, every year I make one big mistake. I wonder what it will be this year?

MITCH: This mistake, is it at a particular time, or can't you tell when it's coming?

STELLA: I can usually feel it coming . . .

BLANCHE: (*from inside the box*) I've always depended on the strangeness of strangers.

STELLA: Or at least after the fact I thought I knew it was coming.

MITCH: Isn't there something you can do to stop it happening?

STELLA: Such as . . .

MITCH: Change the script!

STELLA: Change the script. Ha ha. You want me to do *what* in these shoes? The script is not the problem. I've changed the script.

MITCH: It's a start.

STELLA: Look, I'm supposed to wander around in a state of narcotized sensuality. That's my part. (*Blanche and Stanley speak simultaneously from inside the two largest boxes*)

BLANCHE: You didn't see, Miss Stella, see what I saw, the long parade to the graveyard. The mortgage on the house, death is expensive, Miss Stella, death is expensive.

STANLEY: Is that so? You don't say, hey Stella wasn't we happy before she showed up. Didn't we see those colored lights you and me. Didn't we see those colored lights.

STELLA: And anyway, it's too late. It's already started.

STANLEY: Hey Stella! (*He comes out of the stage right box*)

STELLA: Don't holler at me like that, Stanley.

STANLEY: Hey Stella, Stella baby! Catch! (*He throws her a package wrapped in bloody paper*)

STELLA: What!

STANLEY: Meat.

BLANCHE: (*emerging from the stage left box*) Are we here? Is this the place? Are my necessaries disembarked? How sweet it is to arrive at a new place for the first time. The future stretching out in front of us like a clean, white carpet. There's the stir and rustle of endless possibility in the air.

STANLEY: You don't say.

STELLA: Honey, we're in exactly the same place we started out from.

BLANCHE: Started out? What do you mean started out? You mean we haven't arrived?

STELLA: No, we haven't arrived, but don't worry about that now. You just take it easy.

STANLEY: Something smells fishy around here and it's not me.

STELLA: (*to Stanley*) Now you be kind to my sister. Tell her how nice she looks.

BLANCHE: I can't stand being in between. I just can't bear it.

STELLA: (*to Stanley*) You should try to understand her a little better, she's just different.

STANLEY: Different? You can say that again.

BLANCHE: I have never regretted my decision to be unique.

STANLEY: I'm gonna put an end to this charade here and now.

BLANCHE: (*as Stanley moves to center stage with a trunk and becomes a customs agent*) That my plans of late have gone somewhat awry is the price one has to pay if life is to be superb.

STANLEY: (*to Blanche*) Ticket please.

BLANCHE: (*to Mitch*) Young man, don't I know you?

MITCH: We were engaged to be married.

STANLEY: Ticket please!

BLANCHE: Did I break your heart?

MITCH: No, you broke my leg.

BLANCHE: I must be stronger than I thought.

STANLEY: Ticket please!

BLANCHE: Oh, well, all right, I have it here somewhere. (*She rummages through her bag*) Which ticket do you mean, the one that got me here or the one that will take me away?

STANLEY: Both.

BLANCHE: Oh, well I don't seem to have either at the moment. Although we must have gotten here somehow, we can't have walked, we have a heavy load. However, I present myself as overwhelming evidence that I am actually here.

STANLEY: While we're at it, I'm gonna need your passport.

BLANCHE: Passport? I wasn't aware that we were crossing any borders. What borders?

STANLEY: Passport.

BLANCHE: (*rummaging around*) Passport, passport ... (*Mitch steps forward with her passport and hands it to Stanley*)

STANLEY: (*still staring at Mitch*) Name?

BLANCHE: Blanche DuBois.

STANLEY: That's not what it says here.

BLANCHE: I assure you that is who I am. My namesake is a role played by that incandescent star, Vivien Leigh, and although the resemblance is not immediately striking I have been told we have the same shoulders.

STANLEY: (*looking at the passport photo*) Then who's this here?

BLANCHE: The information in that document is a convention which allows me to pass in the world without let or hindrance. If you'll just notice the message inside the front cover, The Queen of England herself not only requests this but requires it.

STANLEY: You don't look anything like this photograph.

BLANCHE: I believe nature is there to be improved upon.

STANLEY: You're lying.

BLANCHE: Well, that's one way of looking at it.

STANLEY: Is there another?

BLANCHE: You wouldn't treat me like this if I wasn't at the end of my rope!

STANLEY: (*slamming his fist on the trunk*) But ya are Blanche, ya are.

(*Cat screams from Mitch and Stella*)

BLANCHE: What was that?

STANLEY: Cats. I'm afraid I'm going to have to perform an intimate search.

BLANCHE: My body?

STANLEY: Your luggage.

BLANCHE: Stella, how do I look?

STELLA: Fresh as a daisy.

STANLEY: One that's been picked a few days.

MITCH: Look, can't we just scrub 'round the search and get on with the scenes of brutal humiliation and sexual passion?

STANLEY: I'm afraid we have to find a motive in this case, and I believe it's in this trunk. (*To Mitch*) Why don't you mind your own business?

BLANCHE: How dare you speak to my ex-fiancé like that!

STANLEY: Your ex-fiancé?! This man is your ex-fiancé?

BLANCHE: That's right.

MITCH: I told her I loved her and she pushed me down the stair-well, but I forgave her as any decent man would.

STANLEY: That's not what it says in the script. In the script it says you treated her like shit because you're a stuck-up mommy's boy.

MITCH: That's a lie!

BLANCHE: I think I'm going to faint.

STELLA: Is all this really necessary?

STANLEY: Look, have you any idea how many people we have come in here saying they're Blanche DuBois, clutching tiny handbags and fainting in the foyer? I'm afraid I'll have to subject this case to the closest possible scrutiny before I allow any of you to pass any further.

BLANCHE: I see, you want me to come clean by showing my dirty laundry to the world.

STANLEY: You got it.

BLANCHE: I think I'll go into the dressing room and burst into tears.

STELLA: We're in this up to our asses now. There's no going back.

BLANCHE: Hold me Stella, I think I feel a flashback coming on.

(*Lights flash, music plays, a curtain painted like a grotesque piece of torn lace is pulled on stage behind the action, the actors shuffling backward around the trunk*) (And so it was that I set out to prove to the world that I was indeed myself. A difficult enough task, you might say, for anyone.)

STELLA: She threw herself at the feet of an unforgiving world to prove her identity.

MITCH: The answer was somewhere in that trunk.

STANLEY: (*thumping his fist on the trunk as the music and lights stop flashing*) This is gonna cost you, lady. What did you think you were gonna get a free ride or something? (*About to open the trunk*) What do we have here?

BLANCHE: Please open the doors one at a time! If you open them all at once pink things and fur things, dainty things, delicate and wistful things might pop out.

STANLEY: I'll open them one at a time. First things first. (*Music starts. Stanley pulls out a jacket and tosses it to Stella, then pulls out a scarf and throws it to Mitch*)

BLANCHE: I won't take it personally the way you're treating everything I own in the world.

STANLEY: (Let's see, what are little girls made of? (*He sings*) I put my right hand in, I pull my right hand out (*he pulls it out empty and laughs*), I put my right hand in (*he pulls out a dress on a hanger and puts it around his neck*) and I shake it all about.)

BLANCHE: I can't approve of any of this, just as you can't approve of my entire life.

STANLEY: I do the hokey-pokey and I turn myself around. That's what it's all about. So this is what little girls are made of. Tiaras, diamond tiaras. (*He puts a tiara on his head*) And what's this? (*He pulls out a gold bracelet and puts it on*) A solid gold Cadillac. This must be worth a fortune. And what have we got here? A box of valuables. (*He tosses the contents onto the floor*) Love letters, scrap books, newspaper clippings.

BLANCHE: Everybody has something they don't want others to touch because of their intimate nature.

STANLEY: (*singing, as Mitch picks up the newspaper clippings*) I put my right foot in, I take my right foot out, I put my right foot in and I shake it all about ... (*Stanley pulls out a high-heeled shoe*)

MITCH: (*as Stanley continues singing*) There was a time when everyone was trying to get a piece of her. These are the pieces left over, "Tipped for the Top," "What an Angel." Now the angel's in the kitchen, washing out the dishes and picking her teeth.

BLANCHE: (*as Mitch hands her the newspaper clippings*) I don't see how any of this relates to my own life except in the way people perceive my fall.

STANLEY: I put my left hand in ... (*he shakes the box violently from inside*)

BLANCHE: (*ripping up the newspaper clippings*) Tearing ... I hear tearing ... be careful ... the wings, you're tearing them!

STANLEY: They're just animals, lady, what's the matter with you?

BLANCHE: But they've been faithful their whole lives. There are things we don't know here.

STANLEY: Things are different now. (*Still struggling inside the box*) I pull the white-feathered excited body of one swan off the white-feathered excited body of another swan. (*He pulls out a handful of feathers*)

BLANCHE: What right have you to interfere with nature?

STANLEY: (*pulling feathers apart to reveal that they are a boa which he drapes across his shoulders*) And shake it all about.

BLANCHE: Birds of a feather.

STANLEY: I put my left hand in ... (*he pulls his hand quickly out*) Oww, Stella, Stella!

STELLA: What?

STANLEY: I burned my hand.

STELLA: Oh, Stanley, it's just candle wax.

STANLEY: I know but it hurts.

STELLA: Some people think it's sexy.

STANLEY: (*pulling his hand away from her*) I can see where it might be sexy if I knew it was coming. I put my left hand in, I pull my left hand out ... oh, a little cheerleading doll ... (*he breaks off the arm*) the arm is busted .. the rubber band must be broken inside.

BLANCHE: My mother gave me that.

STANLEY: (*dancing the doll on top of the trunk*) And I shake it all about ...

BLANCHE: And before that, it was her mother's.

STANLEY: (*slamming the doll down*) Look, lady, I'm just trying to do my job here.

BLANCHE: Yes, of course.

STANLEY: And my job is to make sure you're not smuggling something personal in this here trunk. (*He reaches into the trunk*) Let's see, what's this? And what is this? (*He pulls out a purse*)

BLANCHE: This contains all of my hopes and dreams . . . this is my hope chest.

STANLEY: Hopes and dreams? Forget it. (*He sticks his hand into the purse*) I put my whole body in, I take my whole body out. (*He pulls out a scarf*) I grab myself a frilly thing and shake it all about. I pin it on my shoulders and I sashay up and down, that's what it's all about. Yes? I put my right hand in, I take my right hand out . . . (*He pulls out his hand covered in blood. Blanche and Stella exit. Mitch enters in fading light to roll away the trunk; music and lights slowly fade out. In blackout*) I am suddenly aware that the atmosphere has changed. It's dark. The night has a thousand eyes and they're all looking at me. They're burning into me, burning into my chest. If I don't sleep now, I never will . . . don't panic . . . the night seems to last forever . . . don't panic . . I'm scared, I'm wrong, the night is making me feel . . . (*The lights return suddenly on a curtain with a painting of an oversized clawed foot of a bathtub and a straight razor lying on a tiled floor. Stella is onstage with Stanley. She is wearing a cheerleading outfit and carries a cheerleading doll*) Vivien Leigh, huh? Okay, that's your story and I'm stuck with it for now. But let's see if you can keep up the deception day after day, week after week in front of me. Let that be a challenge to our relationship. But meanwhile, relax, make yourself at home, have a drink. Tell me about yourself, stuff I haven't heard before, recent stuff like how've you been lately. I got all the time in the world and I'm all ears.

STELLA: Stanley, you come out here and let Blanche finish dressing. (*Stanley exits*) I let her keep her hopes and dreams, just like I let her keep her cheerleading memories. I pretended they were mine as well, came to know them as I know my own face in the mirror. A face that was not a twin of my older sister.

BLANCHE: (*entering stage left in a bathrobe*) I think I handled that really well. It's a tricky business, deception in the face of legal documents. Thank heavens for bathrooms, they always make me feel so new.

STELLA: Blanche, honey, are you all right in there? There was no answer, but I could hear her splashing and the sound of her radio.

BLANCHE: I can always refresh my spirits in the bathroom.

STELLA: Blanche, I brought you your lemon Coke.

BLANCHE: All right sweetie. Be right out.

STELLA: I'll wait out here.

BLANCHE: I don't want you to have to wait on me.

STELLA: I like waiting on you Blanche, it feels more like home.

BLANCHE: I must admit, I do like to be waited on.

STELLA: Well, I'm waiting.

BLANCHE: One day I'll probably just dissolve in the bath. They'll come looking for me, but there'll be nothing left. "Drag Queen Dissolves in Bathtub," that'll be the headline. "All that was left was a full head of hair clogging up the plughole. She was exceptional even in death . . ." I wonder where I'll end up. In the sea, I suppose.

STELLA: I'm waiting, Blanche.

BLANCHE: Just a few last finishing touches.

STELLA: Waiting. Waiting in the wings. Waiting for her to get off the phone.

BLANCHE: You wouldn't want me to go out looking a mess, now would you?

STELLA: Waiting for her to come home from Woolworth's with the new Tangee lipstick. And when I wasn't waiting I was following. I used to follow her into the bathroom. I loved the way she touched her cheek with the back of her hand. How she let her hand come to rest just slightly between her breasts as she took one last look in the mirror. I used to study the way she adjusted her hips and twisted her thighs in that funny way when she was changing her shoes. Then she would fling open the bathroom door and sail down the staircase into the front room to receive her gentlemen callers.

BLANCHE: (colliding into Stella, who drops the doll) My doll, it's broken!

STELLA: (laughingly) No it isn't.

BLANCHE: I did. I broke it.

STELLA: No, honey. You didn't.

BLANCHE: Yes I did. I broke it.

STELLA: (shaking Blanche) No, Blanche, it was already broken.

BLANCHE: I don't know why I'm like this today.

STELLA: (embracing her) Blanche, you know what this reminds me of? My homecoming corsage, remember? Before the homecoming parade, when the band and all the floats were gathered in front of the war memorial. It was your senior year, <u>you were the captain of the cheerleaders, and I was the mascot</u>. And they gave us these big orange and maroon chrysanthemums with ribbon streamers; mine was just as big as yours.

BLANCHE: And I pinned it on your shoulder and you were so proud of its size and excited by the smell of it.

STELLA: I felt every bit as tall and glamorous as the real cheerleaders, the majorettes, the homecoming court, even Miss Mississippi herself. I stood in that November air imagining all the things a grownup woman could be ... and then, that great big old football player came walking across the red dirt and smacked right into me.

BLANCHE: And your poor corsage, it started to bleed, it started to lose its petals one by one.

STELLA: And I started to cry. I threw a god-awful fit.

BLANCHE: You certainly did.

STELLA: My whole life was disappearing with those dropping petals. How was I going to present myself in the same parade with Miss Mississippi, her in her strapless gown and me with a handful of petals. But you put your big strong arms around me and set me right up there on the float with ...

BLANCHE: The beauty queen herself. And there you were, all puffy-eyed and corsageless ...

STELLA: Right next to the great white virgin, with her round bare shoulders and her rhinestone tiara.

BLANCHE: (*As the music starts*) And I took your picture and it was in the papers. (*Blanche takes off the bathrobe to reveal a cheerleading outfit and they sing*)

"*Under the Covers*"

BOTH: When life is unfair, and the world makes you sick
    I know somewhere that's bliss on a stick.

STELLA: Somewhere to go when things are unsteady

BLANCHE: Somewhere to go with cocoa and teddy.

BOTH: Under the covers, the pillows and laces
    We both can share, those soft cotton places

STELLA: Lying together like spoons in a drawer

BLANCHE: Then turning over to have an explore ...

BOTH: Under the covers, those smooth satin covers
We share our dreams

STELLA: Like goose downy lovers

BLANCHE: Tucked in together like girls in the dorm

BOTH: Under the covers everything's cozy and warm . . .

They pull hidden pom-poms from each other's sleeves and cheer:

AMO, AMAS, AMAT
WE LOVE OUR TEAM A LOT
WE'RE GONNA FIGHT FIGHT FIGHT
WE'RE GONNA WIN WIN WIN
WE'RE GONNA BE . . .

BLANCHE: FABULOUS.

Tap dance break.

BOTH: Under the covers, it's you and it's me now
Our pleasure grows, because we are two now
Lean on a pillow and look in my eyes
Spreading our knowledge and sharing our thighs
Under the covers, our fingers exploring
Those hidden dreams, we've found there is something

Stella pulls a hand covered in menstrual blood out from under her skirt.

Mother has maybe forgotten to tell
Tho' if she found out
We'd found out
She'd give us hell.

STANLEY: (*yelling from backstage*) Stella!

BLANCHE AND STELLA: She'd give us hell.

STANLEY: Stella!

BLANCHE AND STELLA: She'd give us . . . (*the song dissolves into laughter*)

STANLEY: When are you hens gonna end that conversation?

STELLA: Oh, you can't hear us.

STANLEY: Well, you can hear me, and I say hush up!

STELLA: This is my house too, Stanley, and I'll talk as much as . . .

BLANCHE: (*interrupting her*) Please don't start another row, I couldn't bear it . . . (*She exits*)

STELLA: I tried to follow her, but I got stuck. Stuck in the bathroom, where I saw myself in the medicine chest mirror. I stopped there and I stared. For three days I stared. I wasn't her little sister. And in the mirror I saw the road split, and I took mine . . .

STANLEY: (*grabbing Stella*) Stella. (*They hug; Stella exits; Stanley goes to the bathroom and starts shaving. The lights dim*) blf os weee

MITCH: (*entering stage right. He carries a painting of a card table, which he places over the front of the square box*) Now and then I reached out to touch his wrists. They glittered with a dozen golden bracelets that matched the large earrings he wore. He was like a shimmering waterfall of gold, his whole front covered with golden pendants that looked like coins. Beneath, he wore a purple semitransparent shift that matched the dark makeup around his large bedroom eyes. There was something both fierce and warm in his face. He was glowing with a pagan intensity that matched the intense feelings brimming up in my heart, which in turn matched the brimming purple wine that was being poured, seemingly without end, into our glittering golden goblets that matched the shafts of golden scorching sunlight that poured through the high windows down onto the banqueting table, where they were scattered in a dozen colors as they hit the gold in the glass. Finally, he rose from his throne, which was covered in a mantle of blue macaw feathers that cost ten dollars per square inch and matched the cerulean blue of the deep-piled carpet reputedly made by the tiny fingers of ten-year-old eunuchs within the forbidden city in Peking. Then he began to dance . . .

STANLEY: (*grabbing Mitch by the shoulders*) You know, a bum like me can grow up in a great country like this and be her lover, which is a hell of a better job than being president of the United States.

MITCH: You're a lucky man.

STANLEY: You know, when I think about her, it's like food, I want to eat her, just put her whole leg in my mouth, or her face, or her hands . . .

MITCH: That's a mouthful!

STANLEY: I feel so hungry when I think of her, I could eat my car, I could eat dirt, I could eat a brick wall. I have to, I have no choice. I have to touch things, and my hands bring them to my mouth.

MITCH: Your big hands!

STANLEY: Feelings grow inside me, and sometimes they fly out of me so fast and then smack, I'm out of control. When it comes to big hands, I have no competition. (*Stanley takes a swig of beer*)

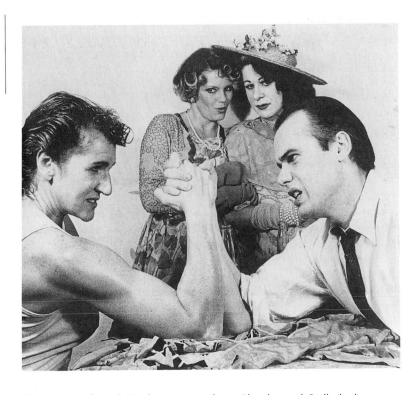

Plate 9   Mitch and Stanley armwrestle as Blanche and Stella look on
Photo: Sheila Burnett

MITCH: When it comes to big hands, she knows she's got your big hands all over her. (*He takes a swig*)

STANLEY: (*challenging him to arm wrestle*) My big pioneer hands all over her rocky mountains.

MITCH: (*taking the challenge*) All over her livestock and vegetation.

STANLEY: Her buffalos and prairies.

MITCH: Her thick forests and golden sunsets.

STANLEY: All over her stars!

MITCH: She's in your hands!

STANLEY: She's in my hands and ... yeeaaa ... (*he pins Mitch's arms down*)

MITCH: That's right! Bite me! Bite me! Suck on me ... oops.

STANLEY: (*pulling away from Mitch*) What are you talking about?

MITCH: Mosquitoes! Biting me, biting me . . .

STANLEY: (*both of them slapping at bugs*) Suck on me, suck on my body!

MITCH: What do you think I'm here for, your entertainment? A Coney Island for you?

STANLEY: A joyride on my ankle! A suck on my wrist! I'll eliminate you! (*He mimes a machine gun and makes a gun noise*)

MITCH: Remove you from my space! Pow!

STANLEY: Away from my body, you aggravating hungry bugger.

MITCH: Bugger off! Away with you!

STANLEY: You're spoiled . . . Splat!

MITCH: You're educated . . . Squash!

STANLEY: You remind me of my fate.

MITCH: You remind me of my immortality! Leave me my blood.

STANLEY: Blood!

MITCH: Bloody sheet.

STANLEY: Bloody night.

MITCH: Blood on your hand!

STANLEY: It's my hand, I'm dealing the cards.

MITCH: (*running after Stanley around the box*) Deal me!

STANLEY: If you want another card I'll hit you with it.

MITCH: Hit me!

STANLEY: When it comes to big hands I got no competition.

MITCH: Take me!

STANLEY: Your shuffle.

MITCH: Cut me in!

STANLEY: Throw your checkbook out the window!

MITCH: Empty my pockets!

STANLEY: I'm a royal flush, I win every time. (*He challenges him to arm wrestle*)

MITCH: (*taking the challenge*) I'm the last sailboat across the horizon before the sun sets.

STANLEY: Nobody can audition for my part. Why not

MITCH: I flop and smash and throw things.

STANLEY: I turn and punch the air!

MITCH: I sweat.

STANLEY: I smell.

MITCH: I smell!

STANLEY: I smell of car oil, I smell of your blood.

MITCH: I smell of . . . cologne!

STANLEY: I'm hungry, ha, hungry! I'm gonna eat rough memories.

MITCH: I'm gonna eat tough dreams.

STANLEY: Digest hard words. Hard, hard words.

MITCH: I'm gonna spit them out!

STANLEY: It's gonna cost you my hunger!

MITCH: I'm gonna pay!

STANLEY: (*grabbing Mitch*) I'm gonna eat my car. I'm gonna eat dirt!

MITCH: I'm gonna eat a tree! Eat your whole leg!

STANLEY: I'm gonna eat the sun and then I'll sweat!

STANLEY AND MITCH: (*in a frenzy*) Bite me! Bite me! Suck on me!

BLANCHE: (*opening the bathroom curtain and entering wearing a man's jacket, pants and cap*) Suck my wrist.

Stanley sings.

"I'm a Man"

STANLEY: When I was a little boy, at the age of five
I had something in my pocket, kept a lot of folks alive
Now I'm a man, made twenty–one
I'll tell you baby, we can have a lot of fun
'Cos I'm a man
Spelled M . . . A . . . N . . . Man
Oohh . . . oowww . . . oowww

All you pretty women, standing in a line
I can make love to you, in an hour's time
'Cos I'm a man
Spelled M . . . A . . . N . . . Man

Dance break.

The line I shoot will never miss
When I make love to you baby, it comes to this
I'm a man

Spelled M ... A ... N ... Man
Oohh ... oowww ... oowww ... owww ...
I'm a man, yes I am, I'm a man ...

STANLEY: (*gradually noticing Blanche has a finger up her nose*) Hold it, hold it. (*To Blanche*) Is there something I can help you with?

BLANCHE: Please could you give me a tissue. I think I've got something stuck up my nose.

STANLEY: Would you like me to have a look?

BLANCHE: Please don't trouble. I think a tissue would probably do it.

STANLEY: (*handing her a tissue*) Here.

BLANCHE: Probably a boogey, I expect.

STANLEY: An acquaintance of mine lost his sense of smell from having a booger stuck up his nose ... better?

BLANCHE: Not really, no.

MITCH: Can I help?

BLANCHE: Oh no, please, it's only something stuck up my nose.

MITCH: Try sticking your little finger in as far as it'll go.

STANLEY: Then blow your nose.

MITCH: Please let me look, I happen to be a doctor.

BLANCHE: It's very kind of you.

MITCH: Turn around to the light please. Now look up. Now look down. Now look up again ... I can see it ... keep still ... (*he twists the tissue and pokes it up her nose*) There!

BLANCHE: Oh dear, what a relief, it was agonizing.

MITCH: (*holding up the tissue*) It looks like a piece of Christmas pudding.

BLANCHE: Thank you very much indeed.

MITCH: Not at all.

BLANCHE: How lucky for me you happened to be here.

MITCH: Anybody could have done it.

BLANCHE: Never mind, you did and I'm most grateful.

MITCH: There's my train ... Goodbye. (*He exits*)

BLANCHE: And that's how it all began, just through me getting a booger stuck up my nose. (*She takes off her cap, turns to face Stanley, then walks away upstage left as the lights dim and music starts. Mitch enters and motions for Blanche to dance with him, as Stanley shuffles a deck of cards*)

STANLEY: Hey Mitch, you in this game or what?

MITCH: Deal me out. I'm talking to Miss DuBois. (*They begin to dance as Stella wanders on*)

STELLA: Look, we made enchantment.

STANLEY: Who turned that on? Turn it off.

STELLA: Ah-h-h-h let them have their music.

STANLEY: I said turn it off!

STELLA: What are you doing?

STANLEY: That's the last time anybody plays music during my game. Now get OUT! OUT! (*The music stops; Stella is laughing quietly*)

STELLA: I guess you think that's funny.

STANLEY: Yeah, I thought it was pretty funny.

STELLA: Well, maybe I blinked at the wrong time, 'cuz I missed the joke.

STANLEY: Oh, so now you're an authority on what's funny.

STELLA: I didn't say that. I said I didn't think that that was funny.

STANLEY: Well, if you know so much, why don't you show me what is funny.

STELLA: Look, I don't want to get twisted out of shape about it, I just didn't think it was all that funny.

STANLEY: Oh, you thought it was just a little bit funny.

STELLA: No, not even a little bit funny.

STANLEY: So, show me!

STELLA: This is ridiculous.

STANLEY: Show me what's funny.

STELLA: You want me to show you what's funny.

STANLEY: Yeah, show me funny.

STELLA: Okay, I'll show you funny ... (*She rips Stanley's sleeve*) That's funny.

STANLEY: That was not funny.

STELLA: You want funny? (*She rips off the other sleeve*) That's funny.

STANLEY: That was not funny.

STELLA: Okay. What about this? (*She rips off half of Stanley's shirt*) Or this? (*She rips off the other half*)

STANLEY: That's not funny.

STELLA: I'll be right back. (*She bustles offstage and comes back with a seltzer bottle, then sprays Stanley*) That was funny.

STANLEY: That was not funny.

STELLA: I'll be right back. (*She comes back with a giant powder puff and powders Stanley*) That was funny.

STANLEY: That's not funny.

STELLA: I'll be right back. (*She comes back with a cream pie. As she nears Stanley, Stanley unexpectedly tips it into Stella's face*)

STANLEY: Now *that* was funny. (*Stanley exits. Mitch enters, pulling a curtain with a painting of a giant orchid. The Cassandra aria from* Les Troyens *comes on loudly, then fades*)

MITCH: The bell sounds and they're both middle weights. They know the rules, and they've been publicized as an even match. 'Ere, you've paid good money to see them, you want to see a battle, you want to see blood. Round One is I Love You, Round Two is You See Me For Who I Really Am. You never see a person more clearly than the first time they lay hands on you. After that, it's all up for grabs. (*To Stella*) He's gonna be back and he's gonna say he's sorry.

STELLA: (*wiping the pie from her face*) Sorry. (*She laughs*) Sorry . . . sorry, sorry. (*laughs*) The Indian women. The Indian women, wrapping their soft bodies in thick silk the colors of a church window. Sari. (*laughs*) I'm sorry too. It makes me laugh. They can't take it back. What the gods give they cannot take back, they can only add to what they've given, to make the gift painful to have. Cassandra! Zeus gave her the gift of the seer, and then she wouldn't have sex with him, but he couldn't take back the gift. He couldn't have her, so he made sure no one would believe her . . . She knew all those men were in that wooden horse, but they wouldn't listen . . . (*laughs*) That's hysterical. It was their loss, that curse! Zeus made a prophetess and then spit in her face. And just what do you think went on inside that horse? Hundreds of warlike men, spitting, smoking, dreaming death in the belly of a fake horse . . . I dream a purple darkness . . . purple . . . the color of the sari . . . darlings. I'm in here. I'm on drugs. I'm braless, shirtless, I'm giggling, I'm lost, I'm in love. I'm stuck in the stomach of a fake horse, can you hear me? I hear you. Cassandra tell me what will happen. I promise I'll believe you! I . . . I'm in love with you Cassandra, you blonde, you seer, you whisperer . . . tell me what's going to happen . . . come here . . . let's make it happen. Please don't, blonde seer. I can't, I'm already married. Take your hands off my breasts, I'm already married. I'm in here. The horse! I'm in the belly of a horse, smoking, shirtless. I'm preparing for a war. (*She begins to strip off her house dress to reveal a tight, strapless dress*) Someone stole my woman, stole her from my house, filched her from history, and I'm here to get her back. I am a powerful warrior. (*She poses like Marilyn Monroe*) Come sweet prophetess, what is going to happen? Tell me, I'm nailed to this story. Cut me down. I'm in here. Can't you see me? I'm having sex with the fortune teller that men don't believe. Sex . . . sex! (*She sings*)

"Running Wild"

STELLA: Running wild, lost control
Running wild, mighty bold
Feeling gay, reckless too
Carefree mind, all the time, never blue
Always going – don't know where
Always showing – I don't care
Don't love nobody, it's not worthwhile
All alone and running wild

Stanley has entered the audience and applauds Stella loudly as the piano starts the intro for Stella's next song.

"Sweet Little Angel"

STELLA: I've got a sweet little angel
And I love the way she spreads her wings
I've got a sweet little angel
And I love the way she spreads her wings
When she spreads those wings over me
She brings joy in everything

STANLEY: (*clapping loudly and talking to the audience*) Is she good or what? She is so good . . . can you believe how good she is? (*Stella stops singing*) Any moment this dame spends out of bed is wasted, totally wasted. (*Stanley runs to Stella and drops to his knees*)

STELLA: I could smell you coming.

STANLEY: You say the sweetest things.

STELLA: Women have to develop a sense of smell. Just in general. Just as a matter of fact. Like in a war. In a war, you learn to smell the enemy. You learn to cross the street. You learn to see through their disguises.

STANLEY: I am not your enemy.

STELLA: No ... but you have many of the characteristics. Not that I go by appearances, just smell and instinct.

STANLEY: What are you looking for?

STELLA: You're tense.

STANLEY: I'm always tense. It keeps me in check, keeps me in balance.

STELLA: It's hard to watch.

STANLEY: That's 'cuz you don't know that it's leading to something.

STELLA: And are you gonna tell me what that is?

STANLEY: It's a fact of life, you figure it out.

STELLA: I already did. I don't have to spend long on the likes of you, not one as experienced as I am. I know that your tension is sexual, and it's a desire that I share in, but not for your pleasure, for my own. I'm lookin' for it, I might not find it in you, I might find it somewhere else, as a matter of fact, and there's nothing you can do about it. You don't satisfy me, you're not real.

STANLEY: Are you saying I'm not a real man?

STELLA: I'm saying you're not real. You're cute. Could be much cuter if you weren't quite so obvious.

STANLEY: Then it wouldn't be me. I am not subtle.

STELLA: Try it, just for tonight.

STANLEY: You mean put it on like clothes? I couldn't pull that off.

STELLA: No, take it off. Take it all off. I want to see what you're really made of. I want to see what it is that makes me want you. That makes me want to have you as I've never had anyone. Strip. Take it off, then we'll talk.

STANLEY: Talk is cheap.

STELLA: I want to see you naked like a baby.

STANLEY: No more talk, let's make a deal.

STELLA: We are partners in this deal. I have my part, you have yours.

STANLEY: I can live up to my end of the deal, how 'bout you.

STELLA: Put your cards on the table, I'm calling your bluff.

Blackout.

STANLEY: Hey, turn on the light!

STELLA: I like it in the dark.

STANLEY: I don't like the dark, I like to see.

STELLA: (*As the lights slowly fade up*) You can see if you get your eyes used to it.

STANLEY: I don't want to get used to it, I'm afraid of the dark.

A low light reveals their silhouettes dancing as the pianist sings.

"Sweet Little Angel"

PIANIST: I've got a sweet little angel
      And I love the way she spreads her wings
      I've got a sweet little angel
      And I love the way she spreads her wings
      When she spreads those wings over me
      She brings joy in everything

      I asked my angel for a nickel
      And she gave me a twenty-dollar bill
      I asked my angel for a nickel
      And she gave me a twenty-dollar bill
      When I asked her for her body
      She said she'd leave it to me in her will . . .

      Well my angel if she quit me
      I believe I would die
      Well my angel if she quit me
      I believe I would die
      If you don't believe me
      You must tell me the reason why.

Stella has pulled off Stanley's ripped T-shirt as they dance. She jumps up and wraps her body around Stanley and throws the shirt to the ground as they exit. Blackout.

ACT TWO

The stage is empty except for the large rectangular box on its side, with the painting of a tub across the front. A dim orange light comes up on Stella standing and stretching in the bathtub in her slip.

STELLA: The fire is keeping me awake. It reminds me of the night Yellow Mountain was burning. All night long I could see Yellow

Read picture

Plate 10   Stanley in the famous Marlon Brando T-shirt pose with Stella
Photo: Sheila Burnett

Mountain burning on my bedroom ceiling. I was afraid that the burning debris would fall from the mountain on to our roof and burn through the ceiling. Meet up with a flicker that was already there, waiting to devour me.

MITCH: (*A light behind the scrim reveals Blanche in a nightgown holding a cigarette and Mitch standing beside her. Mitch lights her cigarette*) There's a shadow over by the window. It's a woman. She's smoking a cigarette. (*Blanche blows smoke into Mitch's face; he coughs*) The smoke is coming my way. Maybe she wants me to go with her. (*Blanches passes around the scrim and crosses to center stage, where she picks up Stanley's torn T-shirt*)

STELLA: The fire has leapt out of control. It's too late, the firemen have all gone home to their wives. Had to hose down their own houses, to protect them from the falling debris.

BLANCHE: (*examining Stanley's shirt*) This shirt smells of success to me. These elements of manhood . . . there's something about Stanley I can't quite put my finger on. I can't put my finger on his smell. I don't believe he's a man. I question his sexuality. His postures are not real, don't seem to be coming from a true place. He's a phoney, and he's got her believing it, and if she has children he'll have them believing it and when he dies, they'll find out. (*She crosses to Stella*) Have you ever seen him naked?

STELLA: (*drinking Coke*) It's the sugar that satisfies me. The cool liquid running down my throat is only temporary. It's when the sugar hits the bloodstream, that's when my heart starts pumping.

BLANCHE: There's something about the way he smells, something about the way he has to prove his manhood all the time, that makes me suspicious. I'm looking at the shape, not the content.

STELLA: (*straddling the edge of the tub*) Don't you love that feeling when you lean against a solid surface and you can feel your heart beating under your body.

BLANCHE: The noises he makes, the way he walks like Mae West, the sensual way he wears his clothes, this is no garage-mechanic working-class boy, this is planned behavior. This is calculated sexuality, developed over years of picking up signals not necessarily genetic is what I'm trying to say.

STELLA: I remember leaning my abdomen against the cold sink and feeling my heart beating between my legs.

BLANCHE: I'm trying to say, what I mean is, perhaps he was a man in some former life. Perhaps he's just a halfway house, to lure you into a sexual trap, a trap well laid, with just the right flavors, just

the right mood to seduce you ... what I'm trying to say is, I think
he's a fag. upins?

STELLA: The thing about Coca-Cola is that one sixteen-ounce bottle
has more than four tablespoons of sugar.

BLANCHE: But now you have the chance to get out. To end this
charade before it's too late ...

STELLA: Enough to keep you up half the night.

BLANCHE: Only someone as skilled as I am at being a woman can
pick up these subtle signs.

STELLA: Enough to curb your appetite.

BLANCHE: I'm well trained, equipped. I know how to talk to him,
to flirt with him, not get involved really, to decorate his arm, to aid
him in his charade, to give him a passing grade.

STELLA: Sugar in a sixteen-ounce bottle.

BLANCHE: (grabbing Stella's hand) I'm the real woman for you. I
can show you satisfaction. A rewarding, cultural life; me and you,
you and me, Blanche and Stella, Stella and Blanche ... You were
such a pretty girl. (Stella pulls away) What day was it that you
changed? You were tipped for the top and you threw it all away.
You were headed upward to the good, right life and suddenly you
changed.

STELLA: Pure sugar, liquid sex.

BLANCHE: Stella, you haven't been listening to a word I've been
saying.

STELLA: (Stanley has come through the audience and is standing
facing Stella and Blanche) The fire is still burning ... my clothes
sticking to my chest just like Mama's dress against her naked belly.
Now why did she stay at the sink so long ... (She walks towards
Stanley) and every day without underwear. (She jumps into Stanley's
arms)

STANLEY: Hey! (Stanley spins her around, then they walk offstage
together)

BLANCHE: Trouble is, Marlon Brando does look gorgeous. And I
know that if I met him at the time he was in that film I'd want to
lick his armpits. I don't suppose he'd be able to open himself up to
that though ... surrender himself. But he does have that big shapely
mouth ... I guess I'm pretty taken with this actor in the film. But
what if the film was life and I could just walk right into it? I don't
suppose he'd welcome me, probably give me a hard time. Just like

he gave Blanche ... I mean Miss Leigh ... and what would she say if this drag queen poured out of the camera lens and blew up to size right there in front of her. Yes, well, she had to deal with Marlon Brando all day and Laurence Olivier in the evenings ... I'd say she had enough problems without me on the set ... I feel like an old hotel. (*Pianist starts the prelude to "Beautiful Dream"*) Beautiful bits of dereliction in need of massive renovation. There's that record again. Have you ever had something stuck in your head for a very long time, like a record playing over and over and every time it stops there's applause, and then it starts all over again ... (*The music stops and Blanche ticks her hand in the tub*) I like a warm bath. It's the warmth I'm after, not the cleanliness. I don't even mind Stella's cheap, common soap ... Oh I did it you know, I did lead the grand life ... chauffeurs, limos. I used to go to clubs and know I was the most attractive person there ... now I don't go to clubs.

STANLEY: (*pulling in the painted vaudeville curtain behind Blanche*) Ha Ha.

BLANCHE: (*with the music beginning again*) Now, here it comes ... the record ... and there's a dark burgundy curtain opening on the stage, and there we are, just me and Vivien ...

STANLEY: HA HA. Did you hear what I said? HA HA HA. (*He exits*)

BLANCHE: (*singing*)

"Beautiful Dream"

> Cold wind blowing through the empty rooms
> Windows broken, floors damp and rotten now
> No sound in the silence
> No step in the stillness
> No warmth in the cold air
> Only shadows moving in the half-light
> Empty lockers, lines of empty hooks
> Vacant showers, all deep in dust now
> Just a modest price bought you paradise
> No one wondered would it last
> Running out of stream, now the beautiful dream
> Has passed.

> No one greets me as I step inside
> Hot and ready for whatever comes my way
> No warm body waiting for me
> No pulse of a warm heart near me
> No strong arms around me
> No one lying warm and sweet beside me

Thought we'd party 'til the end of time
But it's over, seems so long ago now
Down the long parade, see them slowly fade
As they all leave one by one
Running out of steam, now the beautiful dream
Has gone.

So I fill the tub, rub-a-dub-dub-dub
But I still freeze up inside
'Cuz the water's cold
And the dream has grown old and died
Running out of steam
Now the beautiful dream
Has gone.

(The lights fade, the curtain is pulled offstage, Blanche moves to the tub upstage left and climbs in) Bubbles, bawbles, bumholes . . . (*She smells the soap*) Municipal, that's the word. Now I'm going under . . . can't hear the noises at all . . . just the odd humps and hoomps and grinds . . . my hair is floating about . . . whooosh . . . up in the air again. (*Blanche reappears in the tub wearing the bubble dress as a ukelele strums in the background*) Listen . . . there it is again, the record, going around and around and then the applause. Until something replaces that song and that wild applause, I know I'll cling to it. I'll always choose applause over death.

Lights behind the scrim reveal Mitch in fairy costume perched on a ladder and looking down on Blanche in the tub. He is playing the ukelele and singing.

"The Fairy Song"

MITCH: I was sitting on my asteroid, way up in the sky
        When I saw you through the window, and I thought I'd
            drop by
        You were looking sad, bothered and forlorn
        Wondering where your days of youth and beauty all had
            gone.

        Now I don't possess a magic wand, my wings are rather
            small
        As far as fairies go I'm nothing special at all
        But still I've got that something that I know you'll just
            adore
        That special kind of magic, gonna sweep you off the floor.

CHORUS

        I'm a supernatural being, I'm your sweetie-pie
        And I've come here from somewhere far, away up in the sky

I'm here to play a song tonight by Rimsky-Korsakov
And if you play your cards right we might even have it off.

Blanche mouths the words as Mitch continues singing.

Now I was sitting in the bathtub, minding my own biz
When this vision came from outer space and now I'm in a tiz
He was gorgeous, he was handsome, he was eager just to please
And he said that he'd come here so me and him could have a
    squeeze.

I'm a supernatural being, I'm your sweetie-pie
And I've come here from somewhere far, away up in the sky
I'll take you to my fairy dell, in my fairy car
And hang a sign "Do not disturb" upon the evening star.

Dance break, Blanche twirls around and motions Mitch to join her.
They dance.

BLANCHE: *(speaking)* Are you sure that you're a fairy?
           I'd imagined they were blonde.
           And frankly I'm not leaving 'til I've seen your magic
           wand.

MITCH: *(singing)* My wand, alas, I left at home, you'll have to come
        on spec
        But I promise when we get there you can hold it for a sec.

CHORUS

Mitch and Blanche exit. Blanche re-enters with Stella and Stanley,
who resets the table box and holds a birthday cake

STANLEY: *(singing in monotone)* Happy birthday to you, happy
birthday to you, happy birthday . . . Blanche, happy birthday to you.

BLANCHE: What a lovely cake. How many candles are on it?

STELLA: Don't you worry about that right now. Why don't you tell
us one of your funny stories.

BLANCHE: I don't think Mr. Kowalski would be interested in any
of my funny stories.

STANLEY: I've got a funny story, what about this: there's these two
faggots sitting on the sofa, which one is the cocksucker? *(Long pause)*
The one with the feathers coming out of his mouth.

BLANCHE: In the version I heard it was two pollacks.

STANLEY: I am not a pollack. People from Poland are Poles. There
is no such thing as a pollack. And in any case, for your information, I am one hundred percent American.

STELLA: Well, now that we're all getting along so well, why don't you blow out the candles, Blanche, and make a wish.

STANLEY: Be careful what you wish for.

Blanche blows out all the candles. They relight. She blows them out again, but again they relight. As she goes to blow them out again, Stanley brushes her aside and sticks the candles upside down in the cake one by one. Blackout. The bathtub is removed and a painting of an oversized naked light bulb is pulled onstage.

STANLEY: Stella! Blanche! Mitch! It's dark. I'm afraid.

STELLA: Let's play a game. (*She blindfolds him and spins him around*)

STANLEY: This is not funny. Stella. Mitch. (*The lights slowly fade up. Stanley is wandering around the stage blindfolded*) Don't panic . . . I feel these original sins burning into me. I feel I'm never safe. There I am at four a.m. with giant monsters spelling out my life in large slimy letters above my body, just far enough above it to heat it up. To make my skin bead in sweat starting just under my hair, above my forehead, on the back of my neck, on my chest and the back of my knees. Don't panic . . . I was born this way. I didn't learn it at theatre school. I was born butch. I'm so queer I don't even have to talk about it. It speaks for itself, it's not funny. Being butch isn't funny . . . don't panic . . . I fall to pieces in the night. I'm just thousands of parts of other people all mashed into one body. I am not an original person. I take all these pieces, snatch them off the floor before they get swept under the bed, and I manufacture myself. When I'm saying I fall to pieces, I'm saying Marlon Brando was not there for me. (*Pianist starts playing softly*) James Dean failed to come through, where was Susan Hayward when I needed her, and Rita Hayworth was nowhere to be found. I fall to pieces at the drop of a hat. Just pick the piece you want and when I pull myself back together again I'll think of you. I'll think of you and what you want me to be. (*He sings all the verses to a song in the style of the Frank Sinatra hit "My Way," while crawling onto the table with the birthday cake and presents on it. As he gets to his knees on top of the table, one hand breaks through a box and comes out covered in blood, the other hand goes into the cake and then into a box filled with feathers. He sings the final stanza kneeling on the cake*) WHERE THE FUCK IS EVERYBODY?! (*Blackout. After a short pause the lights come up on Stella and Stanley*) What time is it?

STELLA: It's four a.m.

STANLEY: Help me make it through the night.

STELLA: Don't I always?

STANLEY: I'll be tired tomorrow, I'll be tired all day.

STELLA: Don't think about tomorrow. (*They embrace and kiss as the lights fade to black. The lights come up upstage right on Mitch stuffing cake into his mouth*)

MITCH: (*talking with his mouth full throughout*) I think it all started to go wrong when I wasn't allowed to be a boy scout. There were more important things to be done. Vacuuming, clearing up at home, putting the garbage out. I used to get so angry putting out the garbage, I'd kick the shit out of the garbage cans in front. I thought about what I was missing. It gave me a repulsion for physical activity. Swimming was the only exception, and even then it took me a long time to learn, as I was afraid of deep water. Then one day I fell in love with a beautiful young man. He came like a messenger from another world bearing a message of simple physical desire. But it was already too late, for me everything about the body was bound up with pain and boredom. I even used to eat fast because I found it so boring. Soon the boy left. He knew better than to spend his life cooking dinners for someone with poor appetite. Then I was alone. I lived in a small room near a fly-over. I stopped going out except to go to the laundry and get groceries. At night I would lie awake on my bed, and imagine I could hear things. (*The sound of a ukelele from offstage. He opens one of the gift boxes on the table and the sound comes again. He reaches into the box and pulls out a ukelele, then sings a song in the style of "The Man I Love," by George and Ira Gershwin. As he sings, tap-dancing Chinese lanterns – the remaining members of the cast in lantern costumes – enter and begin dancing around him. During the song the lanterns begin running into each other and floundering around the stage. The audience begins to hear them mumbling from under their costumes*)

BLANCHE: Oh, what are we doing? I can't stand it! I want to be in a real play! (*bright light pops on as Stella drops her lantern to the floor*) With real scenery! White telephones, French windows, a beginning, a middle and an end! This is the most confusing show I've ever been in. What's wrong with red plush? What's wrong with a theme and a plot we can all follow? There isn't even a fucking drinks trolley. Agatha Christie was right.

STELLA: Now we all talked about this, and we decided that realism works against us.

BLANCHE: Oh we did, did we?

STELLA, STANLEY AND MITCH: Yes we did!

BLANCHE: But I felt better before, I could cope. All I had to do was learn my lines and not trip over the furniture. It was all so clear.

And here we are romping about in the avant-garde and I don't know what else. I want my mother to come and have a good time. She's seventy–three for chrissake. You know she's expecting me to play Romeo before it's too late. What am I supposed to tell her? That I like being a drag-queen? She couldn't bear it. I know she couldn't. She wants me to be in something realistic, playing a real person with a real job, like on television.

STELLA: <u>You want realism?</u>

BLANCHE: What do you mean?

STELLA: You want realism, you can have it.

BLANCHE: You mean like in a real play?

STELLA: If that's what you want.

BLANCHE: With Marlon Brando and Vivien Leigh?

STELLA: You think you can play it?

BLANCHE: I have the shoulders.

STANLEY: I have the pajamas ... okay, let's go for it. (*Mitch and Stella exit, striking the light bulb curtain. Stanley sweeps the table with his forearm knocking the cake and presents to the floor*) I cleared my place, want me to clear yours? It's just you and me now, Blanche.

BLANCHE: You mean we're alone in here?

STANLEY: Unless you got someone in the bathroom. (*He takes off his pajama top and pulls out a bottle of beer*)

BLANCHE: Please don't get undressed without pulling the curtain.

STANLEY: Oh, this is all I'm gonna undress right now. Feel like a shower? (*He opens the beer and shakes it, then lets it squirt all over the stage, then pours some over his head before drinking it*) You want some?

BLANCHE: No thank you.

STANLEY: (*moving towards her, menacingly*) Sure I can't make you reconsider?

BLANCHE: Keep away from me.

STANLEY: What's the matter, don't you trust me? Afraid I might touch you or something? You should be so lucky. Take a look at yourself in that worn-out party dress from a third-rate thrift store. What queen do you think you are?

BLANCHE: (*trying to get past him*) Oh God.

STANLEY: (*blocking her exit*) I got your number baby.

BLANCHE: Do we have to play this scene?

STANLEY: You said that's what you wanted.

BLANCHE: But I didn't mean it.

STANLEY: You wanted realism.

BLANCHE: Just let me get by you.

STANLEY: Get by me? Sure, go ahead.

BLANCHE: You stand over there.

STANLEY: You got plenty of room, go ahead.

BLANCHE: Not with you there! I've got to get by somehow!

STANLEY: You can get by, there's plenty of room. I won't hurt you. I like you. We're in this together, me and you. We've known that from the start. We're the extremes, the stereotypes. We are as far as we can go. We have no choice, me and you. We're tried it all, haven't we? We've rejected ourselves, not trusted ourselves, mirrored ourselves, and we always come back to ourselves. We're the warriors. We have an agreement ... there's plenty in this world for both of us. We don't have to give each other up to anyone. You are my special angel.

 BLANCHE: You wouldn't talk this way if you were a real man.

STANLEY: No, if I was a real man I'd say, "Come to think of it, you wouldn't be so bad to interfere with."

BLANCHE: And if I were really Blanche I'd say, "Stay back ... don't come near me another step ... or I'll ..."

STANLEY: You'll what?

BLANCHE: Something's gonna happen here. It will.

STANLEY: What are you trying to pull?

BLANCHE: (*pulling off one of her stiletto-heeled shoes*) I warn you ... don't!

STANLEY: Now what did you do that for?

BLANCHE: So I could twist this heel right in your face.

STANLEY: You'd do that, wouldn't you?

BLANCHE: I would, and I will if you ...

STANLEY: You want to play dirty? I can play dirty. (*He grabs her arm*) Drop it. I said drop it! Drop the stiletto!

BLANCHE: You think I'm crazy or something?

STANLEY: If you want to be in this play you've got to drop the stiletto.

BLANCHE: If you want to be in this play you've got to make me!

STANLEY: If you want to play a woman, the woman in this play gets raped and goes crazy in the end.

BLANCHE: I don't want to get raped and go crazy. I just wanted to wear a nice frock, and look at the shit they've given me!

STELLA: (*entering with Mitch*) Gimme that shoe! (*Pianist starts "Pushover" as she grabs Stanley and sings to him*)

"Pushover"

STELLA: All the girls think you're fine, they even call you Romeo,
You've got 'em, yeah you've got 'em runnin' to and fro, oh yes you have.
But I don't want a one-night thrill, I want a love that's for real,
And I can tell by your lies, yours is not the lasting kind.

You took me for a pushover, you thought I was a pushover,
I'm not a pushover, you thought that you could change my mind.

Mitch sings to Blanche.

MITCH: So you told all the boys that were gonna take me out
You even, yeah you even had the nerve to make a bet, oh yes you did,
That I, I would give in, all of my love you would win,
But you haven't, you haven't won it yet.

You took me for a pushover, you thought I was a pushover,
I'm not a pushover, you thought my love was easy to get.

MITCH AND STELLA: Your tempting lips, your wavy hair,
Your pretty eyes with that come hither stare,
It makes me weak, I start to bend and then I stop and think again,
No, no, no don't let yourself go.
I wanna spoil your reputation, I want true love, not an imitation,
And I'm hip, to every word in your conversation.
You took me for a pushover, I'm not a pushover,
You can't push me over, you thought I was a pushover ...

STELLA: (*to the audience*) Did you figure it out yet? Who's who, what's what, who gets what, where the toaster is plugged in? Did you get what you wanted?

STANLEY: Hey Stella, I just figured it out. Wasn't Blanche blonde?

STELLA: That's right. And come to think of it, it was suspicious she didn't have a southern accent.

STANLEY: I knew it all along. The person we've been referring to as your sister is an imposter.

STELLA: Incredible! There's no flies on you Stanley.

STANLEY: What did you say?

STELLA: I said there's no disguising you, Stanley. You're one hundred percent.

STANLEY: I thought you said something else . . . something about flies.

STELLA: Well, come to think of it, there is something in that area I've been meaning to open up a little.

STANLEY: So, you figured it out.

STELLA: Yeah, I figured it out.

STANLEY: And in those shoes. Un-fuckin'-believable! You know what this means?

STELLA: No, what?

STANLEY: This means that you are the only thing we can rely on, because you are at least who you seem to be.

STELLA: Well Stanley, there's something I've been meaning to tell you . . . (*She sings*)

> *You took me for a pushover (All join in) I'm not a pushover*
> *You can't push me over, you thought I was a pushover.*
> *DON'T PUSH!*

Encore.

"I Love My Art"

> *I've been mad about the stage since childhood,*
> *When I roamed the sage and wildwood,*
> *The attraction for the dazzling lights,*
> *Caused me troublesome nights*
> *Now I realize my one ambition*
> *I can make a full and frank admission,*
> *I am madly in love with my art, I love to play my part,*

I love the theatre, I love it better than all my life, and just because
It's so entrancing, the song and dancing, to the music of applause,
I love the stage and all about it, it simply goes right to my heart,
I love the glamour, I love the drama,
I love I love I love my art
I love the glamour, I love the drama
I love I love I love my art

THE END

LESBIANS WHO KILL

DEB MARGOLIN IN COLLABORATION WITH PEGGY SHAW AND LOIS WEAVER

Directed by Lois Weaver
Performed by Peggy Shaw and Lois Weaver
Assisted by Karena Rahall
Musical direction and sound design by Laka Daisical
Costumes by Susan Young
Lights by Howard Theis
Choreography by Stormy Brandenberger
Backdrop artists Nancy Bardawil and Matthew Owen

Originally produced in May 1992 at The Club at La Mama
E.T.C., 74 E. 4th Street, New York

Copyright: Margolin, Shaw, Weaver, 1996

ORIGINAL SONGS
"The Rain Is on the Roof," words and music by Laka Daisical
"Boogey Man," words by Peggy Shaw, music by Laka Daisical

CHARACTERS

MAY (Lois Weaver) ~~June fellows May~~
JUNE (Peggy Shaw)

*The play takes place in a car parked outside the house of May and
June somewhere in the southern United States during a thunder-
storm. The set consists of a front and back seat of a car placed on
stage as if the car was still intact. Behind the seats there is a dark
and ominous painted backdrop of a driveway leading to a simple
cinderblock country house. The porch light is on. The lighting instru-
ments should be placed on stage on trees along the sides of the car
seats to give the effect of a television set.*

*The lights come up on May and June, <u>dressed in clothes from a
forties film,</u> in the front seat of a car, in front of a dark house in
a storm.*

JUNE: We live in a house that attracts lightning, and every time it
storms, May makes us come out and sit in the car. It's because of
the tires, she says they keep us from getting fried. One time she said
she saw a ball of lightning roll into the house, roll around the top
of the stove, the sink, the kitchen cabinet. Smelling hot, looking for
somewhere to land. May said it was looking for us. So we got smart,
we sat in the car. It's not us though, it's the house. The people who
lived here before us, they sat in their car too.

*Blackout. The lights come up in a 'film noir' style on June in the
front seat and May in the back seat. They lip-synch to dialogue
taken from the sound track of a movie in the style of Deception,
starring Claude Rains and Bette Davis, in which a woman shoots a
man. May plays the Bette Davis-type killer and June plays the
incensed and unbelieving Claude Rains-type man. During the course
of the lip-synched dialogue May pulls a gun and eventually shoots
June who falls dead in the front seat. May overdramatizes her shock
at what she's done and throws the gun into front seat, covering her
mouth in horror. Blackout.*

RADIO: (*in the blackout*) Someone sinister may be at work on the
highways of North Florida. So far the trail is eight victims long,
each signpost along the way a bullet-riddled body of a middle-aged
white man. A Citrus County man, missing since June, might be
victim number nine. Investigators are looking for two women seen
driving the missing man's car.

*Thunder and lightning as the lights come up on the front and back
seats of the car. May and June are in the exact positions from the*

last scene, but in different costumes. May is wearing a blue nurse's uniform and June is wearing a blue workman's uniform.

MAY: Guess what I did today.

JUNE: What? What did you do?

MAY: Guess.

JUNE: You quit your job at the hospital.

MAY: No.

JUNE: You planted forsythia.

MAY: No.

JUNE: You leaned over and kissed yourself in the mirror.

MAY: No.

JUNE: What?

MAY: One more guess.

JUNE: Tell me.

MAY: No.

JUNE: Tell me.

MAY: You know.

JUNE: How can I know?

MAY: Because I smell of it!

JUNE: You smell like dirt.

MAY: I washed!

JUNE: Garden dirt.

MAY: That's a good smell.

JUNE: It's okay.

MAY: I killed a guy.

JUNE: In your dreams!

MAY: Stop it! (*She climbs into the front seat*)

JUNE: I like that expression.

MAY: I hate it! (*She accidentally sits on the gun, pulls it out, then hides it under the front console*)

JUNE: In your dreams!

MAY: June –

JUNE: No, I read in a magazine that women say that to men all the time. In your dreams! It means, fat chance! Guess again!

MAY: You wish!

JUNE: Sometime, honey.

MAY: Some other time!

Pause. Lightning and thunder.

JUNE: How much longer?

MAY: You doubt me, don't you.

JUNE: Only that you don't dream. How much longer?

MAY: As long as it takes.

JUNE: What takes?

MAY: Storms are like fits; they take as long as they take.

JUNE: How long is that?

MAY: Storms can do anything. When they've had it up to here they can blow you away.

JUNE: Is it really that bad out there?

MAY: Nah, she's just thinking about it.

JUNE: She's dreaming about it.

MAY: You can want to kill somebody.

JUNE: You sure can.

MAY: You can look at somebody and get sick.

JUNE: You could just throw up!

MAY: You can murder someone in your thoughts, you can murder someone just because of who they are.

JUNE: In your ... thoughts.

MAY: I'm a murderer.

JUNE: A murderer?

MAY: Murderer! Murderer!

May picks up a flashlight as if to hit June over the head. June grabs it and shines the flashlight in May's face in mock interrogation

JUNE: Answer me. If you know what's good for you, you'll come clean. Why'd you do it?

MAY: (*in Bette Davis character*) I didn't do it!

JUNE: You said that before!

MAY: And I'll say it again. I can keep it up as long as you can.

JUNE: Listen, sister, you're gonna fry for this. It means the hot seat for you.

MAY: It does if you can pin it on me, and I don't think you can.

JUNE: I think I can.

MAY: I didn't really kill anybody.

JUNE: (*disappointed*) I thought maybe you did.

MAY: (*as May*) I thought about it. I don't have an alibi. I can't account for my time, for my time during the murder.

June turns off the flashlight and they go back to the previous state

JUNE: It's not that much time.

MAY: Hours pass and you don't get anything done.

JUNE: You pass the time.

MAY: Killing time.

JUNE: So little time.

JUNE: Once I dreamt that she was dying, . . . funny, the dream . . . although she was perfectly healthy, she was dying because death was . . . persistent . . . well organized, and persistent . . . she had, I don't know . . . a problem, like when a sleeper gets tangled up in the bedsheet . . . something tortuous that just waking up would have solved . . . but death was persistent, well organized and persistent . . . she was naked, on her back, pelvis tilted upward, and death was leaning over her, wooing her . . . she protested . . . the tilted pelvis showed resistance . . . she always resisted with that part of herself . . . I dreamt she died that way.

I never told her though. She hates my dreams. She says people make up dreams, that dreams are things people make up during the daytime so they can give themselves credit for great imaginings at night. She doesn't dream she says. She doesn't dream because at night she does things. She does real things. She gardens at night. Often. In March. She gardens all night, on her hands and knees, making Braille readings of the small, fruitless earth outside her bedroom window. She can tell weed from flower by her hands, she always says that. She says weeds were soft, but flowers cut her palms, bite her fingers, draw blood. In the mornings her hands are fluttering with little wounds: mine are white and clean, I've been dreaming.

June turns and shines the flashlight on May who is sorting seeds in the rear window of the car

MAY: I'll tell you the whole truth, just not right now. Later maybe in an hour, or a week or a year, just not right now. (*She assumes the "interrogation position" sitting in the back window of the car*) Yeah I knew him. I knew him but not well. We had fun. I showed him the time of his life, such as it was. But he's gone now and don't you think that is better? You don't? Are you going to take his side? Oh good, good, take his side. Take his whole body, nobody else wanted it I'm afraid. Not now anyway. Maybe later. I'm doing my best, you know that. (*Thunder and lightning; June turns off the flashlight and turns around; May slides back down into the back seat*)

JUNE: Here comes the rain.

MAY: Yeah, you can smell it.

JUNE: All this rain is good for stuff.

MAY: What stuff?

JUNE: Plants.

MAY: You better shut that window.

A big clap of thunder, as June slides over into the passenger seat to close the window. May grabs her from behind.

MAY: Let's take a plane. Fly somewhere.

JUNE: Where?

MAY: I don't know. The Yukon.

JUNE: Where's the Yukon again?

MAY: I forget.

JUNE: I know you do.

Bigger clap of thunder; May frantically crawls over into driver's seat

MAY: Thunder.

JUNE: Do you want to play looks like/is like?

MAY: Yeah.

JUNE: Looks like/is like ... you start.

MAY: Hummingbird.

JUNE: Needle and thread.

MAY: Green lamé.

JUNE: Electricity.

MAY: Precision.

JUNE: Sudden chance.

MAY: Free will.

JUNE: Peeing.

MAY: Peeing?

JUNE: Explanation.

MAY: Not necessarily.

JUNE: You want one?

MAY: Don't know.

JUNE: Yes or no?

MAY: Yes. Looks like?

JUNE: Is like. The flash that lets you know you have to pee.

MAY: That's bogus.

JUNE: How do you know you have to pee?

MAY: I feel the urge to pee!

JUNE: In a flash of speed like a hummingbird at the blossom!

MAY: Not in a flash of speed like a hummingbird at the blossom!
Just an *urge*!

JUNE: Like a flash.

MAY: An *urge*.

JUNE: In a flash.

Thunder.

MAY: Sure. You win. Start another one.

JUNE: Same one, different one?

MAY: Different one.

JUNE: Diamond ring.

MAY: Okay. Hall of mirrors.

JUNE: Prism.

MAY: Spring air.

JUNE: Love.

MAY: Explanation. Looks like or is like?

JUNE: Is like.

MAY: In what way?

JUNE: It's a symbol of love.

MAY: Doesn't count. Symbols don't count. Try again.

JUNE: Okay. Diamond ring ... Ice.

MAY: Ideas.

JUNE: Roller coaster.

MAY: Is like?

JUNE: Looks like ...

MAY: The setting, you mean ...

JUNE: The metal part holding up the stone looks like the scaffolds.

MAY: Good one!

JUNE: Thanks! (*Silence*) Your turn. Same word.

MAY: Crocodile eyes.

JUNE: What?

MAY: Explanation?

JUNE: Yes ... is like ...?

MAY: Looks like.

JUNE: A diamond ring?

MAY: I saw this picture in a magazine. A man took pictures of a river at night where crocodiles swim, some river or other in some country or other and it was just black with brilliant sparklings in it like diamonds, and those diamonds were the crocodiles' eyes reflecting light. And it said they do that in wars, they take night pictures to see enemy eyes.

May's eyes are closed and there's a big flash of lightning.

JUNE: Lightning!

MAY: Sciatica.

JUNE: No, no, I'm not playing.

MAY: Explanation?

JUNE: No! Lightning!

MAY: You saw lightning?

JUNE: Yes!

MAY: Did it hit the house again?

JUNE: Yes. It did!

MAY: Are you sure?

JUNE: Yes I'm sure.

A huge crash of thunder; May hides her face in June's lap.

MAY: Tell me everyone you saw today.

JUNE: I saw a lady and a man.

MAY: Were they in love?

JUNE: They were completely fake.

MAY: Fake, sweetheart?

JUNE: They looked down out of their balcony at the swimming pool, and then they came down in their bathing suits.

MAY: Like Romeo and Juliet!

JUNE: All fucked up!

MAY: Yes all fucked up.

JUNE: I was listening to them. They didn't even know each other.

MAY: And you saw them together on the balcony?

JUNE: Yes ... he was holding her legs in the pool and she said ... where are you from? And ... did you just get in today? And ... what line of work are you in?

MAY: What did she look like?

JUNE: She didn't look like anything. She was thin.

MAY: What else?

JUNE: Just thin and her legs were white.

MAY: Like a church.

JUNE: Just like a church.

MAY: And then what?

JUNE: He showed her an exercise.

MAY: What kind of exercise?

JUNE: I don't know. For your hands.

Big flash of lightning and thunder; May hides her face in June's lap again.

MAY: What about your hands?

JUNE: I don't know.

MAY: Was he paying her? Was she paid, d'ya think?

JUNE: She said she was from a small town and barely knew her father.

MAY: She said that to him?

JUNE: Yes. And he was holding her legs in the pool. And he said *I travel a lot* so she said *what airline did you fly in on?* And he said *United*. And she said *United?* And swam away from him.

MAY: Let's murder him.

JUNE: Kill him ...

MAY: What did he look like?

JUNE: I don't remember.

MAY: You don't remember?

JUNE: Not at all. He was big and old with thick shoulders and white hair and Farina face.

MAY: Picture it, we're having a drink.

JUNE: What are we having?

MAY: Make it a sloe gin fizz.

Blackout.

RADIO: The women are not being called suspects and the slayings are not officially termed serial killings. However, the similarities are so striking that investigators feel compelled to warn the public, particularly middle-aged white men travelling alone. There's a possibility one or more persons are out there targeting these individuals.

The lights come up, June is lying on her back on the front seat with her pants around her ankles. Mary is lying on top of her with her dress unzipped. Time has passed. They've just finished having sex.

MAY: (*spelling the word in the air with her foot*) S ... L ... O .. . E ... I can feel the "e" in sloe with my pussy ... words like SLOE and blackthorn. Fem words, drunk words, dark garden words ... that "e," like a crack, opening me one place to another ... Slow like the speed, is regular ... normal ... in the house, under the light, by the table ... slow ... take it slow ... but the other kind, the dark plum ... the drunken liquor ... the colored bitter, the taste ... the tongue ... is in my garden ... midnight thorn ... snags my fingers like a sniper ... I love that pain, the pain of the thorn

Plate 11   May and June singing "When Hearts Are Passing in the Night"
Photo: Diane Ceresa of Spark Ceresa

in the dark, while I garden . . . men fight wars but I garden in the dark . . . the thorn seeks my finger . . . enters my thumb like a sniper's bullet . . . it comes from nowhere . . . it hurts . . . an invisible fear . . . a way of loving . . . the "e" in sloe . . . I feel it in my sleep . . . I feel it deep where you're empty . . . that "e" in sloe slides on my hand deep where you are empty . . . garden dirt and you on the same hand . . . that's where life comes from . . . dirt and water . . . and heat . . . nights when it's hot . . . nights when the dark doesn't get rid of the heat . . . the heat stays, like an overnight guest . . . call the police . . . tell them a stranger's car is parked in front of mine . . . the heat, my hand in you, stroking the "e" inside you . . .

The theme from a stereotypically romantic movie, like A Man and a Woman comes on the radio. May and June light cigarettes, pour champagne, and begin to sing romantically along with the music as if they were the French lovers in the film.

MAY AND JUNE: (*singing*) When hearts are passing in the night, in the rushing night;
I see two lovers in the night, in the lonely night;
They take a chance that in the light, in the morning light
They'll be together . . . so much in love.

JUNE: (*as the music continues*) What did you mean by that?

MAY: By what?

JUNE: When you said, "Take a lover."

MAY: Oh – if you're not satisfied with me, find someone else to love.

JUNE: But I love you.

MAY: I know. We've been together a long time. Maybe our relationship needs a little spicing up.

JUNE: Oh, you mean splitting up.

MAY: No, it doesn't mean we have to split up. We could just give each other the freedom to have an affair.

Their romance becomes anger as they return to singing along with the music, this time making up their own words.

JUNE: (*singing*)

> I saw you kissing in the night, in the rushing night
> With someone else it wasn't right wasn't really right
> You touched her cheek and held her tight and held her really tight,
> You were together . . . so much in love.

MAY: (*singing*)

> I want to be wild and free
> We've been together, lovers for so long
> I want to have sex with other people, check into a hotel
> It can't be wrong.

JUNE: Okay, you're free. You can have an affair.

MAY: I have something to tell you. I'm already having one.

JUNE: Excuse me.

MAY: I am having an affair.

JUNE: You could have told me.

MAY: I never could have told you.

JUNE: Yes you could.

MAY: No I couldn't.

JUNE: I would have let you if you'd asked me.

MAY: You never would have let me.

JUNE: Yes I would!

MAY: No you wouldn't!

JUNE: Have you, Have you, have you . . . made love with her yet?

MAY: Well, sort of, you know.

JUNE: Does she look like me?

MAY: What?!

JUNE: That was a joke. I feel perfectly fine except I think I'll throw up. And then I'll take all your favorite photographs and cut them in a million pieces and flush them down the toilet. I'll throw money at you in a public place! And then I'll lock your cats out all night long and hope they get lost, and then I'll mix up your seed packets so the wrong thing grows in the wrong place, and then I'll take your snow-globe collection and throw it in the garbage in another county!

MAY: So, what do you want, a divorce?

JUNE: I want one thing, only one thing.

MAY: So, what do you want? A divorce?

JUNE: Oh! Something happens so you've got your boxing gloves, you wanna fight?!

MAY: Soooo, what do you want . . . a DIVORCE!!

JUNE: Don't change the subject! There's one person in this car who's making me miserable and it's not me!

MAY: Oh! Well, it may come as a great surprise to you, but I happen to have a very *sweet* disposition! Ha!

JUNE: Ha!

MAY: That's right!

JUNE: Oh right! All right! Oh, you're right and I'm wrong! You're always right and I'm always wrong! Well, it may come as a big surprise to you but *sometimes* you are wrong!!

MAY: Ooohh!! So now it comes out. Things that have been upsetting you about me. Things that have been *churning* inside of you!

JUNE: *Churning* inside me?! *Boiling* inside me!

MAY: Well, let them *boil* over! I'd be happy to know what's wrong with me.

JUNE: You wanna know what's wrong with you, I'll tell you in a second!

MAY: Yeah, I wanna know what's wrong with me!

JUNE: You wanna know what's wrong with you, I'll tell you in a minute!

MAY: Yeah! I'd be happy to know what's wrong with me!

JUNE: You are a lousy ...

MAY: (*interrupting*) So! What do you want, a divorce?!

JUNE: You want to know what I want!

MAY: Yeah! I wanna know what you want!

JUNE: You really want to know what I want?!

MAY: Yeah, I *really* wanna know what you want!

JUNE: I want you to get out of the car, close the door behind you (*she describes the exit from the stage to the lobby, out onto the street and out of the theatre's neighborhood*) and keep going.

MAY: Fine ... fine! Fine fine fine fine fine! But I want you to remember one thing ... *you* were the one who started this, not *me*! *You* started it! Not *me*!

JUNE: Open the door, get out of the car, close the door behind you ...

MAY: (*interrupting*) Okay! Fine! Fine! But I want you to remember – *you started it! Not me!* YOU! NOT ME!!

JUNE: I'll tell you one more time ... open the door, get out of the car, close the door behind you (*she describes the exit from the stage to the lobby, out onto the street and out of the theatre's neighborhood*) and keep going.

MAY: (*interrupting*) Okay, so long!

JUNE: So long!

MAY: I'm going!

JUNE: Good riddance!

MAY: Goodbye!

JUNE: *Good* it wasn't, *bye* it is.

May leaves through the audience, stops herself and comes back as if to make up and sits back in the car.

MAY: I just wanted to take one last look ... at the TORTURE CHAMBER!!

Blackout. The lights come up on May threatening June with a garden sprayer. She extinguishes June's cigarette with spray. Blackout. Then the lights come up on May and June asleep in the back seat. As May begins to speak she assumes the interrogation position in the back seat window.

MAY: There was a string of them? Not just one? Oh. Oh. On the highway? Ah. Is that what you wanted to talk to me about? Oh. The highway. Unh hunh. Yes, the highway. I love the highway. Oh, the Interstate? Unh hunh. You meet the most interesting people on the Interstate. Unh hunh. I love the Interstate. It leads to all parts of the body of the world! When I'm on the highway I feel like iron in someone's blood. Look at the vein in my arm ... if you got in your car, turned on your flashing red lights and rode it for a while you'd end up in my heart ... in my heart by way of my thighs ... but that's not going to happen, is it? No commercial vehicles on that road, sweetheart. Just pretty girls on motorbikes.

Along that road? What road? Ah, the Interstate. The Florida Interstate. The names of people? The men's names? Dead men's names? I don't know. Open the newspaper, there's a million men's names in there. Let's pick some out! Millions of men. They're everywhere. In the phone book, the Bible, the sports page, the *Who's Who*, the Congress, the Senate, the *Daily News*!

Yes, I did. I know I did. I said I have something to confess, and I do. Lots of things. Like about my hair. Does it look okay? I tried a new hot oil treatment. It said on the box that it surrounds the hair at the shaft and coats it, shoots it full of new life. Is it true?

Do you think it worked? Does my hair look surrounded, shot full of life? Like a stolen car on the Interstate! Ha! Funny how one thing resembles another! I always found that funny!

No, I don't hate men, how could I?

Good, let's! Let's talk about murder weapons! Yes, I'm fully ready to talk about murder weapons! Let's talk about them! You start! What's the matter? Oh! You want me to start? Okay, I'll start. Guns! Guns! They look like the heads of greyhounds.

That's what guns are like! That's what they *look* like! Of course I'm referring to the Ruger P90.45 caliber ACP. It's compact and lightweight and has double action and it's stainless. Like me! Looks like. *Is* like! You see, my friend and I play a game in the car on the Interstate! Yes a game! I love having a gun in my hand ... instead of a slap in the face, you can give a little mortal love bite. And victims never feel a bullet, have you heard that? When you die by the gunshot it's painless, peaceful. There's just a moment of surprise ... have you seen that on the faces of the people you've killed? They just look very, very surprised, and then that's it! Well, the *men* look surprised; the women have come to expect it! Anyway, it's painless to die by gunshot. It's when you *live* that it ends up hurting so much.

Is that what you called me in here to talk about? So, I've talked about it. I have to go now. Do call again, oh yes, do call again. But not now. Later. In a year, maybe. Or in a thousand years.

Or in your dreams. Why don't you call me in your dreams?

May climbs over the seat and begins to sing along with a popular song in the style of "Blame It on the Bossa Nova" playing on the radio. May and June both sing and dance to the song. May plays the part of a murderer and June an interrogator.

Blackout. The lights come up on the back seat. May and June sit in the back seat with their feet up on the back of the front seat.

MAY: Looks like, is like. I'll start. Ummm..m. Puppets.

JUNE: Television.

MAY: Washcloths.

JUNE: Squirrels in trees.

MAY: Explanation.

JUNE: They go inside trees with leaves where you can't see them and move the tree from the inside, like a hand in a puppet.

MAY: Good one.

JUNE: Your turn.

MAY: Same thing or different thing?

JUNE: Same thing.

MAY: Okay. Puppets . . . politics!

JUNE: Newscaster.

RADIO: Most if not all of the victims have been shot. Authorities say they believe that some of the men were killed after stopping to pick up their assailant on the highway. In this case the damsel is turning dragon and slaying the knight.

MAY: (*leaning forward*) Picture it. It's two a.m. . .

JUNE: It is?

MAY: No. Picture it.

JUNE: (*leaning forward*) Oh yeah.

MAY: It's two a.m. and we're driving on Interstate 95.

JUNE: In my car.

MAY: The Buick.

JUNE: Right. My big, beautiful, V-8 gas-guzzling big steering-wheeled Buick Apollo beauty.

MAY: Right. We break down between exits.

JUNE: Somewhere between Flagler and Daytona.

MAY: Right. You picked me up at work and we're on our way to the Last Resort.

JUNE: In my big, beautiful, V-8 gas-guzzling big steering-wheeled Buick Apollo beauty.

MAY: It's my birthday.

JUNE: It is?

MAY: You forgot. I knew you'd forget.

JUNE: I didn't forget. I washed and waxed the car.

MAY: That's no way to wish someone you love a happy birthday, washing and waxing the car.

JUNE: I'm sorry, happy birthday, sweetheart.

MAY: Say it like you mean it.

JUNE: (*putting her arm around May*) Happy birthday, my sweetheart, petunia face, pumpkin pie . . .

MAY: Sing it!

JUNE: (*singing*) Happy birthday to you. Happy birthday to you. Happy birthday, dear Ma-a-y. Happy birthday to you.

MAY: Sing it with feeling!

JUNE: (*with gross exaggeration in tune and gesture*) Ha-a-ppy birthday. Ha-a-ppy birthday. Happy birthday happy birthday, happy birthda-a-ay to you. Happy happy happy happy, happy happy happy happy, happy happy happy happy, happy happy happy happy, happy birthday happy birthday hap-py birth-day, hap-py birth-day, hap-py birth-day to you. Yeah!

MAY: So we break down on the highway.

JUNE: It's your birthday.

MAY: It's my birthday and it's raining cats and dogs.

JUNE: No exit in sight.

MAY: No golden arches on the horizon.

JUNE: It's dark.

MAY: It's cold.

JUNE: Damp. I hear the drip . . . drip . . . drip . . . dripping leaking into the back seat.

MAY: I hear the thump . . . thump . . . thumping on the roof of the car.

JUNE: I turn on the hazards.

MAY: I see my breath on the windshield like little red droplets of blo . . .

JUNE: Headlights!

MAY: Passing.

JUNE: Tailights!

MAY: Trailing into one long red river of blo . . .

JUNE: Headlights!

MAY: Slowing.

JUNE: Stopping . . . a face at the window.

MAY: Rain dripping off a baseball cap.

JUNE: (*in a man's voice*) Well ma'am, what do we have here? Two damsels in distress?

MAY: I sit on my hands.

JUNE: You talk in your best Southern accent.

MAY: Well I don't know. This ole car just won't start.

JUNE: (*in a man's voice*) Well slide over, little lady, I'll start it.

MAY: Greasy hands all over your big Buick steering wheel, grinding the gears as he pumps it, guns it, jerks open the hood, sticks his big hands into your engine, roughing her up.

JUNE: Let's murder him.

MAY: Kill him.

JUNE: Lug wrench.

MAY: Jumper cables.

JUNE: Battery.

MAY: Assault.

JUNE: Distress.

MAY: Dismemberment.

JUNE: (*in a man's voice*) Ma'am?

MAY: Sing it.

JUNE: What are two nice girls like you doing out alone on a night like this?

MAY: Sing it with feeling.

RADIO: Jacksonville police are asking anyone with any information to call a toll-free number in confidence.

JUNE: (*coming out of fantasy*) Confidence.

MAY: Explanation.

JUNE: Is like. Confidence. Like the way a secret looks like one thing on the outside but it has something else on the inside, like a hand in a puppet.

MAY: Bullshit.

JUNE: Fine.

MAY: Start a new one, different word.

JUNE: Heaven.

MAY: The toilet when you have to go.

JUNE: Kissing.

MAY: Water when you're thirsty.

JUNE: Roses in May.

MAY: Weddings in June.

JUNE: Rainstorms in August.

MAY: Sing it.

June begins to lip-synch to the duet then sings it and is joined by May in a tacky romantic duet style. Fake rain begins to fall.

DUET

JUNE: I have no fear
When the sky gets dark above
And I have no doubt
I'm protected by love

MAY: It's the clearest light
While the rain is on the roof
And second sight means
We don't need proof

BOTH: Meanwhile the rain is coming down
The sound keeps us warm
Inside this world
There are no bounds
Here in your arms I'm home
Outside it's freezing cold. Rain, ice, and snow
Doesn't matter how hard the wind can blow
Here in your arms I'm sure
That I'm out of the storm
We keep each other safe and warm
To be right here is all I want and all I need

BOTH: Our eyes won't fail
Cuz we haven't far to see
And our hearts are strong
As we need them to be

MAY: Meanwhile the killer is on the loose

JUNE: Don't worry the rain can't get in

BOTH: No danger shadowing this sky
Here in your arms I'm sure
That I'm out of the storm
We keep each other safe and warm
To be right here is all I want and all I need

Blackout

RADIO: "For two women to kill strangers at random apparently as sport is almost unprecedented," said James Alan Fox, professor of criminal justice at Boston's Northwestern University. Less than five percent of serial killers are female. He could think of only one case involving two women serial killers: a pair of Michigan lesbians who had killed to solidify their love.

MAY: Hurry!

JUNE: Miracles can't be hurried!

MAY: What?

JUNE: I'll be ready in a minute!

MAY: Well, that would be a miracle.

The lights come up on June in back seat standing with a microphone, dressed as Angelica Houston in The Grifters. *The following monologue is accompanied by a recording in the style of Frank Sinatra's "It Was a Very Good Year." May is lying in front seat reading a seed catalogue.*

JUNE: C'mere ... I won't hurt you, I promise ... I'm not going to hurt you, I'm going to kill you ... I read that dying doesn't hurt, it feels good ... you hear a voice, you see a light ... like having someone you love pull into the driveway at midnight ... c'mere, sweetie, I won't hurt you ...

It's strange, isn't it, that I'm going to kill you ... I'm so much softer than you ... so much prettier ... I'm going to take you dancing ... and I'm going to kill you ...

I'm going to kill you in self-defense ... go on ... ask me how I know ... ask me, lover ... ask me how I know ...

I know because I know you ... I know you ... I been rehearsing killing you my whole life ... I was *born* to kill you and everybody like you ... I got your name on a little slip of paper a thousand years ago ... a thousand years ago when the bodies were matched with the souls ... remember me, baby?

C'mere baby, let's dance ... let's dance, sshh! Let's just dance, let's just dance, no talking now ... yes, all right ... all right darling, you lead ... yes, you lead, that's perfect ... perfect ... you lead me ... we take our first steps.

Don't fight me. Let's not fight. Let me dance you a little secret ... and dancers dance in self-defense ... the way I kill ... the way I will kill you, c'mere ...

I think you're tall ... You're tall ... I can't see your face and I don't want to ... I see your chest ... I hear the vespers of your heartbeat ... I got a hold of you, baby ... no, darling, no, I'm not a poet, I'm a killer, don't get mixed up, baby, it's important ...

I'm gonna kill you and you want me to. You want me to sink my clean teeth into your pink lower lip. Pain like music as we dance, dance, dance. Don't stop moving, dance! Dance.

So you see where the self-defense comes in, don't you, love ... I'm defending myself against your voice on my radio, your voice on my answering machine, your saxophone sounds on my phonograph; they manufacture pills for infections you give me on evenings like this, look: keep dancing ... you know what the immediate future is, don't you, I'm going to kill you, and you're asking for it, I'm going to fucking kill you ... Why? Why? Did I hear you ask me why? Did you actually *say* that? O, sweetie, that's kitsch ... *Why?* Okay ... your underpants are too tight ... keep dancing ... your shoes are ugly, your speech writer stinks, your mind is slow, your speech is slurred, your breath is bad, and you're NOT FUNNY! You're just NOT FUNNY!

Okay. (*She takes off the wig and glasses and puts away the microphone*)

MAY: I don't know.

JUNE: Just guess.

MAY: I don't know. I don't have any idea.

JUNE: Sure you do. Just think.

MAY: I don't know!

JUNE: Shall I give you a hint?

MAY: The whole *thing* was supposed to be a hint!

JUNE: It *was*!

MAY: It was not!

JUNE: Frank Sinatra.

MAY: What!

JUNE: Frank Sinatra! Can't you see it now? Frank Sinatra!

MAY: Frank Sinatra!

JUNE: Frank!

MAY: Frank Sinatra!

JUNE: Frank Sinatra!

MAY: Now what the hell in there was going to tell me you killed Frank Sinatra?

JUNE: Don't you remember? "Your voice on my answering machine, your saxophone on my phonograph . . ."

MAY: Like he's the only one who makes phone calls or plays records!

JUNE: I see I can't be subtle when I work with you.

MAY: This is news to you?

JUNE: You do one.

MAY: Okay. (*She draws eyes, nose, mouth, and glasses on her stomach with a marking pen*)

JUNE: I'm ready!

MAY: Okay. Y'ready?

JUNE: Yes! I'm ready.

MAY: Okay. (*The face on her stomach is Ed McMahon; she makes the face talk by squeezing her belly*) Henh henh henh! (M) Laugh again! (EM) Henh henh henh! (M) Music! Music to my ears! You are a specimen! You really are! I'm glad you're here! I'm glad you're sitting next to me! You add so much to my life! (EM) Aw! Henh henh henh! (M) No, you really do, and I'd like to show you my appreciation! (EM) Aw! Henh henh henh! (M) You make me *win*! You make everyone a winner! (EM) That's nice! Henh henh henh! (M) I can't believe it! I won! I won seven thousand and fifty million dollars! (EM) Henh! Henh! (M) Or maybe more! (EM) Henh henh henh henh! (M) I think I'm getting my period.

JUNE: Keep going.

MAY: You already know who it is, right?

JUNE: I've narrowed it down to three possibilities.

MAY: Who?

JUNE: I'm supposed to ask *you* who.

MAY: You're supposed to *guess* who!

JUNE: Well I'd be very glad to if you'd just get on with it.

MAY: Sometimes you stop and question right in the middle of it.

JUNE: It was *you* with the questions.

MAY: I mean "you" in general.

JUNE: Hurry up! I'm losing the thread of the whole thing!

MAY: . . . maybe you know who you're killing, maybe you don't . . . that's the fun of it! You should have to meet everyone you kill

... have a drink with them, a meal ... even in a war ... they should have big parties where everyone meets everyone else!

JUNE: You don't even know who this is?

MAY: I know! I know! I have a very specific individual!

JUNE: Well please continue with it then!

MAY: I'm finished!

JUNE: You didn't even kill him yet!

MAY: Aw, all right! (*She grabs her stomach again*) Golf? Golf? Would you like to play some golf? Bend over you bastard! Bend over and line your putter up with your balls! (EM) Aw, henh henh henh! (M) Do you need help? Do you need my help? C'mon! We'll put them in permanent alignment! We'll go to that great Publisher's Clearing House in God's green heaven. Don't you know who it is yet?

JUNE: Finish it up! Have closure!

MAY: C'mon you bastard! Why don't you go on a diet? I can't even lift you! You're so fat!

JUNE: You're not getting anywhere.

MAY: If you don't like the way I play I'm not going to play!

JUNE: Please?

MAY: No!

JUNE: Kill him!

MAY: No!

JUNE: Put him out of his misery.

MAY: I was trying to!

JUNE: You were just *insulting* him.

MAY: I was trying to *demoralize* him.

JUNE: Demoralizing is different from killing.

MAY: It isn't different!

JUNE: It is!

MAY: Is not!

JUNE: Is too!

MAY: How do you know? Have you ever been killed?

JUNE: No, but I've been demoralized . . .

MAY: Case closed.

RADIO: Police were told by a convenience store manager on Wednesday morning about two suspicious women staying at the Gater Lodge Hotel. They've been staying at the twenty-five dollar-a-night motel in a run-down part of the city since Friday. The women, one blonde and the other brunette, match the description somewhat of composite sketches of the women being sought. Police say if the women turned out to be responsible, it would be something malignantly new under the Florida sun.

May crawls into the back seat. Both May and June begin to get dressed in "Bonnie and Clyde" drag: June in a man's suit and May in a polka dot dress. Blackout.

JUNE: I grew up in Augusta, and I went from Augusta to May. Augusta to May, like a summer going backwards. I was up in Tallahassee where spring comes in January and leaves quick in February as if the cops just came looking for it. I had come down to buy a car. There was this cousin of mine selling a car. I went and looked at the car, agreed to buy it. That night, to celebrate, I took myself to a little tavern near the motel, right on the highway. Bourbon and Coke was on its way from the table to my lips when May walked in. It's trite, meeting someone for the first time in a bar. But this wasn't like that. I stood up. When she walked in, I stood up. Like I had been expecting her. She stood in the doorway for a moment, then walked over to me, laughed and said, "So let's see it." It was a bizarre thing to say. It was a painted-up, bold thing to say. And I had no idea what she meant by it. God, she was beautiful, and her fingernails were dirty. Her hands were sexy like sex itself, they were sticky and young, they seemed to tell a story, and I could tell I was staring at them, I wanted to put her hand in my mouth, and she said it again! "So let's see it." So I took her to see my car. I hadn't paid for it yet. She got in it, backed it up, revved it up to sixty, and crashed it into the cement wall at the end of the street, it was a dead end. A fake dead end. Right beyond that wall was another street. I don't understand Tallahassee. We bought another car and moved here.

The radio returns, playing a couple of phrases from "Just the Two of Us" before they lose the station.

JUNE: Just the two of us in the rain.

MAY: Yeah, so?

JUNE: Like a million years ago in the floods in the ark. Nothing but rain and two of every kind. . . . Two cows . . .

MAY: Two horses . . .

JUNE: Two doves . . .

JUNE: Two mosquitoes . . .

JUNE: Two skunks . . .

MAY: Two killer whales . . .

JUNE: Two vicious mountain lions . . .

MAY: Two broads . . .

JUNE: Shhhhhh.

MAY: (*leaning over the seat with a gun in her hand*) All right, I want all the men in here to back up against the right side of the room.

Blackout. The lights come up on May sitting on the back of the seat in the interrogation position

MAY: Yeah, I went to church. I went to Bible class every Thursday. Not Sunday. Thursday. They said Sunday was a day of rest, but I slept through class so it would have been fine. Fine on Sunday, but they had it Thursday. I used to sleep while the teacher read out loud from the Bible. I'd sleep with my eyes open . . . it was like dozing in front of the eleven o'clock news . . . names and places . . . violent deaths, stories that were supposed to hit close to home. Every once in a while I remember something from the Bible . . . a name just comes up out of the mist . . . like Jehosaphat or Moab. Or something. I think of lightning and no electricity. I like the Bible because it's about people living in the country. Violent know-it-alls, living in the country. It's the wild stuff I like . . . sex in caves among family members to keep the race from dying out. Violent rainstorms without end. Kings. Secrets. The way nothing ever made any sense. Even though the Bible is supposedly about law and order, there never *was* any. Just people screwing and sweating and killing in the country or up on a mountain carrying stones and talking to people who weren't there.

All right, I've had enough! I want all you men on the right side of the room! (*To June*) Let me go! Let me go!

JUNE: Wait, wait.

MAY: Let me go, let me goooo!

JUNE: Go ahead . . . wait, no, easy now, will you? You don't know what you're doing!

MAY: I know what I'm doing!

JUNE: Believe me, you don't know what you're doing!

MAY: What do you know, what do you know about my life? I'm a fed-up tortured soul, but does the world care? It just lays there. Listen, listen, listen to it, it's ignoring me (*she tries to shoot*). The world is ignoring me ...

JUNE: No, no, no, no, let's work this out, huh? Let's not do anything hasty, huh? Think back, when did this all begin?

MAY: When I was born ...

JUNE: Let's not go back that far! When did the real trouble begin?

MAY: I was born in a little town outside of Chicago ... Miami! It was beautiful, the blue sea stretching as far as the eye can see. White-capped waves waving. It was beautiful. I grew up there. I grew up believing I could do anything. Be anything, I could be president, and my father sent me to nursing school.

JUNE: You must have been very happy!

MAY: I was miserable!

JUNE: Of course you were!

MAY: But then I went to work in the county hospital, with all the doctors and nurses rushing back and forth, back and forth, and the elevators going up and down, up and down. Everything going around and around. It was incredible.

JUNE: You were miserable!

MAY: I loved it!

JUNE: Of course you did!

MAY: I'd wake up every morning with a smile on my lips and a chuckle in my heart. Hahahahahahah. Don't laugh! (*She points the gun at June*)

JUNE: Don't laugh! All right! No!

MAY: I was a fool, floating on the flotsam and jetsam of the night shift ...

JUNE: You were overworked.

MAY: You could see me washed up on the shore of an underpaid job ...

JUNE: You were a bum.

MAY: I had no life, just work all night and too tired to do anything else. Coming home in the cold mornings, wind and rain blowing around me ... feet aching ... (*She starts to cry*).

Plate 12   MAY: Don't Laugh!
Photo: Amy Meadow

JUNE: Boohoohoo.

MAY: (*pointing the gun again*) Don't cry!

JUNE: Don't cry!

MAY: It was then that fortune smiled on me . . .

JUNE: Well, it's about time!

MAY: I got a job with a prominent specialist, Dr. Thomas. I worked days, I was in charge. Can't you visualize it? Picture it. Just picture it (*she sings*) the perfect job in a private practice tralala tralala.

JUNE: Tralala tralala.

MAY: (*with the gun in June's face*) Don't sing.

JUNE: Don't sing, no!

MAY: That was Dr. Thomas' song. Dr. Thomas was a spoiled son of a . . . plastic surgeon. But he showered me with things. He showered me with fringe benefits: health insurance, dental insurance, retirement plans, pension plans, paid vacations. But one day he changed . . .

JUNE: He changed.

MAY   He followed me into the ladies' room. I could hear his footsteps coming up behind me. I turned around and there he was! I couldn't stand it anymore. So I said, "Take that (*she grabs June's hat and starts beating her over the head*) and that and that and that!" That's what I said.

JUNE: (*recovering*) You really can talk!

May begins to threaten the audience with the gun.

JUNE: Let's talk. Let's look on the bright side. Wasn't there a bright side?

MAY: Well, there was. The next day he came crawling back to me on his hands and knees begging my forgiveness, he didn't mean it.

JUNE: You misunderstood.

MAY: I made it up . . . then he showered me with things . . . a four-day week, an hour for lunch, a raise in salary . . .

JUNE: Yes.

MAY: But then he changed . . .

JUNE: He changed (*she's aware of what's coming*).

MAY: He followed me into the ladies' room. I could hear his footsteps coming up behind me. I turned around and there he was. I couldn't take it anymore. So I said, "Take that and that and that (*she hits June with her hat and chases her into the back seat*) and that," and I'm glad I said it!

JUNE: (*climbing into the front seat*) You sure can talk. Good riddance to the bum.

MAY: What do you mean calling Dr. Thomas a bum? He was no bum. He was a gentleman. He showered me with things. The newest equipment, computers, electronic thermometers, receptionists, secretaries. He made me nurse of the month. And then he changed . . . he followed me into the ladies' room. I could hear his steps coming up behind me and there he was. I couldn't stand it anymore. I said "Take that and that and that" . . . (*May goes wild, beating up June and following her into the back seat*).

JUNE: (*trying to recover*) I guess you really told him, huh?

MAY: I feel a lot better.

JUNE: Well you got a lot out.

MAY: I feel a whole lot better.

Music comes up and May sits on the top of the back seat with a microphone. She starts to sing. During this song she crawls over the back seat and then moves into the audience.

MAY: You came when I was young
Too young to know
That there's nothing there in the dark
That's not in the light
That's what scares me
Boogie man

What corner of the dark dark house do you hide in
Boogie Man
Are you out there in the dark, behind a tree
With your axe, your chainsaw, your knife or your gun
Boogie man

You're tall and you're strong
What do you want from me
I don't find you attractive
I don't want your body
Boogie man

How do you connect sex and death
How do you why do you fuck what's dead
Army man, street man
Preacher man, relative man

Uncle man, normal man
Boogie boogie boogie boogie man

You are complicit with other men
You don't get it you don't merge
Birth, you don't get birth
You just get dying
Who put you in charge
Who put you in charge of dying
Who made you the boss
Who made you the king
The pres
The vice pres
The senate
The house of boogie man
The supreme boogie man
Dr. boogie man
Pilot boogie man
King of the mountain
Prince of Tides
Silence of the boogie man
JFK boogie man

You're still loose, boogie man
No one turned you in
I'm turning you in, I'm warning you now
I'm turning you in, I'm warning you now

Your time is up
Your game is up
Your dick is down
At the bottom of the heap

Boogie man smile for me
Turn your cheek and smile for me
Who do you hate enough to kill
Who teaches you
Your time is up, I'm warning you now
Your time is up, I'm warning you now
CROSS THE STREET

Don't go out in the dark
Don't jog in the park
Don't fuck, don't kiss
Don't carry a gun
Unless you want it used against you
Unless you want it used against you

You motherfucking cocksucking piece of shit on the end of my boot!

May ends the song with microphone raised in the air. Blackout; the lights come up; June takes the microphone out of May's hand and undresses her as she delivers the next monologue.

JUNE: Once we picked wild raspberries together by the railroad tracks. At night. Ridiculous. She said she knew where they grew, and I loved to make preserves. She said we couldn't go during the day, it was forbidden. Against the law! Of course we went at night ... raspberries ... little clusters of edible garnets ... the darker, the sweeter ... when they're at their prettiest, they're too young to eat ... and the raspberry bramble is so protective of her bower ... thorns ... we brought metal pots ... it was dark, and there was that odd, hot wind, and we crouched down where the trains passed, we were eye level with the train wheels, like being in the mouth of an animal. She forbade me to cry out when the thorns burned my skin, and in the dark I crushed more berries than I picked ... it was torture, not knowing when the pain was going to come, and trying not to scream when it did, and trains kept coming. By morning my fingers were blue with berries and blue with blood and my lips were blue with cold and the horizon was purple as if we'd crushed all those berries against the sky. All those raspberries hidden somewhere in the sunrise ... she washed my hands for me ... sucked the bruises ... even *that* reads like a dream to me, but she says she never dreams. And I believe her.

June leads May back to the front seat and lays her down. Then June takes off her suit jacket, shirt, and undershirt. When she is naked to the waist the lights black out.

RADIO: Ocala police said today that they had arrested a woman believed to be the killer who in the last year had slain as many as seven middle-aged white male motorists whose bodies were found alongside highways of North and Central Florida. The woman is being held without bail. Police said they had not determined her motives, but investigators who interviewed relatives and acquaintances of the woman did say that her relationships with men in her younger years were not the best. (*The lights come up on May and June in the front seat with a white sheet covering their bodies up to their necks*) The commissioner of Florida Department of Law Enforcement said he trusts that the arrest will be a relief to people in the area and that residents could now rest easy.

JUNE: Confession.

MAY: Absolution.

JUNE: Deep sleep.

MAY: Rage.

JUNE: Remorse.

MAY: Revenge.

June stands with the sheet wrapped around her breasts and moves to center stage, where she sings a torch song in Spanish. She begins with this introduction:

JUNE: Buenos noches Madrid. It has taken me a long time to get here this night. But now I am here. This time my lover is in jail. It does not matter what she has done. My heart is always with her. And with your permission I will dedicate this song to her.

On the second verse of the song, May joins June for a Spanish dance with the white sheet. June resumes singing after the dance and May translates the verse into English while she dresses June back into her suit. May gets back into her dress.

JUNE: One night ... there was just this one night ... one night ... it was ... I don't even know when it was ... a little time ago, not a long time ... I looked over at her and I just wasn't sure anymore ... we don't smoke ... we don't usually smoke, but that night we were smoking ... we were smoking feminine cigarettes, I forget the name ... they're long and skinny like tampons ... Maurice or Vavoom or something like that, with a V ... we had the radio on, and a little inlet of that nameless river was opening out in front of us ... she tried to put her cigarette out, but it skipped away from her in a little fit of wind ... you know, when you smoke a cigarette in winter, the wind smokes it with you ... it burns down so fast you don't even know if you really smoked it or not ... and one of the sparks from the end just held the ground and died out real slow ... it looked like a planet very far away in the night sky, dying out like a tiny point against the asphalt ... and we both watched it ... stared at it ... couldn't stop. And when it finally went out, we were afraid to look at each other ... both of us just staring at the point where the spark had been ... afraid to meet eyes ... I knew when I looked at her I was going to see something ... something I had been ... saying no to ... something she knew, and I knew, but we didn't know *together* ... and that's like not knowing at all. ... So finally after a real long time, her forehead and my forehead sort of lifted up ... and when I looked at her ... her eyes ... everything I knew about her and about our daily life ... I wasn't sure about it anymore ... wasn't sure if it was true ... like I had made it up ... or read about it a long time ago and forgotten what I read ... and nothing was on between us except the radio ... and this story about a prostitute from Okala, Florida and death ... and I wanted to slip into that story and I think she did too ... it felt like we were twin murderers with amnesia ... innocent only because we forgot ...

MAY: Then what?

JUNE: Stop.

MAY: Come on ... what would happen *then*?

JUNE: I don't want to talk about it.

MAY: You know you want to.

JUNE: I don't.

MAY: You do.

JUNE: No.

MAY: Picture it.

JUNE: I'm hungry.

MAY: Picturing it's what's so pure.

JUNE: Pure?

MAY: So predictable. So pure.

JUNE: We make them buy us something to eat.

MAY: Where?

JUNE: Oh stop! It doesn't matter.

MAY: It matters, baby. You know it matters.

JUNE: At the diner.

MAY: Which diner?

JUNE: Any diner ...

MAY: Which one ...

JUNE: The one behind the railroad station.

MAY: It's green ...

JUNE: Coke-bottle green ...

MAY: Smoky green ...

JUNE: See-through green. It's breakfast.

MAY: You sit between them ...

JUNE: You on the other side ...

MAY: We order ... we order ...

JUNE: Sausage and eggs and homefries and ketchup and coffee ...

MAY: And Bloody Marys.

JUNE: No!

MAY: No?

JUNE: No Bloody Marys. Too early.

MAY: Too late.

JUNE: Just wrong.

MAY: Right. It's wrong.

JUNE: Right. And then we go to the bathroom. Just you and me.

MAY: The powder room . . .

JUNE: Right! It has one of those bodies on the door . . . metal casting of a lady . . . long legs coming out of a short skirt . . .

MAY: Curly line shows tits . . .

JUNE: Right.

MAY: We go in . . .

JUNE: Right . . .

MAY: And . . .

JUNE: You.

MAY: Me?

JUNE: You say what happens.

MAY: We go in . . .

JUNE: Yeah!

MAY: We . . .

JUNE: We . . .

MAY: We . . . wash up!

JUNE: Wash up! What for?

MAY: We kiss . . . we kiss several times.

JUNE: We kiss for courage!

MAY: Right!

JUNE: We don't even *feel* like kissing . . . we're too *scared* to kiss! We kiss for courage!

MAY: You're absolutely right!

JUNE: We kiss for memory. We kiss before we fall into history.

MAY: We want to be remembered.

JUNE: We kiss to be remembered . . . They'll remember us . . . they'll talk about us . . . we're falling into history . . .

MAY: We're very tired . . .

JUNE: Of course we are! But we're all jazzed up!

MAY: You're absolutely right!

JUNE: And the men are . . . the men are . . .

MAY: Paying the bill! They're paying the check!

JUNE: They're arguing . . . dividing it up! Every cent!

MAY: No, they're not . . .

JUNE: No?

MAY: No! You're wrong! They're looking forward to things! They pay like dreamers!

JUNE: Bullshit.

MAY: Okay! They pay like sleepwalkers!

JUNE: We come back out.

MAY: Giggling . . . the men are smiling at us . . .

JUNE: We get back in the truck . . .

MAY: You think it's a truck?

JUNE: Four-wheel drive.

MAY: Pickup . . . big horsepower.

JUNE: Imagine, measuring things in terms of what they used to be! Horsepower! 250 horsepower! As if a car or truck could be likened to 250 lean, beautiful horses! That would be 1,000 flanks of legs gleaming in moonlight galloping someplace . . .

MAY: Where?

JUNE: What?

MAY: Where next?

JUNE: In the truck . . .

MAY: Then what?

JUNE: That's like imagining people in terms of apes! To say a person, like a really smart person, has 250 ape-power!

MAY: So we're back in the truck . . .

JUNE: You kiss one, I kiss the other . . .

MAY: But you're looking at me . . .

JUNE: You're right . . . I'm in the front seat, kissing this . . . ape . . . and my eyes are open as bulletholes looking right at you.

MAY: I love when you look at me.

JUNE: I'm hungry . . .

MAY: Let's keep going.

JUNE: I'm not interested! I want something to eat!

MAY: Let's go to my garden and pick tomatoes.

JUNE: At this hour?

MAY: What's wrong?

JUNE: It's broad daylight . . .

MAY: So?

JUNE: The garden in daylight is the closest you come to a dream.

MAY: Would you stop with the dreams!

JUNE: I don't believe you.

MAY: What don't you believe?

JUNE: I don't believe you don't dream.

MAY: I don't believe you *do*.

JUNE: And then we kill them . . .

MAY: We abandon them . . .

JUNE: The bodies . . . that's all they were.

MAY: Bodies.

JUNE: Bodies hunting bodies.

MAY: We relieved them by killing them. It was a relief.

May and June sing and dance to a popular song in the style of The Bobbettes' "I Shot Mr. Lee," ending with guns in each hand and pointing at the audience.

JUNE: (*holding the guns in her hands*) What were you thinking?

MAY: I don't know.

JUNE: Were you dreaming?

MAY: No! I was thinking.

JUNE: What about?

MAY: Math.

JUNE: What?

MAY: Mathematics.

JUNE: What about them?

MAY: About ... if you divide a number by zero.

JUNE: What then?

MAY: If you divide a number by zero it's like putting a white sheet over the number.

JUNE: Like it's dead?

MAY: Yeah ... like it died in the hospital ...

JUNE: After an operation?

MAY: Yes ... after an operation ...

JUNE: By a fat surgeon?

MAY: Yes ... a round, middle-aged man with white skin ...

JUNE: Soft white skin when you shake his hand, vulgar soft ...

MAY: As if he never worked ...

JUNE: Rich bastard ...

MAY: And other things ...

JUNE: Tell me.

MAY: There's a number for everything ...

JUNE: A phone number.

MAY: No ... a number ... a number of times ...

JUNE: Of times?

MAY: Yes ... a number of times ... a number of times ... that we'll do things and say things ... let's say ... how many times we'll kiss ...

JUNE: How many times we'll fight ...

MAY: How many times it'll rain ...

JUNE: How many times we'll say how many times.

MAY: Before we ...

JUNE: ... die.

MAY: In Bible class they said the very hairs on your head are numbered.

JUNE: Can I count your hairs?

MAY: No.

JUNE: Why not?

MAY: It would take too long.

JUNE: Please?

MAY: We have no time.

JUNE: We have time.

MAY: No.

JUNE: We have . . .

MAY: No . . . but you can divide me by zero . . .

JUNE: Can I?

MAY: Yes . . . cover me in white . . .

JUNE: Can I cover you in white?

MAY: Yes, please . . .

JUNE: And lay you to rest?

MAY: Yes, please . . .

JUNE: Is there a number how many times I can do that?

MAY: Yes . . . but I don't know . . .

JUNE: You don't know?

MAY: No . . . I don't know.

JUNE: (*to audience*) I'd love to watch her *really* kill somebody. Kill somebody by the railroad tracks in the wind while the trains went by, somebody with a beard of thorns and a crotch as hard and bitter as an unripe raspberry. Y'all know anybody like that?

THE END

LUST AND COMFORT

PEGGY SHAW, LOIS WEAVER, JAMES NEALE-KENNERLEY

Directed by James Neale-Kennerley
Performed by Peggy Shaw and Lois Weaver
Choreography by Stormy Brandenberger
Original music and sound design by Laka Daisical
Set and costumes designed by Annabel Lee
Lighting design by Rachel Shipp

Originally produced in March 1995 by Gay Sweatshop in association with Split Britches, London, and in May 1995 by The Club at La Mama in association with Split Britches, New York. Lighting for the New York production by Howard Thies.

CHARACTERS

*The characters are the performers, Peggy and Lois, who play them-
selves playing various roles, including those based on film characters
and actors such as Barratt and Tony from Joseph Losey's* The
Servant, *Petra and Karin from Fassbinder's* The Bitter Tears of Petra
Von Kant, *Anna Magnani from* Amore, *based on Cocteau's* The
Human Voice. *There are times when they cross clearly in and out
of character and those crossings are noted in the script. Other times
the crossings are more ambiguous and the performers play themselves and the characters simultaneously.*

*The setting is the stage where the performers act out the roles of a
long-term relationship through a set of characters influenced by
popular culture. As the characters transform, the style and color of
the set will change from 1960s English West End theatre to 1970s
German cinema to a cross between a Beckett play and contemporary television situation comedy. There is a conscious use of
theatrical set, props and costumes for the enactment of the relationship just as there is a conscious performing of character. The
opening set consists of a faux marble floor cloth with a mosaic of
two fish in the center. Directly upstage are two fan-shaped folding
screens painted red on the bottom to resemble carpeted stairs cut in
half and placed on their sides. There is an opening between the two
screens which serves as a doorway and each of the screens contain
a panel of scrim which allows some action to be seen from behind.
Downstage left is an old black 1950s typewriter with a large curl
of paper streaming out of the carriage.*

*As the house lights fade the preshow music crossfades into a
recording of Marlene Dietrich singing "I've Grown Accustomed to
Her Face." Halfway through the song the music crossfades to an
instrumental in the style of the opening of a movie sound track. It
is ominous, but innocent. Blackout. The lights come up on Lois
dressed in a glamorous purple gown. She preens and gestures as if
in front of a mirror or silent movie camera. She begins to express
horror as if something is wrong. As she turns to the side in an
arabesque, a leg dressed in men's pants and shoes extends from the
dress instead of her own. Then Peggy slowly comes out from under
the gown dressed in a man's suit. The resulting dance is a struggle
of identities which ends with Lois disappearing, leaving Peggy
holding the empty gown. She throws the gown over the stage left
screen. Blackout. The lights come up on Peggy lying stage right with
the typewriter on her chest.*

Plate 13   The transgender arabesque
Photo: Tom Brazil

PEGGY: (*typing*) Exterior. Night. Aerial view of the beach. Camera pans down through the palm trees which part gently to reveal footprints in the sand. Camera traces footprints to the edge of the ocean. We hear distant music. A party. A drinks party. (*She adjusts the typewriter to her stomach*) At the end of the trail of prints we find a crumpled evening gown lying on the sands. Sudden noise. Shouts. Laughter. (*She puts the typewriter on the floor*) Camera spins 'round and pulls back slowly as a small group of revellers advance to the waters edge. As they pass the camera, they fall silent. Cut to: Front page of the Hollywood Reporter, circa 1956. "Screen Legend and Sex Goddess in Beach Tragedy". How can I write in this position? I need a table.

Lois enters dressed as a manservant, pushing a chaise longue covered in green brocade. In the following section Peggy and Lois play themselves playing with the roles of Barratt and Tony in Joseph Losey's film The Servant. In the role of Barratt, Lois speaks with an English accent.

LOIS: Will this do sir?

PEGGY: Who are you?

LOIS: Barratt, sir.

PEGGY: How did you get in?

LOIS: The door, sir.

PEGGY: What do you want?

LOIS: I came in response to your advertisement.

PEGGY: What adverti–

LOIS: In *The Times*, sir. Is this suitable? (*She refers to the chaise longue*)

PEGGY: It's not a table.

LOIS: But it's a start, sir.

PEGGY: Of sorts.

The phone rings.

LOIS: Shall I answer that, sir?

PEGGY: You'd better not.

LOIS: May I enquire why, sir?

PEGGY: I don't have a phone. (*Pause*) Does that seem strange to you?

LOIS: Oh no sir, not at all.

PEGGY: You'd better sit down.

LOIS: Thank you, sir.

PEGGY: (*breaking out of character*) Jump!

LOIS: (*out of character*) I don't like this game.

PEGGY: Yes you do, you love this game.

LOIS: No, I don't. I hate this game.

PEGGY: (*returning to character*) I'm American.

LOIS: (*returning to character*) Really, sir?

PEGGY: New in town. Just getting my bearings.

LOIS: Of course, sir. Have you come to London to work?

PEGGY: Of sorts. I'm doing research ... I'm a writer.

LOIS: Novels?

PEGGY: Screenplays.

LOIS: Hollywood!!

PEGGY: Yes. I'm a famous Hollywood screenwriter.

LOIS: (*out of character*) What a coincidence. I love the movies. I mean (*in character*), I do enjoy going to the cinema. What film are you working on at the moment?

PEGGY: It's about a famous film star – in the fifties – she has to flee to Europe.

LOIS: How exciting!

PEGGY: She's been summoned to testify. McCarthyism, witchhunts, you know. So she fakes her own suicide.

LOIS: Splendid. Then what?

PEGGY: She changes sex. Mid-Atlantic.

LOIS: How intriguing.

PEGGY: I think so. But you . . . . what do you do?

LOIS: I'm your butler, sir.

PEGGY: Oh, I see.

LOIS: You do, sir?

PEGGY: Oh yes, now I understand. Been in service long?

LOIS: For many years, sir.

PEGGY: Really?

LOIS: Really.

PEGGY: Do you like to work hard?

LOIS: Very much, sir.

PEGGY: Can you cook?

LOIS: I'm something of an expert, sir, if I may say so.

PEGGY: Nothing too exotic I hope.

LOIS: Exotic is as exotic does, sir.

PEGGY: Precisely. Would you like a drink?

LOIS: I don't touch alcohol, sir.

PEGGY: Not even beer? I thought all real men drank beer.

LOIS: Indeed they do, sir. Indeed they do.

The clock strikes.

LOIS: Shall I serve tea sir?

PEGGY: Barratt – you're a real gent.

LOIS: I'm a gentleman's gentleman, sir. (*She exits*)

PEGGY: He does everything for me, he even dresses me. I like it. Why should I worry about it if we're complicit in it? (*Lois enters with a tray and serves tea*) I like him taking care of me and he likes to do it. We appear perfectly normal. He's just one step ahead of me. I love him and if it makes him happy, I'm happy. We've talked about change, but it's just at the talking stage. We try and grow together. That's why it's lasted so long. But it's hard to change. Sometimes he 'lets me' get dressed by myself, but it makes him irritable and he criticises me and picks at me all day. But I do it anyway. (*She starts to exit*)

LOIS: (*out of character*) Where the hell are you going? I mean . . . (*in character*) Can I get anything for you, sir?

PEGGY: I'm just . . .

LOIS: Yes . . .

PEGGY: Going to the little boys room. (*She exits as Lois follows her, watches her off stage and then turns her attention to the typewriter*)

LOIS: (*reading from the curl of paper in the typewriter*) She tried to fight it. She had so much to lose. Wealth. Fame. Comfort . . . and for what? A journey into the unknown. Where would it end? Where would it all end? Pause? Oh . . . pause. (*She pauses, stands, looks to see if Peggy is coming, then continues to read*) Exterior. Night. Somewhere in the North Atlantic. Top deck Queen Mary. Storm . . . We notice a tall figure surrounded by luggage . . . ripping open suitcases and emptying contents over the back of ship . . . jewelled gowns, furs, photographs caught by the wind and whipped into the air. Figure, by now drenched and exhausted, turns slowly around . . . (*Peggy enters and Lois tries to hide the paper in her hand*) . . . close-up. May I enquire if the master is considering a holiday?

PEGGY: I may be. Although I don't see what . . .

LOIS: (*showing the paper*) A cruise?

PEGGY: What? . . . Oh, no that's just . . .

LOIS: What?

PEGGY: What I do . . . You know, I'm a writer.

Lois laughs.

PEGGY: Don't laugh at me. Don't laugh.

Lois laughs louder.

PEGGY: I can be a writer if I want to be.

The phone rings.

LOIS: That'll be your publisher.

The phone stops.

LOIS: Don't worry. They'll ring back. Have some cake.

PEGGY: I'm not hungry.

LOIS: You don't have to be hungry to eat cake. Here (*she offers some on a fork*), try. I baked it myself. (*She feeds her*)

PEGGY: Mmmmm that's wonderful. What a good idea.

LOIS: I knew you'd like it. (*She continues to stuff Peggy's mouth with cake*)

PEGGY: I *am* a writer aren't I?

LOIS: Of course you are . . . At least you can put *that* in your pass-port . . . You should keep a diary. Publishers are always interested in personal recollections.

PEGGY: Won't that take a long time?

LOIS: Oh – about a lifetime.

PEGGY: (*with her mouth full of cake*) Take my shoe off. Go on take it off. Massage my foot.

LOIS: I, er, don't really think . . .

PEGGY: What's the problem: I thought you were my servant.

LOIS: I am, sir.

PEGGY: Then be servile.

LOIS: I think you'll find it's a bit more subtle than that.

PEGGY: Sir!

LOIS: Sir!

LOIS: (*breaking out of character*) I'm not happy with this game. Let's try another one. (*She exits around the stage left screens with the tea tray*) I'll describe it to you. You can write it down and then we can send it out with the shirts to be laundered (*she appears in the doorway briefly then peers over the screens on stage right*) and I'll come back all stiff and clean and you'll love me then won't you?

PEGGY: I need a more comfortable chair.

LOIS: (*disappearing behind the screens*) I should plunder the past. I might turn up something useful. I could inspire myself rather than everyone else. (*She enters through the doorway and returns to character*) Have you considered redecorating, sir?

PEGGY: Brown, plain, masculine.

LOIS: And the bedroom, sir? (*She rolls the chaise longue to stage right with Peggy on it*)

PEGGY: The same. Functional. Nothing too fussy. Comfortable of course.

LOIS: Of course.

PEGGY: Maybe a few cushions.

LOIS: Carpet? (*She exits*)

PEGGY: Rugs.

LOIS: I would recommend wall to wall, sir. To keep out the draughts. (*She enters with a blanket and covers Peggy*)

PEGGY: Perhaps.

LOIS: And curtains. (*She exits*)

PEGGY: Oh yes, curtains. At every window. Closed.

LOIS: All day, sir? (*She returns with cushions*)

PEGGY: It's the light. . . . I suffer from migraine.

LOIS: I see, sir.

PEGGY: You do?

LOIS: Oh yes, sir. There's a small room in the attic, sir. Perfect for a maid. (*She exits*)

PEGGY: A woman?

LOIS: (*from offstage*) They usually are sir.

PEGGY: Is that strictly necessary?

LOIS: If sir wishes to host functions. (*She enters with a glass of beer on a silver tray*)

PEGGY: Functions?

LOIS: Do's, sir. Social events.

PEGGY: Perhaps. One day. When I'm more . . .

LOIS: Established?

PEGGY: Comfortable.

LOIS: In yourself, sir?

PEGGY: In the house, Barratt. In the house.

LOIS: Your drink, sir.

PEGGY: What?

LOIS: Your beer, sir.

PEGGY: Oh . . . good.

LOIS: (*noticing the purple gown on the screen*) I'm sorry, sir. I didn't realize. You have company.

PEGGY: Company?

LOIS: A guest, sir. A female guest.

PEGGY: A woman! Where?

LOIS: Here, sir.

PEGGY: There is no woman here. No woman in this house. Just me . . . and now you it seems.

LOIS: As you wish, sir. In that case may I draw your attention to the article of clothing to your left.

PEGGY: A-a-ah-h! (*She covers her head with the blanket*)

LOIS: I think I'm correct in assuming it's a gown.

PEGGY: Don't touch it!

LOIS: Yes. I was right. It *is* a gown. Shall I remove it, sir?

PEGGY: Burn it!

LOIS: That seems very drastic, if I may say, sir.

PEGGY: Just get rid of it.

LOIS: In that case, sir, I'll fetch the paraffin. (*She breaks out of character and taunts Peggy with the dress*) You've got a guilty secret and I'm not gonna try and drag it out of you. I'm not gonna pry because I'm safer not knowing it and you're safer not saying it. (*She exists to behind the scrim in the stage right screen. The following scene takes place behind the screens*)

PEGGY: (*breaking out of character and exiting to behind the scrim in the stage left screen*) I didn't know we were so concerned with safety.

LOIS: What's with the *we* all of a sudden. What do you mean we? Why are you using this word from the past, from the innocent past, when it was just you and me. There was a time, I was the only one. Now I'm the sad and lonely one.

PEGGY: That's so low using song lyrics. So low.

LOIS: Now when you say we it could mean anyone. You and them. Not necessarily me is included in the we, if you catch my meaning.

PEGGY: Isn't this what we wanted? You're asking for it, you're really asking for it.

LOIS: It's only the secret I'm asking for, despite my reluctance to do so.

PEGGY: I'm not going to tell you.

LOIS: I don't want to know. (*The lights go out behind the scrim*)

PEGGY: (*entering through the doorway in character*) I'd like some . . .

LOIS: (*following*) Toast?

PEGGY: Ah yes and . . .

LOIS: Eggs – bacon?

PEGGY: Did you . . .

LOIS: Freshly ground, as requested.

PEGGY: And the . . .

LOIS: *Times.*

This scene is repeated a little faster each time until Lois completely anticipates each request and Peggy loses the game.

PEGGY: I'd like some . . .

LOIS: Toast?

PEGGY: Ah yes and . . .

LOIS: Eggs – bacon?

PEGGY: Did you . . .

LOIS: Freshly ground, as requested.

PEGGY: And the . . .

LOIS: *Times.*

PEGGY: I'd like some . . .

LOIS: Toast?

PEGGY: Ah yes and . . .

LOIS: Eggs – bacon?

PEGGY: Did you . . .

LOIS: Freshly ground, as requested.

PEGGY: And the . . .

LOIS: *Times*, sir.

*Lois hands Peggy the typewriter, exits and returns immediately with
an oversized pedestal and places it stage left.*

PEGGY: What's this?

LOIS: (*placing a telephone on the pedestal*) A telephone, sir.

PEGGY: I never ordered one.

LOIS: I thought it best, sir, should there be an urgent need for it.

PEGGY: Such as . . . ?

LOIS: An accident . . .

PEGGY: But there won't be any accidents will there, Barratt? That's
why you're here. You're a precaution I've taken. Isn't that so?

LOIS: I might not always be here, sir.

PEGGY: What do you mean by that? You're not going to leave me
are you? I couldn't bear it if you left me. You told me you'd be
here for ever.

LOIS: I won't leave you.

PEGGY: I don't care what you do. Just don't leave me.

LOIS: I won't leave you.

PEGGY: I love you. I've always loved you. Since the day I was born.

LOIS: (*out of character*) I won't leave you.

PEGGY: Why should you leave? You're comfortable, aren't you?
Well paid. A fully equipped kitchen. A large garden.

LOIS: I have an elderly mother, sir.

PEGGY: But what would I do?

LOIS: I'd make sure you were well looked after.

PEGGY: It's got very dark.

LOIS: Time to *shut* the curtains. Oh what shall I do, sir?

PEGGY: Barratt?

LOIS: About the phone, sir.

PEGGY: I suppose it can stay.

LOIS: Very good, sir.

The phone rings.

LOIS: (*on the phone*) Yes . . . Yes . . . everything's perfect. (*She hangs up the phone*) Just the telephone company, sir. Testing the line.

PEGGY: (*typing*) Barratt: about the phone, sir. Tony: I suppose it can stay. Barratt: Very good, sir. Phone rings. Barratt, on phone. Yes, Yes everything's perfect. Close up on Barratt. Cut to Exterior. Telephone kiosk in Knightsbridge. Back of a figure in trench coat. Receiver in left hand, right hand pressed against the glass. Listen, it's time to get rid of her. (*The lights come up on Lois in the stage right scrim, sharpening a knife*) It's pathetic the way she still adores you after all these years. I don't blame you for the way you've grown to feel ordinary about her. She looks like an old man. She's laughable. She's angry, violent, and aggressive, without the real sexual aggression I know you need. She doesn't even own a pair of leather pants. I'll show you a good time. I'll take you to clubs. We'll go to sophisticated places like art shows and movie openings. Come away with me to Spain, yes Spain. I can give you anything she can and more. I'm young and healthy and have a much brighter future. She has such a sordid past. Don't you think she has no friends cause she turned them all in? Just ask her if she is or ever has been a member of the Communist Party. (*The lights go out on Lois*) Just ask her. We'll leak her story to the press. She can't hide for much longer . . . I know, I know . . . everything's perfect. Just tell her it's the telephone company, testing the line . . .

LOIS: (*entering*) Oh, excuse me, sir. I'm sorry to disturb you.

PEGGY: I'm on the typewriter.

LOIS: Yes I realize that, sir.

PEGGY: It's a crucial moment.

LOIS: Yes I'm sorry, sir. It's just that . . .

PEGGY: Could we finish this later?

LOIS: Of course, sir. I'm very sorry, sir. It won't happen again. (*She exits*)

PEGGY: Damn!

LOIS: (*from behind the scrim in the stage right screen*) The rain in Spain stays mainly on the plain. The rain in Spain . . .

PEGGY: What are you doing?

LOIS: Practising.

The lights go out behind the scrim. There are sounds of drilling and hammering.

PEGGY: Barratt ... (*Lois enters unseen and stands behind Peggy*) Barratt ... Bar ...

LOIS: Yes, sir?

PEGGY: What's that terrible noise?

LOIS: It's the men, sir.

PEGGY: What men?

LOIS: the workmen in the cellar, sir. There's some trouble with the foundations. (*She moves Peggy on the chaise longue to downstage center*)

PEGGY: Will it go on long?

LOIS: Quite some time, sir. It's a big job, considering the state of the house when you arrived.

PEGGY: I hope I've done the right thing in coming here.

LOIS: Of course, sir. It looks perfectly acceptable from the outside.

PEGGY: Are they competent?

LOIS: They came recommended. But I'm keeping an eye on them. (*She manipulates Peggy's body into a stereotypical masculine pose*) Watching their every move, studying them carefully. Then I can report back to you, sir. Every detail.

PEGGY: Is that strictly necessary?

LOIS: Oh yes, sir. (*She slaps her on the back, forcing her to sit up straight*) We wouldn't want the house falling down, now would we?

PEGGY: You might bring me a beer.

LOIS: I was just about to, sir.

PEGGY: And Barratt!

LOIS: Yes, sir?

PEGGY: I don't want to be disturbed.

LOIS: Very well, sir. (*She takes the phone off the hook and walks upstage to the doorway and puts on a bloody butcher's apron*) I'll stand behind the screens and wait. I have all the props and costumes I need to pull this off. (*She exits*)

PEGGY: (*standing on the downstage end of the chaise lounge*) I don't cry anymore. I used to cry when I was a girl. Now I don't cry. It feels great. I get mad a lot now. I get so mad that the only way to feel right is to be aggressive. I can't help it. Then I apologize, and that feels good. I can't help it. It feels right. I feel good. I don't know what your problem with me is. This is the way I want to feel. It feels good. It feels right. It's something to strive for. Crying is embarrassing. Aggression makes sense. And I like to fuck. I find I now prefer 'super feminine' women, though I'm sexually interested in too many things now to consider marriage. I don't kiss 'cause then you get emotionally involved. My favorite thing is not to kiss, leave all my clothes on and never, ever stay the night . . . (*She unzips her pants, pulls out a bunch of grapes, takes a classical masculine pose and begins to eat the grapes*)

LOIS: (*entering*) *What* are you doing?

PEGGY: Eating fruit.

LOIS: Which kind?

PEGGY: Oranges.

LOIS: Are you sure?

PEGGY: What do you mean, am I sure?

LOIS: Are you sure they're oranges?

PEGGY: They look like oranges, taste like oranges, smell like oranges.

LOIS: You're sure they're not grapes.

PEGGY: Who mentioned grapes?

LOIS: I did. I mentioned grapes.

PEGGY: Why change the subject, we were talking about oranges.

LOIS: Where are the skins?

PEGGY: What skins?

LOIS: The orange skins?

PEGGY: Oh, you mean the peel?

LOIS: Yes, the peel. Where is it?

PEGGY: I ate it.

LOIS: You ate it?

PEGGY: All of it. It's good for the skin.

LOIS: I know what it's good for. That's not the point. You don't eat grapes 'til the end. Then you gorge yourself.

PEGGY: I'm gorging now.

LOIS: Ha!

PEGGY: Ha?

Plate 14   LOIS: I knew you wouldn't be able to restrain yourself
Photo: Tom Brazil

LOIS: (*Bringing her hands from behind her back to reveal knives
and forks between her fingers like giant silver claws*) I knew you
wouldn't be able to restrain yourself. *I knew!*

PEGGY: It didn't take a genius to work that one out.

LOIS: I make no claims for genius. Call it intuition.

PEGGY: Female intuition?

LOIS: I wouldn't know anything about that, sir.

PEGGY: Then get back to the kitchen.

LOIS: You'll give yourself away, sir, and I won't be able to mend
it. (*She lays Peggy out on the couch like meat on a slab and displays
each body part with the knives and forks*) See these arms? These
arms aren't that big, they're not that developed, can't lift a lot of
weights, but men don't screw with their arms. See these legs? They're
not especially sporty legs, they're a little flabby and they can't run
that far, but men don't screw with their legs. See these hands, they're
not that great. I mean, they can do some damage and have, but it
doesn't matter because men don't screw with their hands. The back

is kind of skinny in comparison with some, it's not all that impressive as backs go, but men don't screw with the backs. What do men screw with? Tell me Tony ole boy, what do men screw with?

The lights fade to blue to give the effect of time passing. A clock strikes. Lois puts the silverware in her pocket.

PEGGY: I haven't left the couch for three days. Or is it four?

LOIS: It's been a week. (*She moves Peggy on the chaise longue to stage left*)

PEGGY: A week! How time flies!

LOIS: How's the screenplay coming along, sir? (*She exits*)

PEGGY: It's dried up. I've no ideas left. (*Lois enters with a blanket and tucks her in*) Thank you. Maybe I'll go upstairs.

LOIS: What for?

PEGGY: Don't know. Something to do. I can't really remember what it looks like.

LOIS: Big. Dark. Cold.

PEGGY: Oh, that's right.

LOIS: Damp. Echoey. Gloomy.

PEGGY: That's enough . . . Talk to me. Amuse me.

LOIS: It's not in my job description.

PEGGY: Anything. Tell me anything. What's happening downstairs?

LOIS: I found the cat eating a kitten but apart from that, nothing new. Just the same old routine . . . I'll get you another blanket. (*She exits and returns immediately with a blanket*) You look cold.

PEGGY: No. I'm fine.

LOIS: Take it. There, that's better. You look ill.

PEGGY: I do feel tired.

LOIS: Overdoing it. Stress. What you need is a nice cup of tea. I'll get us one in a minute. Just let me rearrange these pillows.

PEGGY: No really.

LOIS: Keep still. There. Comfy? Oh dear, there's a smudge on your nose. How funny you look. (*She gets out a handkerchief*) Lick it. Go on. Now keep still.

PEGGY: Ow!

LOIS: Don't be such a baby.

PEGGY: It hurts.

LOIS: Do you want me to kiss it better?

PEGGY: Is that proper?

LOIS: We make our own rules, don't we sir?

PEGGY: I suppose so. I don't know. I can't think. I'm too tired.

LOIS: Time for tea.

PEGGY: I don't want any tea.

LOIS: Yes you do. You like tea.

PEGGY: It's all we do. Drink tea.

LOIS: It's good for you, refreshing, calming.

PEGGY: I don't like it.

LOIS: Yes you do. You do like it. You love it. You drink it with milk and one sugar.

PEGGY: No I don't.

LOIS: You like it with lemon.

PEGGY: I don't.

LOIS: You like it black.

PEGGY: No, I . . .

LOIS: You drink Assam and Darjeeling and Ceylon.

PEGGY: Stop it.

LOIS: And Lapsang Souchong and Earl Grey and especially English Breakfast.

PEGGY: No.

LOIS: You like it iced in summer and in November you drink it with milk and honey.

PEGGY: No.

LOIS: And when you get ill, you drink it with whiskey. (*She loses control*) Yes, you do. You, do, you do, you do. Don't ever tell me you don't like tea again. (*Out of character*) I like this game.

PEGGY: Sure you do, you love this game.

LOIS: But what happens now?

PEGGY: What do you mean?

LOIS: So the movie star moves to London and she takes a manservant and then *he* lives with the drapes pulled and the phone off the hook.

PEGGY: Off the hook?

LOIS: So we won't be disturbed, sir.

PEGGY: Wise, Barratt.

LOIS: Thank you sir, not at all. But, then what? (*She pushes the typewriter toward Peggy with her foot*)

PEGGY: I don't know what you're getting at.

LOIS: Don't you think we could use a maid sir?

PEGGY: A what?

LOIS: A maid, sir, a housekeeper, a woman about the house, some one to pick up ... (*she hands her the typewriter*) you know ...

PEGGY: This isn't helping.

LOIS: What isn't?

PEGGY: This isn't. It's supposed to be firing me up. Instead I'm exhausted, I can't do anything.

LOIS: Go back and sit down. I'll bring you some tea.

PEGGY: Who will?

LOIS: I will.

PEGGY: Do I know you? Have we met?

LOIS: Tea – and cake.

PEGGY: I want coffee. Make it strong. Put three heaping spoonfuls of espresso in the Melita or it's useless to me. I like my coffee strong. Forte. It's gotta give me a slug of energy. Make mine strong. Make mine. Make mine a double espresso.

LOIS: Coffee will make you nervous.

PEGGY: I do have a headache.

LOIS: I'll bring you an aspirin.

PEGGY: I think I'll lie down.

LOIS: It's probably best ... sir. (*She places the phone back on the hook. It rings immediately. Lois watches it as it rings then picks the receiver up and places it back down, cutting off the connection. Sound of wind*)

It must be January, the way this is moving. I stare at the lights and wonder what next? What next? Here we are:

We have a tea set, we have red screens we have marble floors we have a chaise longue, we have a plinth, you have a new typewriter, we have nice suits, there is the . . . purple dress. I could bring you more blankets, bring you cocoa in the afternoons and coffee in the mornings. I could call a doctor if you needed one and they would come and we wouldn't have to pay for it. I could answer the phone for you and screen your calls. I could intercept the police and the FBI and the CIA and the House on UnAmerican Activities Committee. I could be your agent, tie your ties, shine your shoes, be your cover. I could work undercover adjusting the lighting and faking the compliments so you can keep your youthful image. I could laugh at your jokes. Tell me one, tell me one now and I'll laugh. I'll pull the curtains to keep out the wandering eyes of the workmen, the milkmen, my mother, your mother, the next door neighbors. I could just sit here and wait until you're finished. But what next? What next? What next? Something must be coming. It must be . . . it must be January. I haven't seen the light of day since this play started. (*She exits around the stage right screens and enters immediately through the doorway, hovering impatiently over Peggy*)

PEGGY: (*lethargically pecking on the typewriter*) I'm working.

LOIS: I'm helping. Shall I adjust your chair?

PEGGY: No thanks.

Lois moves Peggy on the chaise lounge to stage right.

LOIS: Do you need any more paper?

PEGGY: No thanks, I'm fine.

LOIS: What about a ribbon for your typewriter?

PEGGY: No problem.

LOIS: Need any new ideas?

PEGGY: I'm still trying to capture the sense of power you get when you're loved so completely and utterly that your every need is not only . . .

LOIS: . . . met . . .

PEGGY: . . . but . . .

LOIS: . . . anticipated.

PEGGY: Right.

LOIS: Would you mind if I came a bit closer, sir?

PEGGY: Go on.

LOIS: How about here, sir?

PEGGY: That's fine.

LOIS: You wouldn't mind if I just sat right here, would you?

PEGGY: No, no, not at all.

LOIS: I'll just sit right here. (*She traps Peggy with her arms and leans into her face*) So I'm sitting in January thinking about April. April in Paris, New York in June, October in Berlin. . .

PEGGY: Berlin?

LOIS: Berlin!

PEGGY: What the hell are you getting at?

LOIS: Nothing you need concern yourself with, sir. You look sleepy. Why don't you have a nap?

PEGGY: You're right, I can barely keep my eyes open. But I can't sleep. There's too much work to be done on the screenplay.

LOIS: Leave it to me, sir. (*She pushes her back into a reclining position*) Just leave it to me. (*She walks to the telephone and picks up the receiver*) Hello is anyone there? Anyone out there? Am I talking to anybody? Can anyone hear me? Anyone on the line: Hello? . . . Oh hello, operator? Operator, the number I am trying to reach is 36–26–38. What do you mean there's a member missing . . . a number . . . the exchange? Let me think . . . yes I know the exchange is very important . . . I need time to think. Please don't go, I really need to make this connection. I need to . . . Hello? Hello? Who's this? Oh, hello . . . I'm sorry to call so late in the day, but I need a little assistance here. You see I'm stuck here . . . in this house . . . in London . . . in this play. My name? My name is Barratt. My first name? I don't have one. Do you think that's significant? Am I lacking in some way? Well then, could you give me one?

Karin? That's an unusual name for a man. Not where you come from? Tell me where is that – Berlin! Hello? Hello? Operator, there's some kind of interference on the line, hello? Who's this, who's this speaking . . . oh, hello, my name's . . . Karin. (*Sleazy strip music comes up and continues under rest of monologue as/Lois transforms into a feminine body and voice*)\I've been let down rather badly, could you help me? Yes I am tense. I've tried getting comfortable but it only makes things worse. I'm in a very difficult position here. What position is that? Well the position I was hired for, this part, I'm playing, this role . . . excuse me? Oh . . . what *position* am I in? . . . Well, I am standing at the moment . . . uh . . . oh . . . they are spread already . . . (*she runs her hands along the inside of her thigh*) You have a very sweet voice. I trust it, I trust your voice. You have a 'sacher torte' kind of voice. I would do anything a voice like that asked me to do. Oh, yes anything. What am I wearing? (*She regains a masculine stance*) Just a suit, shirt, tie . . . traditional . . . Yes, yes it is a little constraining. I guess I could loosen it a little. Take it off? Sure. (*She rips off the clip-on tie and throws it upstage*) And the jacket? Of course. (*She slowly slips off the jacket and lets it fall to the stage*) Long sleeve and gold cufflinks . . . cast off? Oh no I bought them myself . . . oh *cast* off . . . All right here goes; anything you say. (*She rips off the sleeves and pulls them slowly down the arm like a stripper would a long pair of gloves*) Yes. Yes, I'll have to be quiet though, . . . I'm afraid . . . no I have . . . I will . . . I am . . . listen. (*She lies on the floor with her pelvis tilted toward the receiver*) Mmmmmm mmmmm, can you hear the zipper? (*She stands up and kicks off her pants and shoes*) That feels much better . . . just socks and suspenders . . . what? All right, I'm lifting the left leg and I'm slipping it in . . . yes I'm slipping it in . . . okay slowly . . . slowly (*she pulls her right sock off with her left foot*) How long will it take? Oh-h. How *long* will it take? Well, how long have you got? (*She laughs and starts to remove the other sock*) Now the other one. I'm lifting my leg . . . What do you mean turn around? You can't see me . . . can you? (*She looks nervously around for an observer*) What do you mean partially? What if I move over here . . . (*she moves center stage*) Can you see me better now? No? How about now? (*She unbuttons her shirt*) No? How about now? (*She rips her shirt off and is naked except for a purple g-string*) You know there is a ritual in summoning up a lover.

First you call (*she puts the receiver back on the hook and the phone rings immediately*) and then I come. I travel long distances just because it's how I make my living. (*She crosses in front of Peggy who has been awakened by the phone*) You should hire me. (*She exits to the scrim in the stage right screens*)

PEGGY: Barratt?

LOIS: (*appearing through the stage right scrim as she dresses in a maid's uniform*) Your job is to fall in love with me.

PEGGY: I already fell in love with you in Italy.

LOIS: It was Berlin.

PEGGY: Berlin?

LOIS: (*in a fake German accent*) Don't you remember? How could you forget so easily?

PEGGY: Karin? . . . Oooh, Karin. (*She stands up*) We haven't played

Plate 15   PEGGY: I'll have to detach myself, like an appliance with
detachable parts. LOIS: Oh no. I want the whole damn Hoover.
Photo: Tom Brazil

this one for a long time. I *like* this game. Come here and kiss me.

LOIS: (*peering over the edge of the screen as she dresses*) Slow down.
First you have to woo me.

PEGGY: Woo you? I hardly know you?

LOIS: Yes, you know, seduce me with poetry, win me over with
tokens of your love.

PEGGY: Can't we just fuck?

LOIS: Later. First you have to get me in the mood.

PEGGY: I could sing to you but I'd need a band.

LOIS: I think I hear music.

*Music. Lois enters as the maid, naked except for a tiny white
pinafore, a long red wig and high heels. Peggy takes off her jacket
and Lois hands her a silk smoking jacket and a microphone. Peggy
begins to sing a song that describes love from the subject's point of
view in the style of "This Guy's in Love with You." Lois clears the*

stage of discarded clothes, moves the pedestal to upstage center between the screens and begins to clear the blankets, cushions and green slip covers from the chaise lounge, revealing a red crushed velvet mattress.

LOIS: (interrupting the song) No, no, no, no, no!!

PEGGY: I'm sorry?

LOIS: You're supposed to be singing to me; to me. The love object. Instead you're singing about yourself. That's so typical of a butch. (She picks up the cushions and blankets in a huge bundle and begins to exit)

PEGGY: Just like a femme to throw a fit . . . never satisfied.

LOIS: Do you want me?

PEGGY: I always want you.

LOIS: Then you'll have to try a little harder.

PEGGY: I'll have to stand back. I'll have to detach myself, like an appliance with detachable parts.

LOIS: Oh no, I want the whole damn Hoover. I want to be sucked up and ground down.

Peggy begins to sing a song that glorifies the attributes of a femme in the style of Tony Bennett's "All the World to Me".

LOIS: (after the first lines of the song) That's better. (Lois exits with the cushions, enters with six large framed photos of her body parts and places them in a semi-circle at the front of the stage. She exits and enters with a round orange carpet and places it center stage, covering the fish mosaic. She falls immediately on the carpet in several cheesecake poses. She notices the chaise longue which is now covered in red velvet, moves it onto the carpet, then falls on the couch in more poses. She notices the pedestal, removes the telephone and climbs up and sits on the pedestal in a final pose at the end of the song. The set has now been transformed to the 1970s colors and style of Rainer Werner Fassbinder's The Bitter Tears of Petra Von Kant. Throughout this next section Lois and Peggy play themselves playing with the roles of Karin and Petra from the same film. In the role of Karin, Lois speaks with a fake German accent.

PEGGY: I'm so glad you came. Are you comfortable? Can I get you anything? A snack maybe – or a drink?

LOIS: (still posing on the pedestal) Maybe later.

PEGGY: As you wish. So, here you are. At last.

LOIS: Yes, here I am.

PEGGY: Talk to me, tell me about yourself.

LOIS: What is it you want to know?

PEGGY: Anything. Everything. You past, your future. What you want to do with your life?

LOIS: Do? I don't want to do anything. Except maybe fall in love.

PEGGY: That's very exciting.

LOIS: Is it?

PEGGY: Oh yes. Though you must have had many lovers?

LOIS: I really can't remember them. I remember cars, and fur coats and holidays, but I don't recall faces.

PEGGY: You're such a tease.

LOIS: Am I?

PEGGY: I find it very stimulating.

LOIS: Do you?

PEGGY: Oh yes. Tell me about your family.

LOIS: All dead.

PEGGY: All. My God.

LOIS: A boating accident. Drowned. All of them.

PEGGY: Not even one survivor.

LOIS: None.

PEGGY: A sister perhaps? Or a brother?

LOIS: None I tell you. They were horribly burnt. Unrecognizable.

PEGGY: So you are alone in the world.

LOIS: In some ways. At least since I left Freddy.

PEGGY: Freddy?

LOIS: My lover of the last fifteen years. But it's over now. Finished. I don't really want to talk about it.

PEGGY: But I want you to.

LOIS: This is neither the time or the place.

PEGGY: (*out of character*) Going somewhere?

LOIS: (*out of character*) I might if you carry on treating me this way.

PEGGY: Let's not quarrel.

LOIS: Well you started it.

PEGGY: You were the one who mentioned Freddy.

LOIS: Only as a reference to the past.

PEGGY: So tell me one thing. This Freddy. (*Back in character*) Is it a man or a woman?

LOIS: (*in character*) Does it matter? What will it tell you? For your information, Freddy was a man when I knew him. Before that? Who knows?

PEGGY: And now?

LOIS: God in Heaven! Should I care? Maybe you're Freddy. Maybe I'm Freddy. It's just a name. You see, you've upset me now. (*She flails her legs in a tantrum on top of the pedestal*)

PEGGY: You must be protected. After what you've been through. You must be looked after while you recover. (*She grabs her legs to calm her*)

LOIS: That's the general idea. I'm cold. Get me a frock.

PEGGY: A frock? But I love what you have on already!

LOIS: It's too cold for this game. Get me a dress. After all it is what you do isn't it. You are an internationally famous clothes designer.

PEGGY: Am I? That's right I am. (*She lets go of her legs so that Lois nearly falls off the pedestal*) And you are?

LOIS: On the brink ... (*she tries to regain balance*) of a fabulous career.

PEGGY: As?

LOIS: (*still struggling*) An icon.

PEGGY: It must require very special qualities.

LOIS: Oh it does. (*She finally regains composure*) On the other hand, with the right wig and clever lighting ...

PEGGY: You're so funny.

LOIS: I am amusing in an unthreatening way and I laugh prettily at the jokes although I don't always understand the punchline.

PEGGY: But you're very intelligent.

LOIS: I am that too. I am also colder than I was five minutes ago.

PEGGY: The dress! I forgot. Forgive me. You can have anyone you want. (*She exits*)

LOIS: (*taking off the apron so that she is naked except for the purple g-string*) Do you have something in purple?

PEGGY: Of course.

LOIS: Skip the underwear. I find it claustrophobic.

PEGGY: But then you'll have nothing to slip into my pocket at the coffee shop. (*She hands her a purple sequined tube dress*)

LOIS: I hate cappuccino.

PEGGY: I would appreciate the gesture.

LOIS: (*putting on the dress*) I exist only for your pleasure.

PEGGY: And I love you. I love you, I love, you, I love you. Life will be different from now on, Karin. Now we have found each other. I will spend every waking hour worshipping you. You will always be safe and I shall always protect you. I could take you apart. (*She lifts her off the pedestal and holds her on her knee with one foot resting on the chaise longue*) Take you apart from the hustle of the crowd to the coffee bar just before you get to the cinema near the square. And somewhere between the espresso and pannetone, between the walk and don't walk, I could stop you just like that. Slip my hand up under your coat and feel your breasts. I know they're there and I reach for them. Don't pull back. Your reaction will draw attention. If you don't look to see who's looking, no one will. Just let me be the guard. I'll watch and touch at the same time. It's your job to keep still. Drink your coffee, chew your cake and swallow. I'll feel the food as it travels down your throat. I'll chew it for you. I'll mix my saliva with yours to aid your digestion. Don't move; you'll attract attention and I won't be able to get the zipper down without being heard. (*She zips up the dress and lowers her onto the couch*)

LOIS: Do you own a television?

PEGGY: Why don't you look at me any more?

LOIS: I'm doing my toenails.

PEGGY: And then? (*She gives her a hand mirror*)

LOIS: I can't read the future. I'm thirsty. Get me a drink.

PEGGY: It's eleven o'clock in the morning.

LOIS: Not in New York.

PEGGY: Martini?

LOIS: Thank you.

PEGGY: Straight up?

LOIS: Of course.

PEGGY: With a twist?

LOIS: Hasn't everything?

PEGGY: You'll put weight on. I say this for your own good. Because I love you.

LOIS: (*looking into the mirror*) Me too.

PEGGY: You do? Say it. Just once. Say it.

LOIS: Say what?

PEGGY: I love you.

LOIS: Yeah, okay.

PEGGY: Okay what?

LOIS: You're fine. I mean (*into the mirror*) I love you.

PEGGY: You are a goddess. Your hair, your eyes, your breasts . . . (*she unties her cravat and signals to Lois that a different game has begun. Lois assumes a submissive position and Peggy blindfolds her with the red cravat*) See these eyes? They see themselves in the mirror. They are mirrors and the desire lies in her own reflection, in the corners upside down in the brain and back out again projected onto you. You know, the way eyes do that. But femmes don't fuck with their eyes. (*She covers Lois's mouth with the cravat*) You see these lips? Quivering, unable to keep still, filling up with tears that drip from the eyes. When she pouts she sees her own reflection. Lips, painted red like blood, dangerous, parting in desire. Knowing how desirable she is to you, knowing that one flick of the tongue will draw you in and capture you, hold you fast, unable to move unless she lets you in. But femmes don't fuck with their mouths. (*She binds Lois's hands*) See these hands? They want what you have. They will grab your things and add them to their own things. They want to hold it all. They think you've got it and they want it. The polish on the nails tells the story of green with envy, signals you all is not as it appears. But femmes don't fuck with their hands. (*She binds Lois's feet as Lois lies on her back*) You see these feet? They don't know which way to move. They move toward you and then back, not being able to make up their minds, changing their direction 'til you go crazy. You reach for them and they're gone, you can't get a grasp on them. But femmes don't fuck with their feet. (*She strad-*

dles her with the cravat stretched across Lois's stomach) See this belly? Held in secure between her hips. It rises and falls with each outrageous threat and violent breath. If you can get close enough you can hear her body doing everything it can to keep down her worst thoughts. You can hear her pounding on her chest 'til it's bruised and she is spent. But femmes don't fuck with their bellies.

LOIS: (*bringing her face close to Peggy's*) I have a guilty secret.

PEGGY: They fuck with your minds.

LOIS: I've got a guilty secret. I keep it in my belly. I pass it off as wind. I got gas, I say when strangers look at me knowingly. I got a stomach ache I say and I don't eat much - my belly's too full, too crowded with all those secrets sloshing around, slipping into my bloodstream and making for my brain. Then I go crazy. I can handle that. I'm crazy, I say. I can't talk to you, I'm crazy.

PEGGY: I'm crazy. Crazy for you.

LOIS: Don't come any closer.

PEGGY: Why not?

LOIS: I've no deodorant on.

PEGGY: I don't care.

LOIS: I do. Anyway I want to read my horoscope. (*She lies on her stomach and looks into the mirror*)

PEGGY: I can tell your future. (*She climbs on top of Lois*)

LOIS: Does it include you?

PEGGY: By your side. Making love to you twenty-four hours a day. (*She pushes Lois down*)

LOIS: Don't you ever get tired?

PEGGY: Not with you, I would spend an eternity in your arms.

LOIS: Oh, just get me another drink. (*She pushes Peggy up*)

PEGGY: So, are we going to have sex now? (*She pushes back down*)

LOIS: Sex? You want sex now? (*She pushes Peggy back up*)

PEGGY: Yes. (*She pushes back down*)

LOIS: (*crawling out from under Peggy and onto the floor*) How can I have sex now when I have such a . . . stomach ache?

PEGGY: Who mentioned you?

LOIS: So you want sex with someone else?

PEGGY: I wouldn't say no.

LOIS: You never could.

PEGGY: I could get excited about sex.

LOIS: But not with me?

PEGGY: Not at the moment, no.

LOIS: Who with then?

PEGGY: Come again?

LOIS: Who do you want to have sex with now, at this moment, if not with me?

PEGGY: No one in particular . . . Anyone.

LOIS: Anyone? So you'd have sex with anyone else, anyone in this whole theatre rather than with me. I'm that awful am I?

PEGGY: Why does my wanting to have sex with someone else make you an awful person? We have good sex.

LOIS: You think so?

PEGGY: Don't you?

LOIS: Not really. Not anymore. Maybe at the beginning . . .

PEGGY: Maybe?

LOIS: . . . at the beginning and oh, I don't know . . . lots of times. Like New Year's Eve. (*She removes her wig and exits, then reappears between the screens and places an orange vanity case on top of the pedestal, then stands behind it and delivers her monologue out of character*) I have a guilty secret. I keep it in my basement. When I was a child I built a house in the basement. It was made from other people's furniture and packing cases. Most of it was covered in green mold, which was appropriate since it was a house of correction. I was the madam, the director, the führer. Other children would come to my house and I would tell them what to do. Binding their legs with their own underwear, I would place them in different positions, silently giving a title to the picture I had created. Sometimes I would stuff a pair of my father's socks down the front of my pants, and if they had performed well I would let them kiss or nuzzle my crotch. I would expose their genitals. I would put sticks between the girls' legs and rocks down the boys' pants. Soon I gave up words and they would know by the look in my eye or the curl of my lip which tableaux to perform. No one ever said no. Not the policeman's son or the preacher's daughter. We all knew I had the biggest dick. (*She staggers back onstage with the wig in her hand*)

PEGGY: Where have you been?

LOIS: Out.

PEGGY: I know that, where?

LOIS: Dancing.

PEGGY: Alone?

LOIS: Some of the time.

PEGGY: Where did you go?

LOIS: A bar somewhere in the city. Then a club.

PEGGY: What kind of a club?

LOIS: (*putting the wig back on and reassuming the character of Karin*) Just an ordinary lesbian fetish club.

PEGGY: Who did you dance with?

LOIS: A woman. A beautiful lesbian boy.

PEGGY: How old was she?

LOIS: About half your age. She was very sexy.

PEGGY: Did she make love to you?

LOIS: No. She fucked me.

PEGGY: Oh God. Why do you tell me these things?

LOIS: You asked. And besides, we agreed not to lie to each other. Shall I tell you the details?

PEGGY: You disgust me.

LOIS: She had me over the seat of her Harley-Davidson.

PEGGY: With the engine running?

LOIS: Of course.

PEGGY: Were you alone?

LOIS: Apart from her friends.

PEGGY: People were watching?

LOIS: There'd be no point otherwise.

PEGGY: Why can't you lie to me. Why can't you tell me something I want to hear?

LOIS: Okay. It's not true.

PEGGY: No? What were you doing?

LOIS: Walking by the river writing love poems to you.

PEGGY: Where are they?

LOIS: Scattered on the waters!

PEGGY: That's very beautiful.

LOIS: Thank you.

PEGGY: Is it true?

LOIS: No, of course not.

PEGGY: (*taking off the wig as Lois falls into her lap*) Can't we take a break from all this? I wish we could just go to a café and have coffee and another coffee and read the paper. And when I'd look up between pages, I'd see you there lifting your cup to your lips. And I'd imagine how sweet they are and how hard they press against mine, like you want to smother me and punch me. And they'll be playing Otis Redding and the coffee will be in those white heavy mugs. And it will be morning and there'll be so much hope and endless time.

LOIS: What do you want?

PEGGY: I want what you want.

LOIS: Not fair, I want you to tell me. I want you to describe it in words that make your mouth go dry.

PEGGY: I want to lock myself up and throw away the key.

LOIS: What else do you want?

PEGGY: I want to feel hopeful.

LOIS: Okay, close your eyes and I'll tell you all the things I'm going to do to you and it will take hours and then I'll ask you to dance.

PEGGY: I feel hopeful already.

LOIS: Kiss me and get it over with quickly. Hurry up. Kiss me godammit. (*They kiss*) There now, that wasn't as big a deal as we thought after all was it?

PEGGY: It wasn't the kissing you that was so powerful. You shouldn't have touched my tongue with yours. That changed things.

LOIS: I just wanted to see if you were paying attention. Are you paying attention? Can you see me? How do I look? I'm dressed. I'm ready. Shall we dance? (*Cha cha music*) She's going to dance with me now . . . you're going to dance with me. (*She moves towards the audience*) You're going to lead and I will follow. (*She kicks over the picture frames*) I will relinquish, surrender, yield, submit. I will be seized in a state of following, in a state of two steps and high heels. I will gaze into your eyes and you will know me. You will see me in the soundness of my shoulders as something that is yours and I will know they belong to me . . . only as they are reflected in your eyes. But watch carefully. Pay close attention as I (*she moves upstage to begin dancing with Peggy*) glide across the floor in a cloud of sequins that appears to be hanging on the arm of a dinner suit. Observe carefully as my foot retreats to leave space for hers. (*To Peggy*) Put your foot there. No there. Put your hand there in the small of my back. No, one hand. You're going to lead me. Don't you know how to lead? Don't make me have to tell you. Can't you read my mind? Try listening. Can't you hear it?

They begin to cha cha in the style of Shelley Winters and Peter Sellers in the film Lolita. *Lois is comic, flirtatious but powerful. Peggy plays the serious male lead.*

PEGGY: (*the music continues as Lois dances around Peggy*) How much floor have we covered? An inch? How long have we been dancing? A second? A minute? Fifty years?

LOIS: Fifty years! And all I got was roses. I wanted pearls and you gave me roses.

PEGGY: Red is not my favorite color.

LOIS: Color me blue.

PEGGY: I sent me your blue note –

LOIS: It wasn't perfumed. I was surprised.

PEGGY: Maybe it wore off crossing the Atlantic.

LOIS: So much is lost at sea. They say the band played on when the Titanic sank. All those notes lost at sea.

PEGGY: When I get old I'll still slick back my hair.

LOIS: When you get old you'll be distinguished, mature, graying around the temples. You'll have on sensible shoes and comfortable clothes. When I get old I'll be cold in my stockings and bare legs. I won't be so steady on my feet and I'll feel foolish in my lipstick. Move a little closer. (*They return to the cha cha; still comic but a bit more desperate*) Listen to it. Feel it. See it. Look how round . . . cha cha cha, I am . . . cha cha . . . how perfectly formed . . . cha cha cha. I wilt at the slightest compliment. I swoon at the sound of my own voice. (*The monologue breaks for a dance sequence in which Lois is determined to seduce Peggy*) My mother always said I would need something to fall back on . . . a couch or a pair of arms and even when I was at my best she said I would have to look like I needed a little help . . . (*they continue the dance*) but pay close attention. (*The cha cha becomes more of a tango in which Lois begins to dominate Peggy and becomes the sexual aggressor. Lois delivers the following monologue over the music when she is on her back on the couch and it seems they are about to have sex)* I've been in this room with you for too long, so long that you've worn out my skin with your glances and caresses, your eyes like a pumice stone. (*Lois stands as Peggy strokes and caresses her*) What if no one else but you ever touches it again what if I never fuck anybody else? What if they don't want me 'cause your hands have mapped out indelible invisible tatoos all over my body. What if you've sucked out my fluids and dried me up like an old crone, brittle bones, faded lips, sagging tits, laugh lines, crow's feet, frog's legs ... (*Peggy kneels on the couch and Lois stands in front and wraps her leg around Peggy's neck in a strangle hold*) You know there's a ritual in summoning up a lover. First you call (*the phone rings*) and then I come ... (*she walks to the orange vanity case on top of the pedestal, opens it, takes out a white European phone, and answers it*) Yes? Yes, everything's perfect. Two hours. (*She hangs up the phone and places it on the floor downstage right*) Untie your shoes quickly. (*Peggy obeys her commands as if preparing for a sexual ritual while Lois packs the photographs and articles of clothing into the vanity case*) Unbutton your shirt. (*Peggy takes off her shirt, revealing a red silk slip tucked into her trousers*) Unzip your pants. (*She does so as Lois walks to the typewriter, rips off a segment of paper, and packs it in the case with the trousers*) Close your eyes. (*Peggy lies down as Lois pushes the couch forward, rolls Peggy off and pushes the couch off stage. She has removed everything except the orange carpet and the white telephone. As Lois takes the vanity case and prepares to leave, Peggy grabs onto her ankles but Lois walks away, leaving Peggy alone in the red slip on the orange carpet with the white phone. The following scene is Peggy playing her own dilemma in the style of Petra in the final scenes in* The Bitter Tears of Petra Von Kant *and Anna Magnani in* Amore, *the film version of Cocteau's* The Human Voice. *Lois can be seen behind the screens, packing and rearranging the backstage props*)

PEGGY: I guess it was a little too far for me to go this time. I should have waited ... I should have gone slowly, I had plenty of time. I rushed it. Funny how a kiss can do that. Before there was no hurry, but once you kiss you have to have more and right away. It changes everything. (*The phone rings. She dives for the phone*) Hello? ... Who is this? ... NO!!!!!!!! (*She slams down the phone. It rings*) Hello? (*She slams the phone down*) I hate you. I hate you. (*The phone rings. She picks it up angrily and then realizes it's a friend*) I'm not hungry! ... just coffee and cigarettes ... I feel fine ... (*She places the phone down. The phone rings*) Hello? Who's there? I'll call you back; no number? ... There must be a number, look again

... Oh God, don't hang up, hello? I can hear the beeps ... yes well get another ... what do you mean in case you can't reach me again, I'll be right here. (*She places the phone down. The phone rings*) Where are you? What do you have on? Are you alone? Can you talk? Why haven't you called me, have you been sick? You sound funny, far away and different ... hello? (*She realizes it's someone else*) No, no, no. Can't you see I'm expecting a call, hang up now! (*She places the phone down on the carpet and paces*) What am I doing to myself waiting for this ... slut ... to phone me? I have better things to do! I can't get anything done. It's all downhill from now, how can I go on? I'm lost, I'm lost ... (*She falls down on the carpet*) ... I'm fine, just fine. (*She gets up and paces*) Goddammit! I'll just go out! (*She starts to exit*) I can't go out! What if she calls? Shit! Shit! I'm paralyzed. She's turned me into a child. I have nothing left, no love, no desire, no passion. I just want to sleep. I want my life back! I want you out of my life! (*She falls down on the carpet*) I have work to do. (*She gets up*) You're driving me crazy and you made me lose my sense of humor. You're crazy. Why else would you behave in such a sick, perverted way. I don't know anymore than when we started ... Why can't you just pick up the phone and make one fucking call to me? I know you can feel me thinking of you. (*The phone rings and stops*) That's it! I'm finished with you. I'm finished with women for good. Women are wicked anyway, everyone knows that. It's a good thing women aren't in political office, the whole world would be blown away by their demented, erratic behavior. I will get you out of my system ... (*She picks up the phone and talks to it*) I'm the same, you're the one who's changed! I hate myself that I've even fucked you. I'm sick of your tears, I'm sick of your drama, I'm sick of your face. How could I ever have loved you! I wish you were dead! How I detest you! Yes, dead!!! (*She puts the phone down*) I felt you at the corners of my mouth. I could taste you right at the back of my throat and deep inside my neck. Without that passion for you I will get old, crumble into a worthless heap of skin and bones and old clothes. But it's hard to die, your body sometimes just keeps you going. I'll have to go to Holland so they will inject me with something 'cause I couldn't go on living without you. (*The phone rings*) Hello? Is that you? You sound funny. Is there someone else there? Where are you? I hear so many unfamiliar sounds, my sweet. (*Music comes up: an extremely sentimental version of a song in the style of "Are You Lonesome Tonight?" Lights come up behind the stage left scrim revealing Lois as she dresses in a pair of pajamas and sings along with the music*) Remember the time we went all night in that great conversation on time, how time goes fast and slow depending on how long it is 'til I see you ... No, no ... I don't mean to make you defensive ... Are you all right? You sound funny, are you alone? Can you talk?

No, I'm not crying, I'm fine really, where will you be later? No I won't call you I just want to know where you'll be. I know that it doesn't help me but somewhere it comforts me ... can't you just give me one more night, only one more, you could pretend that you still want me, would that really be so hard to remember that feeling? No, it's not being fake, it's being kind, you know, easing me out of you. No I'm fine ... What's that noise? A toilet flushing. Where are you? I can hear you doing something else ... can't it fucking wait 'til I get off the phone to you? Can't you concentrate on me for a minute, is that too much to ask? Foolish? I'm not being foolish. What was once considered passion you now consider foolish. No, I'm not obsessed ... yes, I know you like me better when I'm laughing, I hardly have anything to laugh about do I? (*The music and lights fade out on Lois*) Your sun is not shining on me anymore, it's cold here in the shade. No please, I'm sorry. I didn't mean to make you feel bad, really. Don't take any of this personally. I hope you don't take any of this personally. You just sound different, like I don't know you. Maybe I never did. Maybe I made you up. A moment ago you were so tangible, I could feel you and touch you, and now when I reach out there's nothing there, just my hand in the air. (*The phone rings*) Yes, yes, oh it's you. I didn't recognize your voice for a moment. Could you hold on a second ... (*she covers the phone with her hand and waits*) ... Sorry. Now, where were we? (*Lois enters and begins to fold and tie up the screens on either side of the doorway. The backs of the screens, piles of props, costumes, suitcases and trunks are revealed giving the impression of a backstage or basement storage area*) I'm just trying to get a lot of small business details out of the way so I have some time ... No, I haven't had time to think about you. I've been busy with one thing and another and I've been conking out when my head hits the pillow which is unusual for me ... Yes, yes, well I haven't had a chance to miss you really ... Listen, I have someone waiting for me right now so I have to go. Yes I know. I'll call you later. How many times do I have to tell you don't call me here? Don't ever call me here again. Goodbye. Goodbye. Bye. No, I can't talk. What do I have on? I'm not going to tell you. No ... it's over. Bye. (*She slams the phone down. The phone rings.*) Hello ... yes, is that you? It's not a very good connection ... where are you? France? ... how long have you been in France? ... Now? I can't just ... You'll be there three days ... I couldn't possibly ... just like that ... hello? Are you still there? Hello? Can you hear me? ... Of course I'll meet you ... Can you hear me ... Operator, hello, I've just been cut off, can you tell me where ... no ... okay ... but surely there must be a way to trace ... thank you, yes, operator. Goodbye. (*She puts the phone down on the carpet. Blackout*)

LOIS: (*flashing a large flashlight around the set like a searchlight and manipulating her voice as if it's coming from a loudspeaker. Peggy moves around the set trying to avoid the light*) This is it! We're closing in. No hiding any longer. It was just a matter of time and the last five minutes on that carpet was all the proof we needed. We're just outside your window. We can see your every move. We know what you're wearing. Your dry cleaning has given you away. (*She shines the light on the typewriter. Peggy dives under the carpet and moves toward the typewriter, retrieves it and moves back center stage, still under the carpet*) We're closing in. We're coming in your basement. We're unpacking hour crates and looking through your photographs. We have the purple dress. We know everything. Come on. Give it up. Hands up. Surrender.

The lights come up. Peggy sticks her head out from under the carpet, looks around and sits up. (The final scenes are played as a cross between a Beckett play and a situation comedy. Peggy and Lois play themselves, bunkered in their basement of props and costumes, looking for the next roles to play.

PEGGY: Where are the walls?

LOIS: (*Entering, picking up the phone and placing it backstage*) Gone. Tumbled down.

PEGGY: Just now? When I was on the phone. You turn your back for five minutes and everything's different.

LOIS: Not everything. Here, put these on. *She throws Peggy a pair of pajamas similar to the ones she's wearing*) You'll catch your death walking around in your underwear.

PEGGY: Who are you? (*Lois rolls up the orange carpet, revealing the typewriter underneath*) I'm sorry, I know that sounds very confrontational, but it came out like that. Who are you? How did you get in? Have I seen you before? Have they sent you? (*She grabs the typewriter from Lois who is trying to read what she's written*) How can I know I can trust you?

LOIS: Don't you remember me? (*She lifts the carpet to her shoulder and turns upstage, nearly hitting Peggy on the head as she bends down to place the typewriter*)

PEGGY: You seem a little familiar . . .

LOIS: (*exiting with the carpet*) You won't remember me; there were so many people around.

PEGGY: I have a feeling that you're very important to me, just give me a minute . . .

LOIS: You've had plenty of time already. Do you want some coffee?

PEGGY: You're wrong. (*She puts on the pajamas*)

LOIS: Excuse me?

PEGGY: I said you're wrong.

LOIS: Oh, yes, you're right.

PEGGY: I'm usually right. Refreshing, isn't it?

LOIS: (*entering with a pillow and blanket*) Start again.

PEGGY: So you're back. (*Pause*) I'm sorry, it just came out like that. So you're back.

LOIS: Yes.

PEGGY: What do you have to say for yourself? Where have you been?

LOIS: Gone.

PEGGY: Did you have a good time?

LOIS: Yes ... I missed you.

PEGGY: I couldn't remember what you looked like and I had no photo of you. But now I remember, now that I see you.

LOIS: I'm tired. It's like when I used to visit my mother, no matter how I felt when I got here I would always feel exhausted when I saw her and immediately fall asleep on the couch. (*She falls onto the floor with her head on the pillow and covers herself with the blanket*)

PEGGY: I'm not your mother.

LOIS: You bring it out in me.

PEGGY: I dreamt about you.

LOIS: Stay out of my dreams.

PEGGY: Did you dream about me at all?

LOIS: I thought about you once in a while. Do you want some coffee?

PEGGY: Okay. And cake, or no no, wait, a biscuit, the ones with the coconut shreds that stick in your teeth. You have no idea what I go though during the night. For all you know I'll be dead when you wake up. You wouldn't know that I'd gotten the ebola virus, lost all my teeth to that gum disease, opened a show without memorizing my lines and just missed the low interest rates and now had to get a mortgage at nine-and-a-half percent instead of seven. I'm exhausted from all this when you wake up.

LOIS: If there's no coffee, will you have tea?

PEGGY: If I have to. In that case I can't have a biscuit. I'll have cake. Some of that sponge cake you make so well. I'll have tea and cake. It makes more sense. (*Lois starts to get up, then falls back to the floor, unable to stay awake.*) I pretend it's just ordinary to see you and I control myself from smashing your head into my chest to rid myself of the nightmares of losing you in the night while you sleep through it all. (*Lois pulls herself to her knees and begins to crawl towards the doorway*) Could you pass me the paper?

LOIS: Here. (*She throws Peggy a rolled-up newspaper*)

PEGGY: You want to do the crossword?

LOIS: After I've made the tea.

PEGGY: We're growing older and we're spending nights apart. When I first met you, I got down on my knees and said there wasn't enough nights in the rest of our life together and I wanted to spend each one with you. I didn't want to miss one. (*She opens the paper to the crossword*) Okay – hey – it's been done.

LOIS: What?

PEGGY: The crossword. When did you do that? That's not fair. We always do them together.

LOIS: (*entering*) Show me. That's yesterday's paper.

PEGGY: Where's today's?

LOIS: Somewhere –

PEGGY: Where *are* we?

LOIS: It's the same place. It just looks different. More relaxed.

PEGGY: It's a mess. Help me tidy up.

The phone rings.

LOIS: In a minute. The kettle is boiling.

PEGGY: That's not the kettle, it's the phone.

LOIS: Shall I answer it?

PEGGY: I'm not here. I can't speak. I'm too thirsty.

LOIS: I'll let it ring then. (*She exits*)

PEGGY: Whatever. Just get me some tea. Oh yeah, your girlfriend called.

LOIS: My girlfriend called? (*She enters with a deck chair in her hand*)

PEGGY: She wanted to talk to you.

LOIS: What did you tell her?

PEGGY: I told her you weren't here.

LOIS: You told her I wasn't here?

PEGGY: Yeah.

LOIS: Who said you could say that?

PEGGY: I said so.

LOIS: You said so?

PEGGY: Yeah.

LOIS: Yeah? (*They fall into the rhythm of a familiar fight/game*)

PEGGY: Yeah.

LOIS: Yeah?

PEGGY: Yeah.

LOIS: Shut up.

PEGGY: Shut up.

LOIS: Shut up.

PEGGY: You shut up.

LOIS: You shut up.

PEGGY: You shut up.

LOIS: Shut your face.

PEGGY AND LOIS: (*making up*) Awwwwww . . .

Peggy takes Lois in her arms in a ballroom dance pose.

PEGGY: Where are we? (*She sees the deck chair in Lois's hand*) We're at the beach. My God, which beach?

LOIS: Not that beach. The film hasn't been made yet. (*She sets the deck chair up stage right*) Has it? Is that what you were doing while I was away? Making movies? (*She moves to the typewriter and looks at the paper*)

PEGGY: (*pursuing her*) Yes and this is how it ends . . . the butler trips over the cat and plunges down the stairs and is found a week later in a pool of his own vomit. (*She chases her around the deck chair*) The maid is found strangled by her own underwear in the Plaza Hotel in the room of a famous London lawyer. (*Lois picks up the deck chair to shield herself as Peggy chases her stage left*) After stealing the second act, Karen's airplane is found crashed in the Swiss Alps and her dismembered, decapitated body is never recovered.

LOIS: (*hiding under the deck chair*) Is that true?

PEGGY: No, I just made it up.

LOIS: Well then, no cause for alarm. (*She sets up the deck chair stage right facing the audience*)

PEGGY: Which doesn't answer my question.

LOIS: Which is?

PEGGY: Where are we?

LOIS: Work it out. You're the writer. Set your own scene. Describe it to me. (*She sits in the deck chair*)

PEGGY: I can't. I can't describe a place I don't know.

LOIS: Well then describe me. Am I bored?

PEGGY: You're angry.

LOIS: Is there a difference?

PEGGY: I don't know. You've been away. Maybe I could have answered that once but now ... (*she exits*)

LOIS: So what about now? Let's play now.

PEGGY: Don't want to. (*She looks through the props and set pieces "off stage"*)

LOIS: Go on.

PEGGY: No.

LOIS: Why not?

PEGGY: I can't make up now. I can only invent the past or the future.

LOIS: We can imagine.

PEGGY: Your imagination's too terrifying.

LOIS: Not if you write it down.

PEGGY: Then it's history.

LOIS: Then it's a lie.

PEGGY: So how do you record the truth?

LOIS: Whose truth? I'm not looking for truth. I'm looking for opinions. What's your opinion of me?

PEGGY: You want the truth?

LOIS: No! I want your opinion.

PEGGY: That's a different story.

LOIS: Where I come from a story was as good as a lie. Lie was a dirty word. It sounded dirty in the mouth. Maybe that was from the threat of soap. I used to imagine the whole bar in my mouth with the suds dripping down my chin, more afraid of choking on it than of the taste. So if you told a lie it was a story. Maybe that's how I developed my distaste . . . for story . . . like the bar of soap . . . not something I can truthfully say belongs in my mouth.

PEGGY: (*entering with another deck chair and the book* Venus in Furs *and sitting in the deck chair, perpendicular to Lois*) I'll tell you a story.

LOIS: A lie you mean.

PEGGY: I met a princess today.

LOIS: How do you know she was a princess?

PEGGY: She had a long name.

LOIS: Did she have golden hair?

PEGGY: No.

LOIS: Then she's a fake.

PEGGY: She made me feel old . . . and . . .

LOIS: You're not too old. Well you're not too old for me and . . . I'm not too old for you . . .

PEGGY: You did it again.

LOIS: I did what again?

PEGGY: You cut me off.

LOIS: I cut you off?

PEGGY: I don't remember what I was going to say.

LOIS: Oh yeah and why not?

PEGGY: 'Cause you interrupted me.

LOIS: That's because you were taking too long.

PEGGY: You think so?

LOIS: Yeah, I think so.

PEGGY: Yeah? (*They fall into the same rhythm of the fight/game that occurred earlier in this section*)

LOIS: Yeah.

PEGGY: Yeah?

LOIS: Yeah.

PEGGY: Shut up.

LOIS: Shut up.

PEGGY: Shut up.

LOIS: You shut up.

PEGGY: You shut up.

LOIS: You shut up.

PEGGY: Shut your face.

LOIS AND PEGGY: (*making up*) Awwwwwwwwwwwwwwwwww . . .

The phone rings.

PEGGY: That'll be your girlfriend. (*Lois goes for the phone and it stops ringing*)

LOIS: Start again.

PEGGY: What?

LOIS: Let's make a clean slate. Start again.

PEGGY: I'll have to empty my heart. I don't know if I can do that.

The phone rings.

PEGGY: That'll be your girlfriend.

LOIS: (*going for the phone; it stops*) Start again, that didn't work.

PEGGY: I need time by myself.

LOIS: We're in different moods.

PEGGY: Then we probably aren't playing right.

LOIS: Then start again.

The phone rings.

PEGGY: I have more important things to think about.

LOIS: I'll check on the kettle. (*She goes for the phone and it stops before she gets to it*) Who *is* it?

PEGGY: Wrong number. (*The phone rings once and stops*) Wrong number.

LOIS: Wrong number, again?

PEGGY: Thirteen calls in fifteen minutes. It's beginning to worry me.

LOIS: Thirteen! If everything you said was true you'd be two hundred years instead of fifty. (*She exits and searches through "backstage" props*)

PEGGY: Why tell a story unless it's exaggerated? If I feel a relationship was fifty years long, then calling it "fifty years," rather than the fifteen it was, is truth. The calendar is not truth. Everything that goes into that relationship affects how time feels . . . Why not be creative?

LOIS: (*picking up a tennis racket*) Okay, let's be creative.

PEGGY: Sexually?

LOIS: (*peering around from behind the folded screens*) Yeah, you start.

PEGGY: Seducing you, you mean?

LOIS: No, let's change it. I'll seduce you.

PEGGY: How will I know when you start?

LOIS: You'll know.

PEGGY: Are you in the mood?

LOIS: You want the truth?

PEGGY: I know the truth.

LOIS: (*entering with the tennis racket in her hand*) Why do you always say that?

PEGGY: Because it's true.

LOIS: And you exaggerate everything.

PEGGY: I exaggerate everything?

LOIS: Yeah and you can't see past the nose on your own face.

PEGGY: And you're a historian.

LOIS: And you have one thing on your mind.

PEGGY: Yeah?

LOIS: Yeah!

PEGGY: Yeah?

LOIS: (*entering again into the rhythm of the fight/game, but this time the words are barely audible and only the rhythm remains*) Yeah.

PEGGY: Shut up.

LOIS: Shut up.

PEGGY: Shut up.

LOIS: Shut up.

PEGGY: Shut up.

LOIS: Shut up.

PEGGY AND LOIS: Awwwwwww . . .

LOIS: Guess what I brought you?

PEGGY: A nice cup of tea?

LOIS: A tennis racket.

PEGGY: A tennis racket? I wanted a whip!

LOIS: Well then, your serve. (*She hands Peggy the racket*)

PEGGY: No, what I wanted was some commonplace sadism like in French films.

LOIS: So you're not a real sadist?

PEGGY: Of course not.

LOIS: What are you, then?

PEGGY: I'm researching for a screenplay. Obviously, I'll have to invent it myself.

LOIS: You can do that. You're a writer.

The phone rings and Lois is startled.

PEGGY: Relax. There'll be a perfectly reasonable explanation.

LOIS: Someone could be trying to get through.

PEGGY: Who?

LOIS: I don't know. Anyone. Someone . . . Someone could be trying to contact us and repeatedly get the busy signal and will sooner or later get tired of trying and give up, and not bother to call again.

PEGGY: Like your girlfriend?

LOIS: Like the Chinese takeaway.

PEGGY: You're right. (*She exits*)

LOIS: (*moving her deck chair downstage right*) It's been two weeks since we ordered and I'm starving.

PEGGY: (*entering with a blanket and pillow*) There's some jam in the fridge.

LOIS: I ate it. (*She exits*)

PEGGY: When?

LOIS: With a friend.

PEGGY: You slut that was *our* jam.

LOIS: Relax, there's lots of jars in the back. (*She enters with a long string of fairy lights and begins to hang them across the set pieces and props at the back of the stage so that when they are lit they resemble city lights*)

PEGGY: They're full of air. (*She moves her deck chair downstage left and sits*)

LOIS: Air?

PEGGY: From Amsterdam and Hawaii. Berlin, New York ... We had air from London but it got used up when you went away. When I breathed it I could see you singing for me while I lifted you in the air.

LOIS: How high?

PEGGY: As high as I could. We told each other secrets.

LOIS: Where?

PEGGY: In the basement.

LOIS: Were we hiding?

PEGGY: From the guests we'd forgotten we'd invited.

LOIS: What did we do?

PEGGY: We went swimming in the ocean. You wore a purple dress.

LOIS: I didn't drown did I?

PEGGY: Not exactly.

LOIS: What time is it?

PEGGY: Late, I think.

LOIS: I miss having windows.

PEGGY: That's your fault.

LOIS: My fault? How come?

PEGGY: You took the walls down. No walls. No windows.

LOIS: What comes down must go up.

PEGGY: Not necessarily.

LOIS: How so?

PEGGY: Ask your mother.

LOIS: Meaning?

PEGGY: About your father's pajama pants – "What can't get up, can't get out."

LOIS: Start again.

PEGGY: No walls, no windows, no doors.

LOIS: We never had doors.

PEGGY: No door, no locks.

LOIS: No locks, no keys.

PEGGY: No keys, no car.

LOIS: Well, that's that then. No escape.

PEGGY: A car! That's a great idea! (*She moves onto her hands and knees in front of the typewriter*)

LOIS: For what?

PEGGY: The end of the screenplay could be a car chase. For instance, the transgendered movie star, after re-uniting with her lover, the maid, is pursued across Germany by the ... Interpol, the FBI and the CIA and ...

LOIS: The House on Un-American Activities ...

PEGGY: And the House on Un-American Activities Committee and end up ...

LOIS: Going over a cliff.

PEGGY: Going over a cliff!

They look at each other.

LOIS AND PEGGY: Naaaaaaaaawwwwwwwwww!!!

Blackout. Music comes up: A love song in the style of "The Ten

*Commandments of Love." The lights fade up on Lois and Peggy
slow-dancing center stage. They dance in a tender and familiar way.
Early in the dance, Peggy steps on Lois's toes. Lois complains. They
reconcile but as they move back to the dance Lois punches Peggy
in the jaw. Peggy recovers and they resume dancing. Then in the
middle of a twirl, Peggy punches Lois in the stomach. Lois recovers
and they resume dancing. This establishes a pattern of dancing
intercut with fighting that becomes more and more violent and acro-
batic until at the end of the song both Lois and Peggy are lying
exhausted on the floor. Lights come up on the deck chairs down
stage left and right. Lois crawls to the stage right chair and sits. As
she picks up her pillow and blanket she discovers a roll of paper
like the one in the typewriter hidden in the pillow. She unrolls it
and begins to read aloud. Peggy brings a wicker picnic basket from
backstage, sits in the stage left deck chair, pours herself a cup of
tea from a thermos and begins to blow up an inflatable globe.*

LOIS: (*reading from the rolled paper*) Her hands felt like cold steel
when I grabbed onto them. I walked and walked along the river
until I found her in the park, all bold and dark and huge, in the
fading light of an already gray day. Her arm was upraised and I
could see the veins in her forearm. From where I stood her hands
looked enormous, half the size of her arm. Her fingers were worn
out on the edges from so many people touching her. I grabbed her
giant hand where the steel had actually changed color and wanted
her to lift me up and take me to a safe place. Her hand was cold
from the metal it was made of and from the autumn air, and
although it felt strong and solid and hard and capable of lifting me,
it didn't move, it didn't budge, even with my whole body weight
pulling on it. All there was left for me to do was to pull myself up
with the strength of my own body and caress her cold arched back
and ass beneath the folds of material and then slide down onto the
bright grass and sit on the wooden bench by the river and add my
tears to the Thames, to the thousands of tears already churning in
that fast moving river. The waves lapping on that strange dark small
beach along the wall sound like an ocean, covering the loud smacks
of my heart against my chest. My mother told me keep moving. So
I took her with me. I picked her off the bench and it started bells
ringing, all of them including Big Ben. (*There are the sounds of a
riverside park with a bell chiming in the distance*) They wouldn't
stop so I covered my ear with one hand while pulling her across
Trafalgar Square with the other. Pushing and pulling her to Charing
Cross, trying to make sense of her cold steel hands, her desire run
cold. And then throwing myself into the early evening London alley
where every place I knew was shut. In the fake city of London. (*The
fairy lights fade up, resembling the night view of a city from across*

a river) The last boat was at four, the sandwich shop shut at six and she closed at nine for good. I was standing there still open, the saxophone playing "The Girl from Ipanema" competing with the tolling of the bells. I was still open in a city where everything was closed. Time has passed and now I'm ordinary again. Trying to make sense of the phone bills and the passion and the time.

PEGGY: (*taking the scroll of paper from Lois's hand and replacing it with a cup of tea*) Do you know when I was in high school I learned geography on a map that showed that the United States was bigger than Russia.

LOIS: No!

PEGGY: You see, there's a lot of things you don't know about me.

They both sit quietly in their deck chairs facing different directions. Lois sips her tea. Peggy is reading her book. A saxophone playing "The Girl from Ipanema" fades up. Peggy whistles to get Lois's attention and tosses her the globe. Lois settles back in chair, comparing the map of the United States to the map of Russia. The lights fade out and the music fades up as Peggy turns to look at Lois. Blackout.

THE END

BIBLIOGRAPHY

BOOKS AND ACADEMIC ARTICLES

Blair, Rhonda. 'The Alcestis Project: Split Britches at Hampshire College.' *Women and Performance: A Journal of Feminist Theory* 6.1 (1993): 147-76.

Bourne, Betty, Peggy Shaw, Paul Shaw and Lois Weaver. 'Belle Reprieve.' *Gay and Lesbian Plays Today*. Ed. Terry Helbing. New Hampshire: Heineman Educational Books, Inc., 1993. 3–38. Rpt. in *Modern Drama*. Ed. William Worthen. New York: Harcourt Brace College Publishers, 1995. 992–1002.

Case, Sue-Ellen. 'From Split Subject to Split Britches.' *Feminine Focus: The New Women Playwrights*. Ed. Enoch Brater. New York: Oxford University Press, 1989. 126–46.

—'Toward a Butch-Femme Aesthetic.' *Making a Spectacle: Feminist Essays on Contemporary Women's Theatre*. Ed. Lynda Hart. Ann Arbor: University of Michigan Press, 1989. 282–299. Rpt. in *The Lesbian and Gay Studies Reader*. Eds Michèle Aina Barale, David M. Halperin, and Henry Abelove. New York: Routledge, 1993. 294–306.

Davy, Kate. "Constructing the Spectator: Reception, Context, and Address in Lesbian Performance." *Performing Arts Journal* 10.2 (1986): 43–52.

—'Fe/male Impersonation: The Discourse of Camp.' *Critical Theory and Performance*. Eds Janelle Reinelt and Joseph Roach. Ann Arbor: University of Michigan Press, 1992. 231–47.

—'From *Lady Dick* to Ladylike: The Work of Holly Hughes.' *Acting Out: Feminist Performances*. Eds Lynda Hart and Peggy Phelan. Ann Arbor: University of Michigan Press, 1993. 55–84.

—'Peggy Shaw and Lois Weaver: Interviews (1985, 1992, 1993).' *Modern Drama*. Ed. William Worthen. New York: Harcourt Brace College Publishers, 1995. 1003–8.

—'Reading Past the Heterosexual Imperative, *Dress Suits to Hire*.' *Drama Review* 33.1 (1989): 153–71.

de Lauretis, Teresa. 'Sexual Indifference and Lesbian Representation.' *Theatre Journal* 40.2 (1988): 155–77. Rpt. in *Performing Feminisms*. Ed. Sue-Ellen Case. Baltimore: Johns Hopkins University Press, 1991. 17–39.

Diamond, Elin. 'Mimesis, Mimicry and the "True-Real".' Hart and Phelan, *Acting Out* 363–82.

Dolan, Jill. 'Desire Cloaked in a Trenchcoat.' Hart and Phelan, *Acting Out* 105–118.

—'The Dynamics of Desire: Sexuality and Gender in Pornography and Performance,' *Theatre Journal* 39.2 (1987): 156–74.

—*The Feminist Spectator as Critic.* Ann Arbor: University of Michigan Press, 1988. 59–81.

Dolan, Jill. 'Practicing Cultural Disruptions: Gay and Lesbian Representation and Sexuality.' *Critical Theory and Performance.* Eds Janelle Reinelt and Joe Roach. Ann Arbor: University of Michigan Press, 1992.

—*Presence and Desire: Essays on Gender, Sexuality, Performance.* Ann Arbor: University of Michigan Press, 1993.

Hart, Lynda. *Fatal Woman: Lesbian Sexuality and the Mark of Aggression.* Princeton: Princeton University Press, 1994.

—'Identity and Seduction: Lesbians in the Mainstream.' Hart and Phelan, *Acting Out* 119–37.

Hart, Lynda and Peggy Phelan. 'Queerer Than Thou: Being and Deb Margolin.' *Theatre Journal* 47.2 (1995): 269–82.

Hughes, Holly. 'Dress Suits to Hire.' *Drama Review* 33.1 (March 1989): 132–51.

Margolin, Deborah, Lois Weaver, Peggy Shaw and Vivian Patraka. 'Little Women: The Tragedy.' *Kenyon Review* 15.2 (March 1993): 14–26.

Mayne, Judith. 'Lesbian Looks: Dorothy Arzner and Female Authorship,' *How Do I Look?: Queer Film and Video*, Ed. Bad Object Choices. Seattle: Bay Press, 1991. 103–35.

Patraka, Vivian. 'Split Britches in *Split Britches*: Performing History, Vaudeville, and the Everyday.' *Women and Performance* 4.2 (1989): 58–67. Rpt in Hart and Phelan, *Acting Out* 215–24.

—'Split Britches in "Little Women: The Tragedy" – Staging Censorship, Nostalgia, and Desire.' *Kenyon Review* 15.2 (March 1993): 6–13.

Schneider, Rebecca. 'Holly Hughes: Polymorphous Perversity and the Lesbian Scientist.' *Drama Review* 33.1 (March 1989): 171–84.

—'See the Big Show: Spiderwoman Theater Doubling Back.' Hart and Phelan, *Acting Out* 227–55.

Shaw, Peggy, Deborah Margolin and Lois Weaver. 'Split Britches: A True Story.' *Women and Performance* 4.2 (1989): 68–95.

Solomon, Alisa. 'It's Never Too Late to Switch.' *Crossing the Stage.* Ed. Lesley Ferris. London: Routledge, 1993. 144–54.

—'The Wow Cafe.' *Drama Review* 29.1 (1985): 92–101.

Weaver, Lois and Peggy Shaw. 'May Interviews June.' *Movement Research* (September 1991): 4–5.

REVIEWS

SPLIT BRITCHES

Stasio, Marilyn. *New York Post.* 24 February 1981: 18.
Stone, Laurie. *The Village Voice.* 19 April 1983: 105.
Swan, Christopher. *The Christian Science Monitor.* 28 January 1982.

BEAUTY AND THE BEAST

Hartigan, Patti. *The Boston Globe.* 16 February 1988: 62.
Stone, Laurie. *The Village Voice.* 19 April 1983: 105.

UPWARDLY MOBILE HOME

Cumbow, Paul. *Seattle Post Intelligencer*. 20 June 1985.
Pasternak, June. *Guardian*. 24 November 1984: 20.
Solomon, Alisa. *The Village Voice*. 13 November 1984: 95.

PATIENCE AND SARAH

Bruckner, D. J. R. *New York Times*. 10 April 1987: C18.
Day, S. *Gay Community News*. 4 January 1987: 6.
Kendall. *Women's Review of Books* 4.10 (September 1987): 16.

DRESS SUITS TO HIRE

Eddings, A. *Women and Performance* 4.1 (1988): 170.
Pasternak, J. *Guardian*. 30 December 1987: 17.
Stone, Laurie. *The Village Voice*. 12 January 1988: 90.

LITTLE WOMEN

Massa, Robert. *The Village Voice*. 27 June 1989: 100.
Rosmiarek, Joseph T. *The Honolulu Advertiser*. 14 July 1990.
Tallmer, Jerry. *New York Post*. 7 July 1989: 22.

ANNIVERSARY WALTZ

Harris, Hilary. *Theatre Journal* 42.4 (December 1990): 484–8.
Satin, L. *Women and Performance* 5.1 (1990): 189.

BELLE REPRIEVE

Caldwell, Ron. "Kind of Stranger." *Gay Community News*. 8 April 1991.
Clay, Carolyn. "The Kindness of Strangers." *The Boston Phoenix*. 12 April 1991.
Friedman, Arthur. 'Hilarious "Streetcar" Sendup Plays Up Gays' Perspective.' *The Boston Review*. 5 April 1991.
Leondar, Gail. *Theatre Journal* 43.3 (October 1991): 386–8.
Power, Sarah Mee. *Stage and Television Today*. 24 January 1991.
Raymond, G. *Advocate*. 22 October 1991: 70.
Siegel, Fern. *Ms. Magazine* 2.2 (September 1991): 81.
Solomon, Alisa. *The Village Voice*. 19 February 1991: 59–62.
Udovich, Mim. 'Brass Menagerie.' *The Village Voice*. 5 March 1991.

LESBIANS WHO KILL

Hart, Lynda. *Theatre Journal* 44.4 (December 1992): 515-18.
Russo, Francine. *The Village Voice*. 19 May 1992: 106.
Siegel, Fern. *Ms Magazine* 2.2 (September 1991):81.

LUST AND COMFORT

Brantley, Ben. 'An Old-fashioned Couple, Except Both Are Women.' *New York Times*. 17 May 1995: C14.
Dieckmann, Katherine. 'Awwwww.' *The Village Voice*. 6 June 1995.

Schloff, Aaron Mack. 'Companion Pieces: Peggy Shaw and Lois Weaver Bring Their Longtime Love to the Theater.' *Lesbian and Gay New York*. 4 June 1995: Arts, 18.

Williamson, Tellery. *Theatre Journal*. March 1996: 102–4.

VARIOUS

Holden, Stephen. Review of *You're Just Like My Father*. *New York Times*. 26 May 1994: G19.

Kingsburg, M. Review of *An Evening of Disgusting Songs and Pukey Images*. *Gay Community News*. 25 October 1980: 15.

Maslin, Janet. Review of *She Must Be Seeing Things*. *New York Times*. 13 April 1988: C20.

Solomon, Alisa. 'The Strangeness of Strangers.' *The Village Voice*. 19 February 1991.

Stone, Laurie. 'Interview with Lois Weaver and Peggy Shaw.' *The Village Voice*. 28 June 1988, 33: 30.

Walsh, Winifred. 'Upwardly Mobile Home Interview.' *Baltimore Evening Sun*. 2 February 1988: B3.

Weaver, Lois and Peggy Shaw. 'May Interviews June.' *Movement Research*. Fall 1991: 4.

Write in gumming for LWK
dolic

Expand rep to Bell's chat in SB.

Del Some Friend.